A Guide to

HUNTING PENNSYLVANIA WHITETAILS

Tom Fegely

ISBN   0-9643278-0-5

Published by: B & T Outdoor Enterprises
            P.O. Box 518
            Coopersburg, PA 18036

Printed in the United States of America
by: Gilliland Printing, Inc.
     215 North Summit
     Arkansas City, KS 67005

DEDICATION

To Betty Lou, my friend and companion at home and in the deer woods.

TABLE OF CONTENTS

ACKNOWLEDGEMENTS

A project such as this, requiring painstaking research and many years of gathering information, photographs and keeping up with happenings indoors and out affecting deer and deer hunting, is not done on a whim.

The initial interest in doing a book on Pennsylvania deer hunting was sparked a decade ago. But other matters -- not the least of which were daily deadlines for newspaper, magazine, TV and radio projects -- kept that spark from igniting into full flame. Then, last January, when snows piled deep outside the office window and deer nibbled corn from the pile I'd scattered there, I wrote the first word. That was followed by many hours at the computer and dozens of letters, phone calls and visits to the library.

My wife, Betty Lou, an integral part of the project, kept the embers burning. Spring brought travel and an increased load of deadlines, and another lull in the operation. In mid-summer, we began devoting every spare minute to gathering information on public hunting lands, scrutinizing photo files, making dozens and dozens of phone calls and picking up all the loose ends which eventually filled this guide.

Many others also played supporting roles. At the top of the list is Kay Richey, whose talents in layout with her Macintosh computer are unmatched. Ditto for Keith Kaeppel who was responsible for illustrations and layout of the entire County Profiles section.

Gathering what often turned out to be conflicting information on game, forest, park and federal hunting lands, as well as game laws and statistics, was a job made easier by my friend Bruce Whitman, the Game Commission's public information agent. Add to that a laundry list of folks from other agencies too numerous to mention.

Thanks also to the editors of Pennsylvania Sportsman, Pennsylvania Game News, Buckmasters, Harris Publications and Outdoor Life for providing their blessings in using bits and pieces of information previously published in their magazines.

Invaluable also, are the many memorable days spent at Green Tree Lodge in Carbon County and with Wayne Pocius and friends at Mountain View Camp in Bradford County and other deer camps across the state. They were sources of information, inspiration, unique experiences and photos galore.

Thanks, too, to our friends in the Outdoor Writers Association of America and Pennsylvania Outdoor Writers Association for their help over the years. A special thanks also goes to Tom Gresham and Jameson Campaigne for their advice on the business end of self-publishing and marketing books. And to Bob Bell, former Pennsylvania Game News editor, who rejected my first article and bought my second way back in 1968. Along with that rejection came a letter of encouragement and some invaluable advice which I've not forgotten.

Mostly, thanks to my wife for her assistance and constant encouragement without which this book might still be bytes on a computer screen.

......T.F.

FOREWORD

Deer hunters have roamed Pennsylvania searching for whitetails long before William Penn gave our state its name. Deer were food. Food was survival. There was little enjoyment associated with deer hunting.

Modern hunters still pursue deer, driven by a powerful heritage and strong tradition. But today deer are hunted for more than food and they nourish more than our bodies...they enrich our spirit as well. These days deer hunting is more enjoyable. Pursuing whitetails connects us to the living systems of our landscape and bridges us to a past that many have forgotten. The animal is timeless; the tradition is priceless. At least for now.

Pennsylvania has more deer and deer hunters than ever before. In fact, deer hunting in Pennsylvania represents the largest single participatory recreational event in the world. Each year well over a million of us hunt whitetails in Pennsylvania, and we hunt them in almost as many different ways. But it isn't a numbers game; deer hunting is made up of personal experience. It is an incredible phenomenon.

Despite this rich heritage, no one has adequately recorded our story. Parts and pieces have been written about deer hunting in Pennsylvania, and literally tons of books have been published about deer and deer hunting throughout the country, but until now sportsmen of Pennsylvania have only a piecemeal record of our deer, our hunters, the places we meet and where to find new hunting grounds.

With *A Guide to Hunting Pennsylvania Whitetails* Tom Fegely corrects that shortcoming. More than any Pennsylvania writer, Tom has pursued deer throughout their range. He's traveled the U.S. and Canada in pursuit of them. I know Tom as a hard-working, busy, intensive guy and his work and passion for the outdoors requires him to be away a great deal of time. But come deer season you'll find him "back home," for his first love is the Pennsylvania whitetail and deer camp.

This book is more than a guide. Tom combines all the magic of the deer woods and shares it with us in his usual, friendly way. He has given us something that is as old as the hills and yet as crisp and new as a frosty November morn.

The timing for this book is perfect, although any time is a good time to talk and read about deer hunting. As I collect my thoughts and write these words, it's the eve of another deer season in Pennsylvania. Tomorrow the hunt is on and, for me, there is no other animal I would rather hunt...or see...or talk and read about...than the white-tailed deer. And there's no other place that I enjoy all those things more than here in Pennsylvania and my Potter County deer camp.

Thanks, Tom, for sharing with us your thoughts, experience and advice.....as we join you in "Hunting Pennsylvania Whitetails."

Lou Hoffman
Editor-In-Chief, *Pennsylvania Sportsman*

PREFACE

Why another deer book?

Surely enough titles are on the market and dozens of magazines, some devoted specifically to whitetails, stand sentry at newsstands.

Since 1976, when I began my tenure as outdoors editor of The Morning Call in Allentown, I've fielded countless letters and calls from readers on every conceivable aspect of the outdoors. Many -- indeed, most -- focused on deer and deer hunting.

Some 1.1 million Pennsylvanians hunt deer, unmatched in any other state. They're an insatiable bunch. If not actually deer hunting, they talk or read or argue about deer hunting. Even in summer they find excuses for weekend "work party" visits to deer camp.

In September they patrol back roads spotlighting deer, previewing what will be available in the local deer woods at the start of the bow and gun seasons. They live for opening day, often leaving home after eating Thanksgiving dinner to "get ready." They devour news of changing deer laws, season revisions, spread word of local buck "legends" that someone's seen or shot, read countless magazine articles, attend post-season "buck clubs" or are found on the range all year long firing muzzleloaders, scoped shotguns and sweet-shooting rifles or aiming bows and arrows.

In all my travels for whitetails, nowhere have I seen the overall passion and devotion to deer as here in Pennsylvania. For some it's a family affair. For many it's a lifestyle.

Then, too, we need to recruit new hunters, young and old, to the ranks. Many of them are in need of guidance and, unable to find mentors to lead them gently into the sport, may seek other avocations.

That, alone, is reason enough for a book devoted entirely to hunting in the Keystone State. I've not taken up precious pages with details not pertaining to the Pennsylvania scene nor does this guide enter into analysis of topics to which entire books have been devoted.

Rather, it's as the title implies -- a guide. It's a reference on where to go, how to get started, how to make the most of the seasons afforded Pennsylvanians and out-of-state guests and where to get specific information, with addresses and phone numbers galore.

It's my hope, also, that readers will page through this book when they need a dose of "buck fever." I've tapped the minds of some well-known hunters who patrol the state's deer woods and looked back at game laws and deer hunters of the past. It's also illustrated with photos of some of the state's biggest bucks -- both wall-hangers and others running wild and free.

It is only fitting that the book begins with an essay on the aura of deer camp and ends with a visit to these "palaces in the popples," where hundreds of thousands of men, women and kids spend time and make memories.

I hope you enjoy and benefit from this book, sharing with me this venture into Pennsylvania's whitetail country.

Tom Fegely
October 10, 1994

PART
I
WHITETAILS
And Whitetail Hunters

Chapter 1

DEER CAMP
A Pennsylvania Tradition

Deer camp.

The words ring magic in hunters' ears.

On the eve of opening day, windows in deer camps all across the state will glow as woodsmoke from seldom-used chimneys curls into the night-sky.

Deer camp is a place occupied for a only a few days each fall while holding a place in the minds and hearts of hunters all year long. On the hottest days of August and the most frigid nights of February, hunters sip iced tea or steaming coffee and talk of deer camps past.

I vividly recall my first deer camp experience in Sullivan County in 1959. It was here I got my first taste of the spirit and camaraderie of the hunt. Consider it a move toward manhood if you will — a male bonding as old the hunt itself. A tentative acceptance into the clan.

And more.

For one, to be a good deer camper you've got to be able to take a joke. Like someone hiding your hunting license. Sure panic.

Or taking a portrait of you perched in the outhouse. Sheer embarrassment.

Or some clown sneaking into the cook's bedroom and turning his clock ahead three hours.

That happened at one Cameron County camp I know. The cook climbed from bed, dressed, switched on the coffee pot and began frying eggs and pouring pancake batter. Problem was, it was only 2 a.m.

It took him and the rest of the crew a few sleepy-eyed minutes to realize what had happened as they staggered about wondering where the night had gone. The unhappy campers grumbled and returned to their bunks, vowing to find out who did the foul deed.

But they never found out and no one ever "fessed up," although there were a few prime suspects.

Funny how time can mellow such happenings. What was cursed in December becomes hilarious in July.

Of course, the essence of deer camp is seeing old friends and loved ones. Sons, brothers, parents, college friends and others taken afar by jobs and marriages are brought under one roof in buck season.

The firm handshakes. The smiles. The jokes. And reliving past hunts, of course.

While deer camp memories are strong, details somehow meld and blur over time. That's why, many years back when I hunted with a bunch of Lehigh Valley friends at Greentree Lodge in Carbon County, we began a tradition that makes history of deer camp happenings. It's in the form of several scrapbooks.

Who was there and who shot what?

Who bagged the biggest buck in 1971?

Who got lost in Lime Hollow?

Whose treestand was gnawed off by a porcupine?

Included are jokes and barbs. The camp menu. The lucky campers who filled their tags each year. And pictures. Lots of pictures.

When Lou starts bragging about the monster 8-pointer he shot in 1967, someone pulls out The Official Scrapbook. It shows Louie proudly posing with a small Y-buck.

"Oh yeah," he admits sheepishly. "Guess it grew a bit since then."

It matters little whether deer camp is a rustic cabin in the backwoods, a motorhome, a leaky tent lit by Coleman lanterns or a plush lodge tucked away in a mountain retreat. The surroundings may vary but the smells and spirit are the same.

Hoppe's No. 9 strokes the nostrils as it did 35 years ago. Morning coffee wafts through the bedroom, making alarm clocks unnecessary. A restless night dreaming about big-racked bucks is nipped by the roar of sizzling bacon in the camp kitchen.

Nervous jokes break the tension. More teasing. Checking for extra shells. Now where did I put that drag rope?

Someone sets bare feet on the porch to check the sky, then offers a forecast. Nervous chatter grows as the magic hour draws near, until the cabin finally falls silent as hunters head to their chosen stands.

You nestle against a familiar tree and await the deer hunter's dawn — none so special as on opening day.

Oh yes, every once in a while someone shoots a buck. But that's the bonus.

Deer camp is more than anything an escape. A celebration. A joy. An initiation. A reminder of what life and good times and buck hunting and friends are all about.

The nostalgic times take on new meaning as one moves along the trail from rookie to graybeard.

For hundreds of thousands of Pennsylvanians, it just doesn't get any better than this.

And what better way to start — and end — a book of tribute to Pennsylvania's deer and deer hunters than to honor its richest tradition?

Deer camp.

It's often possible to tell the sex of a deer that bedded in snow. Often, upon standing, a deer will urinate. If the yellow splashes are scattered chances are it was a buck, particularly at or near rut time. A doe's urine path is usually more confined to a single spot.

How far do deer travel from their birthplaces? Surprisingly documented cases of bucks and does being killed 90-170 miles from where they were born have been recorded.

"Forkhorn," Y-buck" and "crotch buck" are all slang terms used by deer hunters to describe a (2x2) 4-pointer.

Most hunters know that a deer chews its cud but not many can describe what the "cud" really is. It's a wad of vegetation eaten earlier, about the size of a small orange, that's regurgitated into the gullet when a deer is at rest. It's a back-up system for helping masticate and digest foods that may have had to be eaten "on the run."

The hairs on velvet-covered antlers are believed to act as sensors in protecting the growing bone. The erect hairs "feel" obstructions as the deer attends to its daily rounds which may include everything from feeding in a thorny thicket to crawling under barbed-wire fences.

Few living tissues grow as fast as antlers. A buck's velvet-covered rack will grow about one-quarter inch a day. Elk antlers grow twice as fast, or about a half-inch per day.

A deer's antlers grow from the outside in, like a tree. The velvet lays down the bone on the outside, accounting for its gradual growth throughout the summer. Horns, such as on pronghorns, sheep, goats and cattle, grow from the inside out.

A deer's eye pupils open considerably wider than that of a human, allowing up to nine times more light to enter and increasing their acuity after dark.

Hunters pose for a photo at Shoemaker's Camp in the Iron Run area of Clinton County circa 1910.

Chapter
2

LOOKING BACK

Charting a course for the future is largely dependent upon the past. And no where is there a richer and more colorful history of whitetail hunting and management than right here in Pennsylvania — from the first game law more than 270 years ago through the ever-changing realm of special seasons and bonus doe licenses of the past decade.

Today, deer numbers in the state match the populations of the early 1930s, approximately a million. But it wasn't always that way. Venison was the "beef" of pioneers and Indians, the source of buckskin coats and antler tools. Market hunters and others later shot them by lantern-light (called "jacklighting"), with snares, gun-traps, dogs and by any other workable means.

Though exploitive, don't compare that to the poachers of today. Back then it was simply a way to make a living. Venison was a big city treat, selling in Pittsburgh markets for a mere two cents a pound.

Add to that an insatiable lust for wood and wood products during which much of the state was cleared. Stripped mountains, erosion and fires continued to wreak havoc with whitetails and other wildlife for many years.

By the turn of the 20th Century deer had become rarities. From 1906 through 1924 nearly 1,200 deer were stocked from Michigan, Maine, New Hampshire, New Jersey, Ohio, Kentucky and a few from Pennsylvania breeders, hauled on railcars to their new homes. For 16 years doe hunting was banned.

The stocking efforts and work to protect deer by law were successful, although not without cost. Natural succession brought regrowth of seedlings and saplings, all within reach of whitetails. By 1930 the state hosted an estimated million deer.

Then came the crash. As forests matured to pole stage, producing minimal food, deer competed for what was available. Two severe, back-to-back winters in the mid-1930s caused mass starvation. To further nip deer numbers, doe season became an acceptable, although controversial, management tool.

Since that time a variety of changes, in both deer management and hunting

In 1930 Pennsylvania had about as many deer as today.

laws, have been set. Some are controversial. Others are widely accepted. And they keep changing as they promise to do into the challenging 21st Century.

Following is a brief chronological history of whitetail hunting, deer laws and management in yesterday's "good old days" — and now.

1681 — Charter granted by King Charles II of England to William Penn to found a colony in the new world, later to become know as Penn's Woods or Pennsylvania.

1683 — Hunting is permitted on all lands under William Penn's charter; first bounty is established, 10 and 15 shillings for wolf scalps.

1721 — Pennsylvania's first game law enacted to protect deer from January 1 to July 1; fine of 20 shillings established to penalize violators.

1730 — Pennsylvania Rifle (later to be falsely dubbed the Kentucky Rifle) developed in Lancaster, York and Lebanon counties.

1850-1885 — Venison and other game becomes standard fare on free-lunch counters in better saloons in Philadelphia and Pittsburgh.

1867 — Last native elk killed in north-central Pennsylvania.

1873 — Use of dogs for deer hunting outlawed.

1878 — Sunday hunting of game is prohibited.

1896 — Pennsylvania Game Commission established.

1905 — Pennsylvania becomes the first state to protect black bears; buckshot banned for deer hunting.

1906 — Fourteen game protectors are shot at with three killed, three seriously wounded, one slightly injured and one citizen killed while aiding a game protector.

1907 — First deer are stocked — 50 from Michigan; Pennsylvania becomes the first state to ban the use of automatic guns in hunting game; only bucks legal game with 300 harvested.

1909 — Bucks declared legal only "with horns visible above the hair."

1913 — Resident hunting law enacted, calling for a $1 per year license fee; bucks declared legal with "antlers two inches above the hair."

1917 — Law passed making it unlawful to hunt from an automobile; camp limit for deer established; night hunting of all game animals, except raccoons, forbidden.

1919 — Legislature passes law to permit the Game Commission to purchase property to be known as "State Game Lands."

1920 — First State Game Land tract purchased in Elk County — 6,228 acres, for which the commission paid $2.75 per acre.

1921 — Bucks declared legal "with antlers four inches above the top of the skull."

1923 — Landowners are given the right to kill deer for damage to crops; first special doe license established and commission given the right to establish antlerless deer seasons; Legislature makes it illegal to "kill bucks unless with two or more points on one antler or with an antler at least six inches long from the top of skull;" first open season on elk brought from Yellowstone National Park and private game propagators.

1925 — Deer law amended to declare a buck illegal "unless it has two or more points on one antler."

Spike bucks with antlers of 4-inches or longer were legal in 1921.

1928 — First statewide season on antlerless deer except in 16 counties which were closed; only deer that exceeded 50 pounds (field-dressed weight) legal.

1929 — Bow and arrow legalized for hunting game.

1930 — First issue of official Game Commission publication, "Pennsylvania Game News," published in mimeographed form.

1931 — Elk given complete protection; maximum per acre purchase price for gamelands set at $10; first open season on both bucks and does with only spike bucks protected; kill recorded at 24,796 bucks and 70,255 antlerless deer.

1936 — Sales of timber from state gamelands authorized.

1937 — Maximum purchase price per acre for gamelands increased from $10 to $30; archery preserves first established, one each in Forest and Sullivan counties; bounty removed on wildcats (bobcats).

1939 — Guns discharging .22 or .25 caliber rimfire cartridges prohibited for big game hunting.

1940 — Record deer harvest set at 186,575 — 18,056 from Elk County alone.

1942 — Hunters urged to donate deer skins to make vests for members of armed forces; licenses made of vulcanized fiber instead of aluminum.

1949 — Resident hunting license fee raised from $2 to $3.15.

1951 — Special season authorized for deer hunting with bows and arrows (Oct. 15-27) with $2 archery tag needed; county quota system authorized for issuance of doe licenses, 60 percent of tags issued by county treasurers and 40 percent by the Department of Revenue in Harrisburg.

1953 — Bucks declared legal "only with two or more points to one antler or spike three inches or longer."

1956 — Maximum authorized purchase price per acre for state gamelands raised from $30 to $100.

1957 — Hunting of deer of both sexes authorized for bow hunting season; special antlerless license requirement dropped.

1958 — Commission inaugurates firearms and hunter safety education program with N.R.A.-qualified instructors; Safety Zone program created with cooperation of private landowners.

1963 — Hunting license fees increased from $3.15 to $5.20; junior license fee set at $3.20, $25.35 fee for non-residents.

1964 — Six-day antlerless deer season initiated in Southeastern Pennsylvania; winter archery season established in certain sections of the state (expanded in 1967).

1965 — Millionth acre of state gamelands purchased; establishment of deer record program in cooperation with Pennsylvania Outdoor Writers Association.

1967 — Record buck harvest set at 78,268; first statewide winter archery season set.

1969 — Hunter safety training made mandatory before youth under 16 can purchase a license.

1973 — Cost of antlerless deer license increased to $2.35; compound bow legalized (later rescinded).

1974 — First flintlock-only season established on certain state gamelands; 65 does and four bucks harvested in three-day hunt.

1977 — Record 146,078 buck/doe harvest set; winter deer feeding adopted stressing population control (winter feeding permitted only under extreme conditions).

1979 — Flintlock season extended statewide; deer management system improved by incorporating carrying capacities of varied forest types.

1980 — Deer hunters required to wear at least 100 square inches of fluorescent orange on head or chest and back (later increased to 250 square inches on head, back and chest combined).

1981 — Record reported flintlock harvest of 8,246 whitetails.

1982 — Mechanical release for bowhunters legalized.

1985 — Record 161,428 buck/doe harvest set; record bow harvest of 7,467.

1988 — Record buck kill of 163,106 and record all-time buck/doe harvest of 381,399; bonus deer tag (leftover doe permits) program begun.

1989 — Record buck kill of 169,795; record all-time buck/doe harvest of 388,601; record allocation of 806,100 doe licenses; archers break all-time record for fifth consecutive year with harvest of 11,008 whitetails.

1990 — "Second bonus" doe permit program starts.

1992 — Pilot program for harvesting antlerless deer during buck season on approved lands in four counties.

1993 — Fall archery season expanded to six weeks; elk herd expands to 205, highest ever; Pilot Deer Damage Program (during buck season) expanded to 16 counties; all hunters required to purchase doe tag to harvest antlerless deer.

1994 — Game Commission approves deer control permit system allowing year-around culling by certified persons in suburban municipalities; harvest of antlerless deer (with proper license) on Deer Damage Areas during buck season expanded to all counties; state gamelands acreage approaches 1.4 million acres; Pennsylvania again leads nation in hunting license sales with 1,173,428.

Appreciating the evolution of deer laws and conservation attitudes of our grandfathers and great-grandfathers provides us all with a perspective of where we've been — and where we're going.

Velcro is a welcome high-tech fastener for everything from tent flaps to sneakers. But to a deer hunter it can be the item that spoils the day. The sound of a velcro pocket flap being pulled open can alert a deer at 100 yards. Either choose hunting clothes without velcro or sew cloth over those already on your coat or jacket.

Ever stand in a store and scratch your head wondering what length shoelaces are needed to replace the frayed ones on your hunting boots? I have. Here's a way to solve the dilemma. Multiply the number of eyelets on one side of the boot by eight. For example a boot with eight pairs of eyelets will require laces about 64 inches long.

Chapter 3

BIOLOGY and BEHAVIOR

What Every Hunter Should Know About Whitetails

Books could be written about the life of the white-tailed deer.
And hundreds have.
It's no secret that the most successful hunters are also students of the whitetail. They read more than merely "how to" articles and spend the off-season patrolling the deer woods, usually with camera or binocular in hand, unraveling the mysteries of this complex animal.

SCIENTIFIC CLASSIFICATION

The Pennsylvania whitetail is scientifically named *Odocoileus virginianus borealis*, from Greek roots. The genus name, *Odocoileus*, means, "hollow tooth," in reference to the depressions in the crowns of the molars.

The species name *virginianus* is derived from fossils found in caves of Virginia. Hence, the name (once more commonly used) Virginia whitetail.

All whitetails in North and Central America share the scientific name but scientists have further classified them into subspecies, 30 of which range from southern Canada, through most of the U.S. and into Mexico and Central America. Here, and in much of the Northeast, the *borealis* subspecies was originally found. It's considered the largest of the subspecies.

Although it's only occasionally heard today, the *borealis* subspecies is generally known as the "Michigan deer." However, reintroductions of whitetails from other states in the early 1900s, including Michigan, Maine, New Jersey, Ohio, New Hampshire and Kentucky, accounted for the import of both the *virginianus* (same as the species name) and *borealis* subspecies, which are now heavily interbred.

PHYSICAL CHARACTERISTICS

In any talk of deer sizes, only averages apply. Some Pennsylvania bucks exceed 200 pounds and others barely reach 125 pounds. Of course, genetics is one reason for the differences but food is more important. Farm country whitetails with access to crops most of the year — "corn-fed bucks," hunters call them —

The average Pennsylvania buck stands less than three feet tall at the shoulder.

will grow to larger sizes than Northcentral deer which are more highly competitive, subject to severe winters and destined to lesser quality diets.

In Pennsylvania, the average adult buck weighs 140 pounds and stands 32-34 inches at the shoulder. Most hunters, quizzed as to a deer's height, will guess much higher.

Run a tape from nose tip to tail base and a buck will average 70 inches. The tail vertebrae add another 10-12 inches but the long, brown and white tail-hairs make it seem a lot bigger — especially when one runs off following an errant shot.

Of course, deer weights vary with the seasons. At winter's end a buck weighing 135 pounds might well exceed 175 pounds by rutting time.

In summer, deer grow a thin, reddish coat which is shed, hair by hair, and replaced with a darker and heavier coat of hollow, insulating hairs for winter.

Every hunter with more than a couple seasons under his or her belt has learned that deer have excellent eyesight. Flick a hand or move your head and the jig's up. However, as wary as they are, deer seem not to recognize objects that do not move. I've had does as close as 10 feet as I pressed my back against a tree, while dressed in abundant blaze orange.

Unlike us, and many other predators, deers' eyes are located on the sides of the head, angled slightly toward the nose. The placement provides them the ability to see nearly full circle. It's believed a deer can see 310 degrees without moving its head. When focusing on an object both eyes are used, permitting three-dimensional perception.

Despite their excellent eyesight, I've been able to stalk surprisingly close to lone deer feeding in fields and forests. When their noses are on the ground they're focused on feeding. Before lifting the head, they'll usually jerk the tail which is the signal for you to freeze.

If a deer sees you and you don't move, it will often go back to feeding. But if it's even slightly suspicious, it will feign feeding, then quickly jerk its head upward to see if the object of its attention has moved. It's a game deer hunters love to play.

It's standard knowledge that deer see the world in shades of gray. However, recent studies at the University of Georgia and the University of California indicate blue and yellow may stand out vividly to deer while reds and oranges blend with greens, good news to Pennsylvania hunters required to wear at least 250 square inches of the fluorescent color.

No "news" to anyone is that deer have an extraordinarily acute sense of hearing. Like radar antennae, they swivel their cupped ears to catch even the slightest snap of a twig or the scrape of a hand against tree bark.

Whenever a deer's hearing sensitivity is reduced, such as when high winds cut across the woods and fields, they'll become nervous and cautious. Not only is their sound sense and direction adversely affected but they also have a more difficult time locating wind-borne scents.

Which brings us to another subject of near-constant attention by hunters — scent.

SCENT

The white-tailed deer's world of smells is every bit as important as what it sees. More deer have probably been alerted to hunters' presence via their noses than their eyes and ears.

Of course, deer smell not only humans but use their phenomenal scenting abilities to communicate with one another throughout the four seasons. Deers' noses are the sensitive instruments used to pick up every odor—from other deer, predators and humans — carried in the breeze. A buck will also be seen *flehmening* (often improperly called "flaming"), especially during the rut. It stiffens its neck, raises its nose and curls its upper lip, testing the wind. The act traps the molecules of a doe's scent on the epithelial lining of the nostrils and the Jacobsen's organ, located atop the palate, in the mouth. The act is used primarily to detect urine smells and determine whether or not a doe is in estrus.

The next time you have the opportunity to check out a deer close up, spend a few minutes locating the following scent glands, each with a different function.

Interdigital glands

The interdigital glands are located between the hooves of all four feet. Spread the toes on your next kill and look for the small, sparse-haired sac which, to my nose, emits a "sour citrus" smell although others have described it as a "foul, rancid odor." The "cheesy" excretions from the sac aid deer in trailing one another and noting the presence of others in their territories.

The scent evaporates and loses its strength over time, which is why bucks trailing does, or even predators following a deer's trail, can tell about how long in the past it was made.

It's believed that running deer emit more scent than when walking, as the hooves are splayed. It's also been ventured that deer pounding their front feet when disturbed, as when in a face-off with a hunter but not certain what they're looking at, will create a detectable interdigital scent in the air to alert others that something's amiss.

Metatarsal glands

The metatarsal glands are set on the outside of a deer's hind legs, between the feet and knees. They're readily visible as white, oval patches, of hair tufts surrounding the small, hairless pores.

The total function of these glands is the subject of disagreement among biologists. Some believe its purpose is to leave scent on the ground when bedded. Others say its function has nothing to do with scent, rather a method for deer to detect vibrations in the earth from nearby movement.

Tarsal glands

The tarsals are probably the best-known glands among hunters. This is the most important "communication" gland and hunters (bowhunters in particular) should be aware of its location and function.

It's found on the insides of a deer's hind legs, on both bucks and does. The tufts of elongated hairs are readily visible, especially on rutting bucks as they become dark and oily.

Glands beneath the skin are connected to hair follicles which transfer the fatty secretions, called *lactones*, to the hairs. It's believed this is the "fingerprint" of whitetails, individualizing animals as to sex, age and physical condition.

During the rut the frequent urinating over the glands, especially when a buck tends a scrape, individualizes his trademark odor. The same holds true for does, which allow urine to run down their legs at estrus time. Bucks sometimes rub their tarsals together while urinating, performing sort of a mating dance.

The odor from a tarsal gland is enhanced when a deer, buck or doe, becomes excited. Specialized muscles make the hairs stand erect, further releasing scent into the air. It also serves as a visible signal to other deer with which it may be traveling.

The odor of a buck's tarsals is most evident during the rut and I, as many hunters, have experienced a "reverse," of sorts, in being able to smell their presence. On one occasion I located a bow-killed buck in a thicket as the breezes carried the blackened tarsal's scent to my nose.

Proper use of commercial and natural tarsal scents has accounted for both bow and gun-hunter's success in Pennsylvania hunting seasons.

Pre-orbital glands

The pre-orbital gland's secretion is one many hunters have noted but, perhaps, didn't identify as anything more than a deposit at the lower corners of the eyes.

Also called the lacrymal glands, these are tear ducts located in front of the eyes.

Check out a whitetail mount from a skilled taxidermist and the narrow slit below the eyes, where the glands are set, can be readily seen. The yellowish or whitish, waxy secretion is often visible on live deer.

It is believed the pre-orbitals emit scent which bucks will rub on overhanging twigs and ground vegetation.

Forehead glands

Forehead glands are a relatively new find among both biologists and hunters, although their function isn't fully understood. Many hunters have witnessed bucks making rubs, almost always brushing their foreheads against the scarred bark. Limbs, saplings and leaves will also be rubbed similarly.

The skin in the region contains scent glands which often discolor the forehead, staining it dark. Deer visiting a rub will first smell the area, lick it and deposit their own forehead scent. The deer I've watched are seldom in a state of excitement, unlike the aggressive scraping of antlers on a bush or tree, but seem to be carefully and purposely depositing their scent.

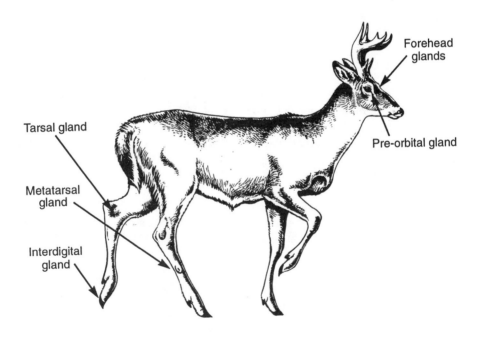

Forehead glands

Pre-orbital gland

Tarsal gland

Metatarsal gland

Interdigital gland

POPULATION DYNAMICS

As evidenced by the phenomenal growth of deer populations in suburbia over the past couple decades, deer are capable of rapidly expanding their ranges and maintaining a high reproduction rate in suitable habitat.

Predation from wolves and mountain lions is a thing of the past and even Pennsylvania's "new wolf," the coyote, seems to have little impact on population control. Hunters, secondly vehicles, are the main limiting factors throughout the state. Add to that winter mortalities, disease, fawn deaths and other accidents.

Currently the Pennsylvania Game Commission is attempting to control deer numbers by establishing density goals in each county (Pennsylvania's version of management units). The desired density goals per square forested mile (see In Brief items in county profiles) is largely controlled by doe license allocations and hunter success rates.

Overpopulation accounts for delayed breeding ages, low fawning rates, fawn mortality, winter losses, low weights and small antler sizes.

WHITETAIL SOCIETY

The whitetail is obviously a social animal, preferring to be in the company of others of its kind. However, like many people, small groups are preferred over large gatherings. In winter feeding areas deer numbers may exceed 100 at one place, largely due to available food.

More common is the "matriarchal" group of a "boss" doe, her fawns of the year and her yearling female offspring. Young bucks go their own ways much earlier than their sisters. Forget the Disney version of a big-racked buck, submissive doe and a couple Bambis napping in the summer woods.

On many occasions several generations stay together in a family group, although they don't necessarily travel together at all times. In May, pregnant does become solitary and later bear, then nurture, their fawns throughout the next few months. By late summer loose family groups again unite.

Bachelor bucks, which travel together summer through early fall, determine hierarchy as the rut period approaches. Simple antler-testing often decides which buck rules and which are sub-dominant. Bucks of near-equal sizes, however, may get into full-fledged donnybrooks, often resulting in injury and, occasionally, death.

HOME RANGE

The ranges of individual whitetails vary from season to season and within the diverse habitats which make up the state. While most Pennsylvania whitetails do not "migrate," studies show long distance movements, as much as 50 miles, during winter in the vast, contiguous tracts of forest composing much of the northern tier.

Smaller shifts in home range, which average 500 to 3,000 acres, are the norm. Rutting bucks and yearling fawns breaking off from their mothers exhibit the greatest range shifts.

FOOD CHOICES

Pick up any hunting magazine devoted to deer and surely you'll find an article or two on scouting and locating feeding areas. Problem is, deer are catholic in their diet choices, consuming a variety of plants.

The wise hunter will pattern these changing food sources and adapt his or her stand or still-hunting locations to what's "ripe" at a particular time of the season.

Deer, like cattle, are grazers. That is, they're adapted to feeding on grasses and herbs and will choose non-woody plants when and where available. But they're also browsing animals, nipping leaves, buds and twigs as the wander, particularly in winter.

Clearcuts are prime examples of good whitetail country where the most varied menu is available. Seedlings and newfound, sun-loving plants on the forest floor entice deer from the deep forest and offer excellent places to hunt.

Grasses make up much of the spring diet followed by herbaceous plants (forbs) in summer and mast and fruits in fall. Winter brings a natural reduction in food intake with grasses, forbs, honeysuckle and other browse which hold leaves late into the year. Woody browse is sought when snows prevent grazing. In agricultural regions, corn, alfalfa, winter wheat and other crops are tapped, as they are throughout the growing season.

Like humans, deer become selective when a variety of foods are available. They make choices from whatever menu's at hand, although not all deer have a wide choice of entrees. Succulent plants are preferred over hardened vegetation, although a Penn State study revealed that woody stems make up about one-fifth of the whitetail's diet throughout the year.

Of course, every hunter knows the beginning of bow season brings whitetails to oak ridges like hummingbirds to sugarwater. All acorns are consumed but deer show a decided preference for the sweeter white oak. Other commonly consumed carbohydrate and protein-rich mast and fruits include apples, beechnuts, blackberries, blueberries, cherries, dogwood, persimmon, hickory nuts, grapes and pears, among others.

At best, deer are opportunists with a taste for a wide variety of foods. Some, such as red maple, offer better nutrition and are more widely utilized than rhododendron or other foods eaten when food is scarce and competition high.

A cooperative Penn State-Pennsylvania Game Commission study yielded the following plants found in stomach content samples of wild whitetails. Some, of course, showed up more abundantly than others. But they're all part of the Pennsylvania whitetail's diet.

If you stumble when walking and your shotgun or rifle dips into the mud or snow, never continue without first checking the barrel for blockage. Unload the the gun and work a thin twig through the muzzle until you're certain all's clear. Not doing so could result in a splintered barrel and serious injury.

Woody Plants

Apple	Grape	Pitch pine
Arborvitae	Gray dogwood	Privet
Ash	Greenbriar	Red oak
Aspen	Hawthorn	Red cedar
Beech	Hazelnut	Red maple
Birch	Hemloc	Rhododendron
Blackberry	Hickory	Rose
Black cherry	Honeysuckle	Sassafras
Black locust	Jackpine	Spruce
Blue beech	Juneberry	Sugar maple
Blueberry	Larch	Sumac
Cherry	Mountain laurel	Sweetfern
Chestnut oak	Mulberry	Teaberry
Coralberry	Oak	Tulip poplar
Crabapple	Orange	Virginia creeper
Deerberry	Partridge berry	White pine
Dogwood	Pear	Willow
Elderberry	Persimmon	Witch hazel
Elm	Pine	

Non-woody Plants

Aster	Ground cherry	Sheep sorrel
Bellwort	Indian pipe	Speedwell
Canada Mayflower	Liverwort	Spikenard
Cinquefoil	Mayapple	Spring beauty
Club moss	Milkweed	Trefoil
Cohash	Panic grass	Violet
Crown vetch	Plantain	Wild geranium
Dandelion	Pokeweed	Wild mustard
Goldenrod	Ragwort	

Commercial Crops

Alfalfa	Clover	Soybean
Apple	Corn	Strawberry
Bean	Lettuce	Timothy
Cabbage	Oats	Tomato
Cantaloupe	Potato	Wheat
Carrot	Rye	

Deer begin raiding cornfields
long before bow season.

The sweet white oak acorn is the
whitetail's favorite.

Fawns are born following a 200 to 205 day gestation.

REPRODUCTION

Yearling bucks will depart their mother's home range in September, acting like their fathers and other older bucks during the rut. Pennsylvania bucks become sexually mature their first fall and sexually active at 18 months but many fail to breed during their first year due to competition from older bucks. Some doe fawns will go into their first estrus period at seven or eight months and, if bred during the post-rut, produce fawns in mid-to-late summer the following year.

The age and health of a doe determines her reproductive capacity. Simply, does living in prime habitat produce more fawns than those in poor range. As a doe matures she stands a better chance of bearing twins or even triplets. According to Game Commission studies, young does will produce a larger percentage of male fawns than do older does.

Bucks are ready to mate in October but it's the doe who determines the exact time. Bucks regularly tend small groups of does in November, chasing after them relentlessly. Hunters sometimes interpret this as watching a doe "in heat" when she's actually fleeing the buck because she's not yet in estrus. As the estrus period, which lasts only 24 hours, approaches, bucks will stick tightly to them.

Following breeding the buck will often stay with the doe for several hours and more. Then he moves on to seek other receptive females, rogue that he is.

The gestation period is typically 200 to 205 days. Considering the mid-November peak of the rut, most births occur at the end of May and beginning of June. But some are born earlier and others later.

Does unbred during their short receptive period will again come into estrus 28 days later. Fawns resulting from such matings are born later in summer than the norm. On rare occasion, as I experienced in Bradford County on the gun season opener in 1989, spotted fawns will be seen well into fall.

Although few people ever witness it, fawn mortalities can be quite high. Besides accidents and predation from bobcats, coyotes and free-running dogs, does stressed by the rigors of winter enter the spring in poor condition and will give birth to fawns weighing less than the typical five to seven pounds. Small, weak fawns may not be able to stand and nurse or nutritionally-stressed does may not produce sufficient, butterfat-rich milk. If a deer is weak and malnourished in winter, the embryos may be resorbed, a natural "abortion," of sorts.

ANTLERS

The sizes and general shapes of antlers depend upon two factors — heredity and diet.

Even a buck with the genetic potential to produce a heavy 10-point rack won't have much more than a scraggly adornment if it can't find nutritious foods — especially those rich in phosphorous and calcium. For a trophy to grow a big, heavy rack it needs both the hereditary traits and the right foods. Often soil is the determining factor in an area's reputation for big-racked bucks. In my Lehigh Valley homeland, for instance, there's prime limestone soil for producing big antler growth.

Genetically deficient bucks, no matter how well fed, simply can't produce trophy-size antlers.

The soft, fuzzy covering on bucks' antlers from spring through the start of September is composed of live, sensitive skin with rich supplies of blood vessels throughout. Should a deer somehow injure the velvet it will bleed, as would an injury to any other part of the body.

While bucks may charge through thickets in fall, in summer I've watched them move cautiously through thickets, taking special care not to tangle the sensitive velvet in briars or hit them against saplings.

One writer adequately described the summer buck as being "as cautious as a matron with a new hairdo."

By early August the fast-growing antlers are large and the size and shape of the mature rack can be foretold. By the end of the first week of September a buck's rising testosterone level causes the velvet to die and dry, peeling off in strips. The chore may be performed in 24-48 hours when aided by rubbing the rack on shrubs, bushes and trees.

I've been privileged to observe whitetails with long, bloody strands dangling from the antlers one day and the next day the same animal was seen with nary a trace of velvet.

I've also listened to hunters discuss the phenomenon, claiming the peeling velvet (like the chapping skin following a sunburn) becomes itchy and bothersome although I've never bought this reasoning. As the skin is dead and nerve endings have been severed, there's no way a buck can feel the dead velvet.

My guess is the hanging strands are simply bothersome and the buck will remove it the only way it can, by rubbing against something. These early rubs are not to be confused with the aggressive rubbing on trees and low-hanging branches later in the season, as the rut approaches.

Freshly-peeled antlers are white but with subsequent rubbings they become stained, sometimes turning dark brown and a few, which may pick up tannic acid stains, approaching a brownish-black by November. Lthers retain their tan color.

When the blood in the vessels no longer flows, the antlers no longer grow. What you see then is what you get in the hunting seasons -- with a bit of good fortune, of course.

It's usually not until a buck's second summer that spikes appear. In its first year, as a fawn, it will be a "button buck." Bumps on the head of a small, antlerless deer sneaking by your stand reveals its sex. Often such deer will be in the company of others, probably siblings and its mother. Research shows that a deer with all the elements going for him can produce an initial rack of 4-8 points.

Not surprisingly, people who don't hunt or aren't otherwise exposed to wildlife harbor fallacies about antlers. Time and again I hear references to the number of points on a deer's rack being an indicator of its age — like rings on a tree. Of course, that's untrue.

Some hunters continue to harbor the old belief that antler loss is caused by freezing weather. If that were true, few Pennsylvania bucks would still be holding their headgear by the end of the buck season

The pituitary gland is the control mechanism that starts antler growth in spring and puts a stop to it in the early fall, causing the velvet-covered bones to solidify and lose the soft blood-rich outer covering. The gland's activity is stimulated by the amount of daylight hours. Once the fall breeding season is over the decreased activity of the pituitary gland, triggered by the diminishing number of daylight hours, causes a drop in the buck's testosterone level. At this time a layer of cells at the pedicle (where antlers join the skull) begins to dissolve into granular form.

According to Leonard Lee Rue III, who has probably written more about deer than any other author, the granulation process is phenomenally rapid. In his book, *The Deer of North America*, Rue writes: "One day the buck's antlers are so solid they could not be broken off if you hit them with a pipe. The next day, after granulation sets in, one or both antlers may drop off by themselves."

On occasion, a deer will be seen or shot that has an unusual antler formation. Tines droop over the eyes, moose-like palms appear or a maze of tangles create a truly unique rack. This sometimes happens when an antler is damaged while still in the velvet stage, as growth is occurring.

Not all non-typical bucks have been subject to antler damage, however. In fact, most non-typicals receive their genes from parents with the code for such racks in their ancestry (does included). As with all rack shapes, genetics plays an important role, with genes from the doe as well as the buck influencing antler structure. Although does don't typically grow "horns," they do have a genetic effect on the sizes and shapes of their son's racks.

Like Samson, a buck's personality changes abruptly when it loses its head adornment. Starting in December for some and stretching as late as March and even early April for others, the granulation process will occur and in a moment the stag that ruled the woodlot will be just another "bald" whitetail. Its aggressiveness will diminish along with the weight on its brow. It will not produce testosterone until new antler growth begins, reaching the peak level of testicular activity in fall.

| Blood-rich velvet nourishes antlers in spring and summer. | The amount of daylight, not temperature, triggers antler loss. |

ANOMALIES

In any wildlife species anomalies — deviations from the norm — occur. Whitetails are no exception.

Every once in a while a hunter will harvest an antlered deer, then discover he or she has shot a doe. At one time a Game Commission biologist estimated that one of every 18,000 antlered whitetails were females. Additional studies indicate the frequency of "rack does" may be as common as one in 2,500-4,000.

Deer color has also been an object of interest among hunters for centuries, particularly white deer. Albino animals lack natural pigments, showing pink eyes as no coloration masks the blood in the eyes. Studies show albinos are ill-equipped for long-term survival with poor eyesight a side effect.

Some white deer are not truly albinos, rather mutations. They're normal in all ways, including black noses, dark hooves and brown eyes.

More common in Pennsylvania are piebald deer, sometimes called "calico deer." Splotches of varying degrees of white throughout the body are taken by hunters each year.

On occasion the opposite of albinism occurs. "Melanism" causes the pelage to be totally black. Although rare, the production of melanin, the pigment causing dark color in black squirrels and other species, is over-produced in such animals.

This buck is not a true albino. Note that its eyes and nose are of normal color.

Chapter
4

DOE HUNTING
and
DEER MANAGEMENT
Back To The Future

When I was a kid, whetting my appetite and interest in deer hunting, I'd listen closely as my father, uncle and their friends argued over whether or not does should be legal game.

Those opposed (and most were opposed in the 1950s, as I recall) claimed that for every doe killed the following year's population is reduced by three. One doe + two fawns = three deer, they reasoned.

Others (the minority, as I recall) countered that deer in the "big woods" country to which they traveled each year for buck season could not live with too much competition, especially in severe winters when the snowmelt brought rotting carcasses in every spring seep in the northern tier.

My hometown then, only a couple miles from where I live today in southeastern Pennsylvania, had only scatterings of deer. They weren't rare by any means but surely not as common as today. The sighting of a big buck, any buck, brought plenty of chatter at the country store or the local taproom and before long everyone knew "Homer saw a big 8-pointer cross Limeport Pike last night."

Then, harvesting antlerless deer in the farmland and woodlot region might well have been counterproductive. Today, of course, all that has changed with not enough hunters having access to far too many deer.

In the spring of 1994, following the infamous snow and cold in which an estimated 20,000 deer succumbed, testimony from sportsmen's groups at a Game Commission meeting also focused on doe harvests. Some called for a reduction of doe licenses in portions of the Northcentral Region. The Unified Sportsmen of Pennsylvania asked for more; they urged commissioners to suspend the doe season in parts of the commonwealth where deer numbers were down.

That was countered by a wildlife biologist from International Paper Company asking the agency to restore allocation numbers (which were targeted for reduction over previous years) in several northern counties. He was supported

**More than 20 deer per square mile of forest will have
detrimental effects on the food base.**

by David deCalesta, research biologist for the U.S. Forest Service in Warren County, who argued that "once deer get above 20 per square mile they begin to destroy their food base and begin to starve to death."

"If antlerless season is dropped, just for one year as many hunters have asked, the deer herd will soar from 1.1 million deer pre-season to about 1.6 million," said deCalesta.

Pennsylvania Farm Bureau spokesman Mel Eckhaus voiced similar opposition to any doe license reduction, stating that such a move "would devastate farmers."

At the same meeting, representatives from the Pittsburgh and Philadelphia areas urged the commission to work with them to reduce deer numbers in the suburbs. One request suggested a year-around season to placate the homeowners whose losses of ornamental shrubs and garden plants, as well as the increased chances for vehicle collisions with deer, are intolerable.

If farm and forest interests have a problem, consider that related by David Robertson of the Pennypack Ecological Restoration Trust in Montgomery County.

"Our trust lands have about 150 deer per square mile and zero forest regeneration," he told the commissioners. "We need both new programs for urban deer and immediate increases in the number of antlerless licenses."

What happened? After considering all testimony, including that of commission biologists, commissioners increased 1994 doe license numbers by 32,000.

The point of all this is that wildlife management through the ages has become a highly complex, scientific and sociological issue. Yet, the conflict "caused" by does, specifically how many should be targeted each year, remains a Pennsylvania "tradition."

But today simply being against or for shooting does is no longer the major issue. Rather, how and how many does should be taken annually is at the core of discussions.

The commission continues to hone scientific deer density goals in each county based on the amount of forested acreage, forest type (seedling, pole timber, saw timber and non-commercial lands) and current estimated deer numbers. Doe tag allocations in each county are then based on whether or not it is desirable for a population to increase, decrease or remain steady. Instituting new management techniques has yielded high doe harvests statewide.

Of course, bringing down doe numbers in most parts of the state wouldn't have been possible without some major changes — the bonus for the sportsman being liberalized hunting opportunities.

The 1993-1994 season saw a major change in the utilization of doe licenses, one that brought about increased harvests without raising allocation numbers dramatically. That's when all hunters drawing doe tags were permitted to use them in any season in which antlerless deer are legal. Previously, regular doe tags (purchased in the initial application period) became invalid when a hunter shot a buck. Under the new system, in which a successful applicant is given a separate ear tag for a doe, shooting a buck no longer invalidates the permit.

Also, beginning in 1993, licenses were issued in August for the first time, making it possible for the growing number of bowhunters (more than 317,000 in 1993) to tag both a buck and doe (with a the county tag in possession).

In the first year of the program archery doe harvests jumped from 6,827 to 26,816. Total bow and gun harvests ballooned 23 percent from 198,065 to 243,343 The figure includes kills tagged with regular, first bonus and second bonus permits.

The winter of 1993-1994 accounted for a mortality of more than 20,000 deer although most made it through in good condition.

Liberalized doe hunting opportunities began with bonus permits in 1988.

"We're pleased to see that the program had an impact on increasing deer harvests in some of the problem areas where actual density numbers are well above habitat carrying capacity," said Bill Shope, a Game Commission deer biologist.

In addition, a Deer Damage Area program which opened more than 107,000 acres of private farmlands to the public was continued. While somewhat successful, posted lands adjacent to deer-ravaged croplands made it difficult for hunters to locate deer in the late winter hunts.

A pilot program for drawing hunters to these lands was extended statewide in 1994. There, a hunter holding a valid county doe tag is now permitted to harvest a doe in addition to a buck during the two-week gun season.

Farmers suffering economic losses are encouraging the commission to provide them with depredation permits for additional deer removal. Add to that suburban townships which may now apply for permits to shoot deer any day of the year by a small core of certified hunters.

Is the program to move deer numbers toward carrying capacity working?

Cal DuBrock, chief of the commission's Bureau of Wildlife Management, believes it is.

"Many folks perceive fewer deer but there are still a lot of deer out there," said DuBrock. "The program is working."

The winter of 1993-1994 didn't cause excessive mortalities because "deer numbers were closer to the goal entering winter and were able to survive" due to lack of competition for available food, DuBrock said.

"I believe we have been underestimating the number of deer in the state," DuBrock added. "Our doe kill last year (1993) was 13 percent over our projection."

Farmers and foresters generally agree with DuBrock. Many hunters don't. Others continue to argue that county management units should be expanded to units linked by land use and ecological similarities.

Which brings us back to the scenario at the top of this chapter; that on-going controversies over doe hunting haven't really changed all that much. Today the numbers are different as are the rules, and sociological influences as well as biological decisions enter the equation.

The argument over doe hunting goes on and will probably continue to do so as long as 1.1 million men, women and kids head to the deer woods each fall.

Some things just don't change.

Contrary to the belief of some rifle hunters, the path of a bullet never rises above the line of the barrel, or bore. But it does rise above the shooter's line of sight as both open sights and scopes are adjusted to allow for a bullet's natural drop, or trajectory. Blame the confusion on drawings showing a bullet "rising" through the shooter's sight line. Actually the barrel is tipped slightly upward which accounts for a bullet crossing the line of sight about 25 yards away, then dropping back through the line of sight as gravity pulls it downward anywhere from 50-300 yards away, whichever distance the hunter chooses to be "sighted in."

In most hunting calibers, a bullet will print at 25 yards at approximately the same spot it will hit a target 220-230 yards down range.

Bucks maintain strong ties throughout most of the year, except during the rut. Often they rub against and preen one another in a non-sexual way, in a sort of male bonding behavior.

The hair on deer grows backward in all places except the brisket, where it grows forward.

Chapter
5

IT'S THE LAW
Deer Hunting's Rules and Regulations

Having hunted waterfowl, upland birds, deer and other big game in 26 states over the past couple decades, I've learned one important facet of pre-hunt preparation — to do my homework.

Game laws vary dramatically from state to state as do license costs, season dates and the many rules and regulations within game laws. In recent years the Pennsylvania Game Law has become increasingly complex. In my job as outdoors editor of a major eastern Pennsylvania newspaper, I receive several hundred calls annually about everything from doe licenses to whether coyotes may be hunted during the deer season or the legality of spotlighting deer during the archery season.

Many of these questions are answered in this chapter.

It's the hunter's responsibility to learn game laws before setting foot in the field. Ignorance of the law isn't a valid excuse for infractions, although it is frustrating when a hunter believes he or she has operated legally only to find that a law has been broken.

Following is a brief guide to varied aspects of Pennsylvania deer hunting of which sportsmen should be aware.

Hunting seasons

Although dates change from year to year, deer seasons in Pennsylvania are typically scheduled as follows:

* Archery season begins the first Saturday in October.
* Buck season starts the first Monday after Thanksgiving and runs an additional 11 days, Sundays excluded, ending on a Saturday.
* Antlerless deer season typically runs for three days, beginning the Monday after the close of buck season.
* The late archery-flintlock season begins the first legal hunting day after Christmas and runs through mid-January.

* The special season on Deer Damage Areas begins with the late bow-muzzleloader season and continues approximately a week longer.
* Legal shooting hours are from one-half hour before sunrise to sunset.

License costs

Licenses (with exceptions as noted) are available from local issuing agents, county treasurers, the six regional Pennsylvania Game Commission offices and the main office in Harrisburg. Or they can be purchased by mail (on proper forms) through the Pennsylvania Game Commission, License Div., 2001 Elmerton Ave., Harrisburg, PA 17110-9797 for the cost of the license desired plus $1. Call (717) 787-4250.

Resident Junior	Ages 12-16	$ 5.75
Resident Adult	Ages 17-64	$12.75
Resident Senior	Ages 65 and older	$10.75
Senior Lifetime Resident	Ages 65 and older	$50.75
Nonresident Adult	Ages 17 and older	$80.75
Nonresident Junior	Ages 12-16	$40.75
Archery Permit	All ages	$ 5.75
Muzzleloader Permit	All ages)	$ 5.75

*Muzzleloader firearms and/or bows and arrows may be used during the regular firearms season without muzzleloader and/or archery licenses.

*Senior Resident and Lifetime licenses are available to hunters who will turn 65 by December 31 of the license year. They're available only through commission offices.

*Licenses are valid from July 1 to the following June 30th, inclusive. They must be worn, clearly visible, on the middle of the back.

*A resident applicant must show satisfactory proof of residency, such as a valid driver's license, when applying for a hunting license. A Hunter Education Card or license from a previous year must also be shown.

Antlerless deer licenses

All hunters wishing to hunt antlerless deer must possess county permits. The initial application period for such licenses begins, by mail only, the first Monday in August. Bonus tags (leftover doe licenses) are sold later, traditionally two weeks after the initial application date for "first bonus" licenses and an additional two weeks later for "second bonus" tags. Non-residents may apply for doe licenses beginning with the second application period.

Each doe permit consists of a license to be displayed on the back and an ear tag and harvest report card.

The exception is muzzleloader hunters who must relinquish their doe license applications (issued to others when the regular license is purchased) when a muzzleloader stamp is purchased. Muzzleloader stamps must be bought prior to the day before doe permits go on sale.

The trade-off is that muzzleloader hunters with unfilled regular (buck) tags may hunt antlerless deer in any county but must tag their kills using the unfilled tag on the regular license. Blackpowder hunters may apply for bonus licenses, however.

Bonus permit applications are contained in the digest accompanying the sale of all regular licenses. Bonus tags permit a properly licensed person to take additional antlerless deer during any season in which does are legal game.

Antlerless deer licenses ($5.75) are available only through county treasurers' offices. The exception is Philadelphia and Potter counties, for which the respective regional offices handle the application process.

*Applications must be sent in the official pink envelopes issued by license issuing agents. All others will be rejected.

Landowner licenses

An eligible landowner who owns 80 or more contiguous acres open to public hunting in a cooperative access program with the Pennsylvania Game Commission, or an immediate family member living in the same household, is entitled to a Landowner Hunting License.

Eligible owners of 50 contiguous acres or more are also entitled to one antlerless deer license at the regular fee.

First-time hunters are required to complete a Hunter Education Course.

Junior licenses

Persons under 17 must present a written request to the license issuing agent, signed by a parent or legal guardian. Eleven-year-olds who have successfully completed a Hunter Education Course may apply for licenses if they will turn 12 by December 31 of the license year. The legal hunting age is 12, however.

Youth ages 12-13 must be accompanied by an adult (18 or over) member of the family or by a person serving in place of the parent. Youngsters 14-15 must be accompanied by any adult age 18 or older. Adults "must be close enough that verbal guidance can be easily understood" while afield, according to Game Law.

Hunters 16 or older may hunt alone.

Replacement licenses

If a license is lost, a replacement may be purchased by application to any issuing agent (preferably by the agent from whom the original license was purchased) or at any Game Commission office. Cost is $5.75.

Lost doe licenses can only be replaced (at original purchase cost) by county treasurers who issued the original tag.

Hunter Education Courses

A person who has not held a hunting license lawfully issued in this Commonwealth or another state or nation or does not possess a certificate of training shall be required to attain accreditation in a Hunter/Trapper Education Course before a hunting license is issued. Regardless of age, persons who have not previously owned hunting licenses must take and successfully pass the 10-hour course. Such courses are offered throughout the state, usually by local sportsmen's clubs, by trained instructors. Most sessions are scheduled from spring through fall. Check local newspapers for course offerings or call the toll-free numbers of any of the six regional offices for information.

Handguns

A Sportsman's Firearm Permit or a license to carry a firearm is required to carry a handgun, concealed or in a motor vehicle, while hunting in Pennsylvania. The latter licenses are issued by county sheriffs or chiefs of police. Applicants are required to appear in person to obtain authorization to carry a handgun.

The Sportsman's Firearms Permit is issued only by county treasurers. The permit does not permit the carrying of a loaded handgun in a vehicle nor to carry it at any other time than while hunting or traveling to or from a target range.

Carrying a loaded handgun while spotlighting or after having taken the lawful deer limit is prohibited.

Safety orange

Anyone hunting deer during the regular firearms seasons for deer must wear at least 250 square inches of fluorescent orange material on the head, chest and back combined. Bowhunters must wear an equal amount of the safety material during the latter two weeks of the fall archery season, when small game hunters are afield.

Jeff Heller of Kuhnsville was dressed head-to-ankle in camo-orange when he filled his Columbia County doe tags. The minimum hunter orange requirement is 250-square inches.

Safety zones

It is unlawful to hunt within 150 yards of any occupied residence, camp, industrial or commercial building, farm house or farm building, school or playground without the permission of the occupants. This provision applies across property lines. While many lands open to hunting are posted with Safety Zone signs, their absence does not suggest the distance law does not apply.

Possession of road-killed deer

Pennsylvania residents may possess deer killed by motor vehicles at any time of the year. A permit must be secured from the Game Commission within 24 hours after taking possession of the deer.

Firearms and vehicles

It is illegal to hunt from a vehicle, shoot at deer on a public road or right-of-way open to public travel, shoot across a road (unless the line of fire is high enough to preclude any danger) or alight from a vehicle to shoot, unless the shooter is at least 25 yards from the road.

Live ammunition in the chamber or attached magazine is illegal in any vehicle, parked or moving. Nor can a loaded gun be propped against or rested on a vehicle.

For the purpose of transportation, muzzleloaders are considered unloaded when all powder is removed from the flash pan or the percussion cap has been removed from the nipple.

Spotlighting

Spotlighting deer is a popular recreational activity throughout much of the state. It is permitted until 11 p.m. each day throughout the year except during the regular buck and doe seasons. It is unlawful to spot deer while in possession of a bow-and-arrow or firearm.

Also, casting the rays of a beam onto any building or farm animal is illegal.

Bait hunting

While legal in some states, baiting is outlawed in Pennsylvania. Such an infraction carries a fine and court costs plus loss of hunting privileges for one year if game is not killed and two years if a kill is made. Artificial or natural baits include hay, grain, fruit, nuts, salt, chemicals, minerals or other items deemed edible attractants.

In addition, hunting is not permitted on areas in which "baits" or supplemental foods had been placed 30 days previous.

Scents and lures

Up until the early 1990s the Game Law, strictly interpreted, made it illegal for hunters to use natural or artificial scents or lures (food, estrus, urine or other scents) while hunting, although the law was never rigidly enforced.

The fine line between scent-use and baiting had hunters in a quandary for a time. However, the commission has since clarified the law, making it legal to use scents while hunting.

Damage from treestands

Hunters using portable or permanent treestands are breaking the law if, on public or private property, trees are damaged while constructing or using a stand or climbing device. The law goes so far as using or "occupying" a treestand (which someone else may have placed) which has damaged a tree.

This law does not apply to landowners building or otherwise using treestands on their own properties or others who have received written permission to use or construct treestands.

Mistaken kill

Any person who mistakenly kills a deer (shooting a doe during buck season, for example) shall immediately remove the entrails and deliver the carcass to a Game Commission officer in the county where it was killed. Deer must be tagged before removal from the area where taken. For turning in the mistaken kill, the hunter will be permitted to pay only a portion of the established fine for the infraction, at the Wildlife Conservation Officer's discretion.

Special Regulations Areas

All of Allegheny County in southwestern Pennsylvania and Bucks, Chester, Delaware, Montgomery and Philadelphia counties in the Southeast are designated Special Regulations Areas.

Rifles are not permitted here although muzzleloaders, manual or semi-automatic shotguns 20 gauge or larger loaded with buckshot or slugs and bows-and-arrows may be used. Bowhunting-only is permitted in Philadelphia County and buckshot may not be used in Allegheny County.

In recent years, gun seasons in these counties have been very liberal. For example, in 1994 the deer seasons ran from November 28-December 17 and December 26 to January 21 with required antlerless licenses. Antlerless deer (with valid county doe permits) may be taken throughout all deer seasons, including the two-week buck season.

Hunters may purchase up to four bonus doe licenses for these counties, unless other licenses are held for counties outside the special areas. Only one application may be sent in the initial (early August) application period and only one bonus license application may be sent two weeks later. However, beginning in early September (dates vary from year to year) hunters may buy, over-counter or by mail, extra licenses.

Deer Damage Areas

Beginning the day after Christmas (except Sundays) and running through the third week of January, designated properties throughout the state registered with the Game Commission are open for antlerless deer.

Hunters are required to have valid county doe permits to hunt these lands. The lands are posted with special green signs.

Lists of cooperating landowners are available by sending a self-addressed, stamped envelope to the regional office in which the county is located. Request only locations of participating farms in the specific county or counties which will be hunted.

Legal bucks/does

Bucks are legal game as long as they hold two or more points on one antler or have a spike at least three inches long.

"Antlerless" deer are defined as having no antlers or one or two antlers less than three inches in length.

Camp rosters

It is unlawful to hunt deer in groups of 25 or more persons.

If five or more hunters from a permanent camp cooperate to drive deer, they must maintain a roster in duplicate. The drive leader must carry one copy and another must be posted at headquarters and remain displayed for 30 days following the close of the season.

The roster must include license year, name of camp or hunting party, location, township, county, name of each party member and hunting license number, firearms caliber and for all game harvested, the date, weight, number of points (if applicable) and dates of arrival and departure.

Persons participating in drives or in any way aiding another licensed hunter, junior or senior, must have a valid Pennsylvania hunting license. A person driving deer for another person during the antlerless deer season must also have an antlerless deer permit for that county.

Any person who has harvested a deer may continue to take part in the hunt as long as he or she does not carry a loaded firearm or bow with a nocked arrow.

Tagging, transporting and reporting

Deer must be tagged immediately after harvest and before the carcass is moved. Tags attached to buck (regular license) and doe licenses must be filled out according to instructions on the tags and attached to the ear of the animal. It must remain attached until processed and when taken to a taxidermist.

The tag must be attached while transporting the carcass, although unmarked parts of deer carcasses need not be tagged.

Issued with each license is a big game harvest report card which must be completed and sent to the Game Commission within 10 days after the harvest. A photocopy may be used.

Pennsylvania hunters are notorious for their non-reporting of harvests, hampering deer management efforts by agency biologists who must calculate estimated buck and doe kills each year. Reporting rates are only about 50 percent.

Coyotes and foxes

Coyotes may be hunted during the regular antlered and antlerless deer seasons as long as hunters hold a valid license with an unused deer tag. It is not legal to hunt coyotes during these seasons if deer tags have been utilized.

A furtaker's license is not needed to hunt coyotes although it is needed to hunt foxes. However, it is not legal to hunt foxes during the hours in which deer may be legally hunted.

Wayne Pocius' Bradford County buck with its ear tag in place.

The coyote today inhabits every Pennsylvania county and may be taken during the deer season.

The white-tailed deer is the carrier of brainworm, a minuscule parasite acquired by eating vegetation on which small slugs and snails are present. The parasite is then passed on through a deer's feces. While the brainworm is fatal to elk, moose and mule deer, it's seldom fatal to whitetails.

Two to five year old clearcuts offer excellent whitetail habitat, especially during the hunting seasons. Not only do they have a good supply of grasses, forbs and browse but deer are more difficult to see in the thick growth, thereby holding them when hunters are prowling the surrounding forest. If you find a standing tree amid a clearcut, install a portable stand. It could prove to be an untapped hotspot.

Carrying a video camera along on deer hunts is becoming as popular as taking snapshots back at camp. For some hunters in one-deer states, it stretches the hunting time whenever a friend is accompanied and the happenings are recorded on tape. The biggest annoyance in watching such videos is shaky camera movement. For $40-$50, a video tripod with a "floating" head can be purchased. It's the most important accessory for recording those memorable times without triggering "motion sickness" in the eventual audience.

It's not necessary to cut the scent glands from a deer's legs after it's been killed. There's no way the glands can come in contact with the venison and even if it happens somehow, the lack of blood flow in the meat will prevent it from imparting any disagreeable taste to a steak or roast.

Fancy putting your favorite deer hunting story into words and trying to have it published? Or would you like to put together an interesting video to show your hunting friends. Or write and self-publish and outdoor book? This and more is detailed in "Selling the Outdoor Story" -- A unique, 371-page handbook written by 52 of the country's best-known outdoor writers. How to write and sell articles, books, photos, videos, radio and TV shows and more fill its pages. Get it for $15 postpaid from: OWAA, 2017 Cato Ave., Suite 101, State College, PA 16801.

PART
II
GETTING STARTED
Bullet, Ball and Bow

Chapter
6

THE RIGHT STUFF
Getting Started Bowhunting

Since 1986 an additional 50,000 Pennsylvania bowhunters have joined the ranks of modern-day Robin Hoods.

At last count more than 317,000 bowhunters purchased the $5.75 tags in Pennsylvania, topping any other state in archery interest and participation. And don't think the bowhunting industry hasn't noticed. Archers bring a steady supply of business for the many stores and shops in the Keystone State dealing in bows and related paraphernalia.

Not only are thousands of new hunters taking up the bow every season but "oldtimers" are updating their gear, yet another boost for the bow-and-arrow industry, all of which know the importance of getting their products in the hands of Pennsylvania's archers.

Thirty years ago picking a bowhunting outfit presented few questions. Choices were meager. Dealers who knew what they were doing were few and scattered. But not today. Now more gear than ever fills the walls of sporting goods stores and the pages of outdoor catalogs, presenting most novices with a head-scratching dilemma.

Most important in any archery shopping spree is getting valid advice on choosing "the right stuff." The wrong match of bows and arrows or sights and releases has led more than one newcomer down the path of despair.

So you want to be a bowhunter?

Where do you start?

Sherwood Schoch of Reading first recommends going to the people who are not only in the business of selling but also know their products and how to use them. Specifically, he advises visiting an archery pro shop.

"More manufacturers are training their people today than ever before," said Schoch, owner of a well-known archery equipment distributorship in Reading. "We go into the stores for training sessions so that our dealers know how to use the equipment on their shelves. We consider good education every bit as

Rudy Blomstrom checks the draw length and anchor point of a fledgling archer.

important as selling a good product."

"A pro shop includes information and education with its product," said Schoch. "You don't get that with every store just because they sell bows and arrows. It may cost a little more at a pro shop but the service and advice you get with it is invaluable."

Studying and handling a selection of rifles before making a choice is a relatively basic operation, but not so with bows.

My personal mentor years back, Rudy Blomstrom, was a pro shop owner in Bethlehem who took me under wing from the initial measuring for draw length to choosing the proper arrows and sighting in and refining my gear. Included in the "deal" were a couple hundred shots over a period of weeks at the 20-yard range in the shop's basement.

When I decided to change sights, he took back my unscarred purchase and credited it toward another. You won't get that kind of service at the X-Mart.

"All good bow shops have indoor or outdoor ranges of one kind or another to give the buyer a chance to shoot the bow," said Schoch. "There are so many errors the new shooter can make — from getting a bow with the wrong draw length to getting disgusted because he can't make an arrow fly straight simply because he's using the wrong grip."

If you can shoot a bow before buying it, under the tutelage of a knowledgeable salesman, you're half way home, Schoch believes.

Consider that one compound bow may have three variations of draw lengths, a half-dozen different wheel sizes and several grip shapes or arrow rest designs. Learning which combination is for you comes with experience — the experience of a bow shop staff person.

Dick Weaknecht of Weaknecht's Archery in Kutztown knows the business well. With sons Rick and Jim, he's run his Berks County specialty shop and mail order business for over 30 years.

"People who come in here today are a whole lot better educated about equipment than ever," Weaknecht mused. "There's so much more available today to learn about bowhunting but there's also a whole lot more to learn about."

"If there's one bit of advice I can give it's that anyone investing in equipment for the first time should decide how much he or she has to spend," Weaknecht suggests. "If I know someone can only bankroll a Ford Escort I'm not going to try to sell him a Lincoln Continental."

There's nothing wrong with inexpensive bows, Weaknecht assures, agreeing with Schoch that today's choices and their quality far surpass the selections of just a few years ago.

Visiting bow clubs, many of which shoot paper target or 3-D ranges practically every weekend, is another good way to familiarize yourself with the variety of gear on the market. Most shooters are friendly and willing to answer any questions you may have.

So where does a new convert to archery begin? What's in store for the person who's done his or her window-shopping and is now ready for the first step into the bow season?

Follow these 10 "Shopping tips" from Schoch and Weaknecht.

Dick Weaknecht helps a young bowhunter choose the "right stuff." Archery pro shops, such as Weaknecht's, are scattered across the state.

(1) Have a reliable person measure your draw length. This is the distance from the bottom of the arrow nock to the front of the bow when the arrow is drawn. About three-fourths of an inch is added to permit broadhead clearance at full draw.

(2) Buy the best you can afford. Today's "low end" bow line is far better than the "high end" was just 10 years ago. Set a limit as to what you can spend for a bow and add some extra for other necessities. Don't be embarrassed to admit your billfold holds $200 and not $500.

(3) Test several bows at the pro shop range to determine that subjective feature of "feel and comfort." Your most comfortable draw weight will be established at this time. All compounds can be adjusted in a range of 10-15 pounds. Start with a comfortable draw weight and work up to greater weights as your muscles develop. If you don't want to tackle the job of readjusting the bow when necessary, take it back to the pro shop from which it was purchased. It only takes a few minutes to do the job.

(4) Stick with prominent brand names. Companies stay in business because of past successes and consistent production of time-tested products. Be wary of product names you haven't seen in ads, articles or being used by fellow archers.

(5) About the only mandatory accessories are a sight system, quiver, shooting glove, tab or mechanical release and, possibly, an arm guard. Try different release types before making a decision. The arm guard keeps the bowstring from slapping against your forearm or catching on your sleeve and causing erratic flight in the arrows. A bow sight is also a good investment, depending on the shooting style you wish to develop. A simple 3-pin sight is a basic addition to a bow. Some archers also use peep sights to further refine their shooting. Again, it's an individual choice.

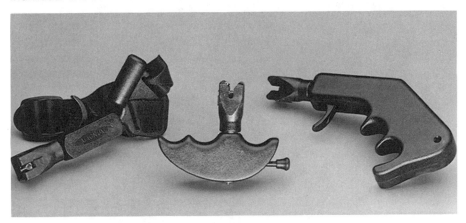

In recent years release aids have grown in popularity.

(6) Be forewarned against "over-accessorizing." That is, the modern archery market is saturated with sights, releases, quivers, silencers, stabilizers, rests, field points, broadheads, range-finders, carrying cases and plenty of gadgets and gimmicks. Reliable bow pros won't try to sell you something that's too intricate or advanced nor items you don't need for getting started. Many accessories refine

shooting skills and may mean the difference between being an adequate archer or a skilled bowman. But don't get hung up on high-tech items just because you see other more experienced archers using them on the local range.

(7) As you wouldn't go afield with a .270 Remington and 30-06 ammunition, so, too, arrows must be matched to bows. At one time wooden arrows were all that was available but now aluminum is the most widely used material with graphite, fiberglass, carbon and various composites also on the market. A bow shop pro will know the proper weight and length of the arrows you'll need along with matching broadhead and field points. Arrows built to shoot from a 40-pound bow won't perform with a 60-pound bow.

Arrow-making is another valuable service of a pro shop.

(8) Also buy a backstop for backyard target practice. A wide array of target butts made of rope-grass, ethafoam, burlap-covered impact material, mattress foam and old-fashioned (but effective) haybale backstops are available. Some targets, such as ethafoam, can take the slicing of broadheads but most are meant for use with field points.

Pick up a few of the multi-colored paper targets to pin to the butts and backstops. Or make your own with paper plates and felt-tip markers. Paper animal targets are also widely available.

Later you may want to invest in a life-size deer target such as those manufactured by McKenzie, Delta, Buffalo River, Game Tracker and others. But start out with paper targets before going to the 3-D prey.

Randy (left) and Chuck Bernhard pluck arrows from a 3-D target at the Izaak Walton Archers' range near Allentown. Hundreds of similar courses across the state offer realistic bowhunting practice.

(9) Another big advantage of dealing with a pro shop rather than buying gear at a discount house, where the clerk probably doesn't know a broadhead from a bullhead, is the prospect of going back if (a) you have additional questions or (b) your equipment isn't performing properly.

(10) Before my initial trip to a bow shop I'd garnered enough information from friends to feel competent and confident in choosing the proper gear. I wasn't afraid to ask questions, regardless of how "stupid" they may have seemed.

"That's what we're here for," said Weaknecht. "It's a pro shop's business to make sure a customer goes out of here with equipment that will perform."

Numerous bow specialty outlets are scattered across Pennsylvania — from shopping center stores in the suburbs to home businesses in dusty country basements.

They're a newcomer's best bet for assuring that first shot at a whitetail is made with "the right stuff."

Are your arrows flaring off the target upon release? Maybe you're squeezing the bow too tightly. Some archers who do well under the relaxed conditions of range shooting become tense when deer are in their sights. A heavy grip torques the bow at the moment of release, sending the arrow off to the left. Lefties will send their arrows off to the right.

During my introduction to bowhunting, my instructor frequently used the terms "porpoising" and "fishtailing" in reference to arrow flight. Not giving the terms much thought, I assumed they meant the same thing. It took a couple sessions before I finally realized that porpoising describes up-and-down arrow wobble while fishtailing indicates a side-to-side wobble. Porpoising, incidentally, is usually alleviated by changing the nock-point position. Fishtailing is often caused by a poor release, improper spine weight or the fletching striking the rest upon release.

Camouflage face masks are standard items for many bowhunters but rarely found on the faces of gun hunters. Yet, the human face is second only to movement in attracting the attention of deer. When hunting in thick understory where a deer might be encountered at close range, a mask may mean the difference between being detected and getting a shot.

The late Fred Bear (left), Pennsylvania's native son and the world's best-known archer, and cinematographer Wally Taber, who once traveled the state showing his hunting and fishing films, share a bowhunt.

Chapter
7

FAVORITE GUNS and LOADS

Like deer camps and deer hunters in Pennsylvania, firearms used for deer have changed over the years.

As a farm-country kid, my first "deer gun" was an old Ithaca double-barrel with which I also tended to pheasants, squirrels and cottontails. I never shot a deer with it but the old "twice-barrel," which a Pennsylvania Dutch neighbor jokingly called it, was confidently carried afield each December, loaded with a pair of "punkin' balls."

Shotguns are now mandated in the state's Special Regulations Areas and available with rifled barrels and scopes that make them surprisingly accurate at 100 yards or more — a long shot from the old smoothbores many deer hunters used in years past. More on them later.

In the mid-1980s *Pennsylvania Game News*, the popular monthly publication of the Pennsylvania Game Commission, surveyed readers on their choices of deer hunting calibers. To no one's surprise, it was discovered the 30-06 was then the most widely used caliber carried by deer hunters. A nationwide survey would probably have yielded a similar finding.

Today the 30-06, originally a military cartridge, may have slipped a bit in popularity. But not all that much. Now there are plenty more calibers and rifles from which to choose. The wide array of guns designed to appeal to whitetail hunters may create some confusion for a fledgling deer hunter wanting to get into the sport or simply seeking to update his or her equipment.

I won't claim for a second to be an authority on rifles, or on any particular type of firearm for that matter. But in making my full-time living as an outdoor writer since 1976 and having spent countless hours afield with a variety of hunters, I'm always curious as to their choices of guns and loads.

Some will be seen carrying rifles with enough knock-down power to incapacitate a buffalo while others opt for more "tamable" guns and cartridges. "Brush guns," chambered in 30-30 or the old .32 caliber Remingtons and Winchesters, were once the solid (and affordable) choices of most Pennsylvania hunters. I vividly recall those early days at my dad's deer camp in the late 50s and early 60s, Tall Maples Hunting Lodge in Sullivan County. Most of the guns lining the rack were pump or lever-action 30-30s and .32s or military converts handed down from one generation to another.

There's nothing wrong with using them today, of course, as my kids all started out with my Remington .32, a Winchester 30-30 or a Winchester .35. My wife killed her first deer with a 30-30 Winchester, preferring it over my Model 700 Remington 30-06 as its size and weight was more to her liking and made for a more comfortable fit.

Since then she's graduated to the Model 7 Remington 7mm-08 which I doubt she'll ever give up. The former "wildcat" caliber is a relative newcomer to the deer hunting scene and seems to be growing in popularity. Weighing just over six pounds, it's the perfect choice for the young hunter or woman. That's not to say men shouldn't consider it. The 140-grain load traveling at 2,800 feet per second is a dandy flat-shooter and may well be the "perfect" cartridge for medium game (although Betty Lou also cleanly dropped a 500-pound Colorado cinnamon bear with it).

Remington's Model 7 7mm-08 weighs only 6-1/2 pounds.

John Plowman, a Game Commission legislative liaison, took his first buck in 1972 with a venerable 30-06.

Choosing a deer gun is foremost a personal matter. Considering more rifles are produced for deer hunting than any other purpose, there's a wide choice of new and used guns from which to pick. The only limit may be one's pocketbook.

Excellent choices for Pennsylvania hunting are the aforementioned 7mm-08 and 30-06 calibers. Add to that the .243 Winchester, .270 Winchester (my personal favorite), .300 Savage and the .308 Winchester, among others. Each caliber offers two to five commercial loads from which to choose.

Experienced shooters like nothing more than to spend hours arguing which calibers are best for deer and I have no intention of getting into that scuffle here. Suffice to say there's a big choice of firearms for "up close" shooting as well as reaching out and touching game with their flat trajectories.

As for rifle types, the solid performances of bolt-actions have made them the choice of most whitetail hunters. Lever-actions are steeped in hunting tradition across Pennsylvania but have declined in popularity since WWII. Pump-action rifles are also carried by many hunters, although they can't match the hardiness of a bolt-action. Semi-automatic rifles for deer are not permitted in Pennsylvania.

SHOTGUNS

The growth of deer populations in suburbia and the ban on rifle use in some counties has brought about new interest in shotgunning among both hunters and rifle/ammo manufacturers. It's a good bet even more localized areas will go the shotgun-only route in years to come.

No longer must a deer hunter shoot an erratic smoothbore, then wonder where a slug is headed beyond 35 yards. Rifled barrels and specialized loads have made shotgunning for whitetails a highly efficient proposition.

During my school teaching days in Corning, New York in the mid-1960s, I drooled over the flashy Ithaca Deerslayer in the window of a sporting goods store. I'd drop by and shoulder it every so often but my meager salary kept me from purchasing it for local hunting, which required the use of shotguns then, as today, in the southern tier of the Empire State.

The 12-gauge, Model 87 Deerslayer (Don't you love that name?) is still popular. It's available in both pump and autoloading models. (Note: While semi-auto rifles are not permitted for Pennsylvania deer hunting, semi-auto shotguns are legal.)

The resurgence of deer shotguns has also brought a cadre of new slug-shooters on the scene. They include the Winchester Model 1300s (including a 20-gauge ladies/youth gun), Mossberg 12-gauge Trophy Slugster, Browning's BPS Deer Special, Remington's Model 870 pumps, SP-10 Magnums and 11-87s, and others.

The shotgun I carry when heading south of my Lehigh County home into the Special Regulations Area is the Remington 11-87 topped with a Simmons 2X Pro Diamond scope. With a one-in-24-inch bore twist and a slug choke, it maintains super accuracy and plenty of knock-down power from 50 to 100 yards.

Of course, the old "punkin-ball" has been replaced with rifled slugs and newer sabot slugs, in both 2-3/4 inch and 3-inch, 12-gauge loads. Some manufacturers also make .410, 16-gauge and 20-gauge slugs. Velocities reach 1,400 to 1,500

Waterways Conservation Officer Bob Steiner and Pennsylvania Game News columnist Linda Steiner used shotguns for these cross-border deer taken in southern New York.

The Remington Model 870 Wingmaster shotgun with rifled deer barrel features the unique cantilever scope mount.

feet per second at the muzzle and deliver 1,600 to 2,300 foot pounds of energy at 50 yards, with variations from one slug type and manufacturer to another.

I've had good luck with two loads, both capable of punching 3-inch groups off a benchrest at 100 yards with scoped sights: Remington's Copper Solid sabot slug and Winchester's Hi-Impact sabot slug loads. Sabots are plastic, slotted cylinders into which the slug is seated. The slug separates from the tight-fitting sabot upon firing, providing maximum energy retention.

Remington's all-copper load is similarly accurate. The nose sections of the unique non-lead bullet expands more than double upon impact, then separates for additional penetration.

The Winchester Hi-Impact sabot slug expands greatly because of its hollow-point design.

Scopes with large objective lenses permit greater light gathering features, especially helpful at dawn and dusk.

Buckshot is the choice of some, albeit few, shotgun hunters. In the Southeast Special Regulations Area buckshot is permitted but it's banned in Allegheny County surrounding Pittsburgh. Occasionally, special hunts in suburban parks may also require the use of buckshot. It's a short-range load, available in OOO, OO and O sizes (.36, .33. and .32 caliber, respectively). Anyone using buckshot should make certain he or she has patterned several loads before going afield. While some users claim effectiveness out to 50 yards, that seems to be stretching things with injured and lost game the result. Keeping shots below the 35 yard mark is arguably best.

Of course, your regular shotgun may also serve double-duty as a deer gun. Hastings, of Clay Center, Kansas, specializes in replacement barrels for shotguns. The Hastings Paradox holds a one-in-34-inch twist and is available for most Remington, Ithaca and Browning shotguns. Many gun manufacturers also offer their own replacement deer barrels which can be purchased through local dealers.

HANDGUNS

Handguns are legal for whitetails in Pennsylvania although a special permit is needed to carry them afield (see Chapter 6).

Don Lewis, *Pennsylvania Game News*' legendary gun columnist, recommends sticking with 41 Magnums or larger for Pennsylvania whitetails. He also cautions against putting too much faith in the popular .38 Specials and .357 Magnums.

"A lot of Pennsylvania handgunners use both cartridges for white-tailed deer," Lewis writes in his book, *The Shooter's Corner* (Pennsylvania Game Commission; 1989), "but success with them requires ultra-precise bullet placement."

He adds: "The most powerful handgun cartridge falls far short of equaling the power output of even the old 30-30 Winchester cartridge. I feel it's utter nonsense to even suggest using a handgun beyond approximately 100 yards."

Certainly there are exceptions. While not a typical "handgun," Remington's XP-100, which I've used on Texas whitetails, is a highly accurate, long-barreled (14-1/2 inches) handgun which has been around for more than 30 years and gaining new fans each year. Holding a handsome laminated, hardwood stock, the bolt-action guns are chambered in eight calibers including the 7mm-08 and 35 Remington. The barrel is tapped for scope mounting.

Experienced handgunners know their limitations as they've spent many hours on the range. Most top their pistols with scopes and choose their loads carefully. Handgun hunting for whitetails is not a venture which should be undertaken on a whim.

OTHER DEER GUNS

While percussion muzzleloaders are not permitted during the special flintlock-only season, they are legal in all other gun seasons. Both sidelock and the newer and phenomenally accurate in-line frontloaders offer popular options.

Replica sidelocks and in-lines are fired with percussion caps. I've taken big game, including whitetails, with my CVA 50-caliber caplock and the sabot-bullet-shooting 50 caliber Knight Hawk from Modern Muzzle Loading in Centreville, Iowa. Looking like a modern rifle but loading like Old Betsy, the "hybrid" in-line muzzleloader is highly accurate out to and beyond 100 yards. Topped with a 4x scope and loaded with a .45 caliber, 260-grain, Speer pistol bullet seated in a plastic sabot, it and others from White, Gonic, Traditions, CVA and Thompson-Center are the most accurate and reliable of front-stuffing guns.

While scopes are not legal on flintlocks in the special winter season, in all other seasons they are permitted — and recommended — on muzzleloaders.

SCOPING YOUR GUN

While we won't get into all the details of scope mounting and sighting (the information is available in most deer hunting books and magazines), suffice it to say that most Pennsylvanians choose either standard 4x scopes or variables in 2-7x or 3-9x powers.

For shotguns and muzzleloaders, lower power scopes from 2x-4x are most widely used. Check out the lighted "red-dot" scopes which are especially helpful in low-light conditions. The smaller red-dots are perfect for handguns, muzzleloaders and shotguns.

Scope costs can run as little as $30 to more than $500. The best advice when shopping for one is to buy the best you can afford. The low-priced scopes of today are as good or better than the high-priced brands of 25 years ago.

Chapter 8

MASTERING THE FINICKY FLINTLOCK

Like the longbow of the archery purist, the flintlock is the choice rifle for many muzzleloader shooters. For some, its use is dictated more by necessity than intrigue as Pennsylvania law mandates flintlocks-only during the late season.

In a Pennsylvania Game Commission hunter survey in the late 1980s, opinions were evenly divided on the legalization of percussion or "cap-lock" rifles, as are permitted in other states.

Guns with both types of firing mechanisms may be used in the regular gun seasons but, up until 1994, flintlocks continued as the sole arms for the "primitive" season. Muzzleloader hunter numbers have ranged from 45,000 to more than 125,000 over the past 15 years, with a dramatic drop in flintlock hunters in 1993. That's when organized blackpowder hunters urged the Game Commission to keep things status quo, opting not to become part of the new doe licensing system.

Whether the decision was wise or not remains to be seen. But surely the drop in blackpowder hunter numbers hasn't helped their "political" influence with the commission.

That being as it may for the time, it's obvious the flintlock is more than "just another" muzzleloading rifle. While the more popular percussion or "caplock" is far from foolproof, the flintlock can be doubly "persnickety," as the Pennsylvania German gunmakers who fashioned rifles in the 18th and 19th centuries probably referred to them.

I'm first to admit I've made my share of errors with the flintlock. But experience is the best teacher. If the experience comes at the expense of an escaped trophy buck, even more attention is made to perfection on the next hunt. On one memorable occasion my flintlock failed to fire due to a cocked flint (which I later surmised) and kept me from bagging a beautiful 10-pointer (at 25 yards) on a special hunt at the Middle Creek Wildlife Management Area in Lancaster and Lebanon counties in 1990.

I'd rather forget about that one, though.

Following are some "flintlock basics" for the "pilgrim" seeking to enter the late season blackpowder ranks.

Flintlock basics

It's necessary here to explain the method by which a flintlock operates.

The gun's cocking mechanism consists of a screw-tightened jaw holding a sharpened piece of flint. A patch of leather is inserted in the clamp for a firmer grip on the flint. When the trigger is nudged, the hammer falls swiftly with the flint striking a steel surface (the "frizzen") resting atop a shallow powder pan.

Upon impact, the frizzen snaps open, exposing the priming powder. The sparks light the priming powder, in turn sending a spark through the flash hole adjoining the pan.

At least that's how it's supposed to work. When it does the gun fires.

If it's nipped in the bud, that frustrating click is the only sound. Equally frustrating is the click followed by *pfffft* — the sound of igniting pan powder — and a puff of smoke.

All this happens only inches in front of a shooter's eyes, the anticipation of which can be quite disconcerting. The prospect of that flash of light and heat is the Achilles' heel for most newcomers to flintlock shooting, whether the gun fires or not. Add to that the minuscule lag time between ignition of the priming powder and the main charge.

While most shooters claim it's this micro-second delay that causes them to flinch, one experienced flintlock shooter claims otherwise.

"It's not possible to flinch in the time between the flash of powder and the gun going off," according to Dave Ehrig, a well-known Pennsylvania writer/lecturer and the author a book on building the Pennsylvania longrifle. Most "flinchers," Ehrig explains, "tense up as they're squeezing the trigger."

Ehrig said only five to seven one-hundredth of a second passes between the external powder's ignition and the firing of the gun, barring misfires, of course. But even misfires, preferably on the shooting range, teach lessons. Many flintlock shooters flinch even when the gun doesn't go off.

"It's the sign of a mindset when a person flinches," said Ehrig. "Mastering the flintlock means spending enough time shooting to feel comfortable with the gun. And that means more than just three or four shots before the hunting season."

Narrowing the odds

Through experience, flintlock shooters learn to the narrow the odds in Murphy's flintlock law, thereby lowering the prospects of misfires.

For one, black powder is highly corrosive and can quickly foul a flash hole (also called the "touch hole"), preventing the spark from ever reaching the internal charge.

It's recommended that both range-shooters and hunters carry a pick with which to probe the touch hole each time pan-powder is changed. The pick may be anything from a piece of firm wire embedded in an antler tip to a simple paper clip. I keep a twist of piano wire attached to the zipper pull on my hunting coat or vest

Only 5/100th to 7/100th of a second elapses between the external powder's ignition (top) and the gun firing (bottom.)

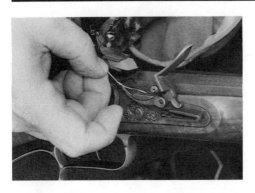

A thin wire is used to ream the touch hole.

so as to avoid the need to prowl around the possibles bag each time I want to use it.

Flintlock aficionados like Ehrig recommend using only enough priming powder to half-fill the pan. Clearing a space between the touch hole and the powder is also advised. Accomplish that by tapping on the breech opposite the lock.

Ehrig uses 3F (FFFg) powder instead of the next finer grain in wet weather.

"The 3F works nicely and allows you to carry only one charge," explains Ehrig, although the larger 3F grains may ignite a touch slower than the finer 4F powder. "It also doesn't seem to absorb moisture as quickly as the glazing is a bit thicker than on the fine grain powder."

Keep your powder dry

"Keep your powder dry" was often the parting words of mountain men heading in opposite directions after a rendezvous or a perchance crossing of paths.

It's also good advice today.

Foul weather is the flintlocker's number one enemy. Percussion firearms will also be influenced by humidity and rain or snow but extra care must be given to a flintlock as the powder is exposed to the elements.

To make matters worse, black powder is inherently hygroscopic. That is, it's water-loving and will quickly cake when moistened.

Hunters have come up with an intriguing variety of ways to keep their powder dry. I've seen them use makeshift covers of aluminum foil, plastic wrap, garbage bags and slices of innertube rubber over the locks. But simplicity and common sense is most effective.

"I always carry the gun under my armpit with the muzzle pointed down," Ehrig explains. "That's a natural way to carry any rifle and when it's raining or snowing the water will run down the barrel away from the pan. The lock area is also protected and kept from direct rain."

Ehrig changes powder several times a day in dry weather, every half-hour if humidity or precipitation is of concern.

He advises: "When you consider you're only losing five to seven grains each time you clear the priming pan, it's not worth losing the chance at a deer just because you wanted to save a few cents worth of black powder."

Some purists go so far as to apply a sealant of beeswax at the jointure of the pan and frizzen to prevent water from penetrating.

Several companies make oiled leather lock covers to shield the ignition area but most are ineffective in heavy downpours. Water trickling down the barrel and gathering in the pan will instantly spoil a hunt.

Deron Erney protects the pan from snow with an oiled leather cover.

Pick a quality flint

Another item demanding special concern is the flint. Specialty muzzleloader shops and mail-order houses such as Dixie Gun Works in Union City, Tennessee and Mountain State Muzzleloading Supplies of Williamstown, West Virginia offer several types, among the best of which is the black English flint.

"The black English flint is the best I've found," explains Toby Bridges, a longtime friend, blackpowder authority and author of "Advanced Muzzleloader's Guide" (Stoeger; 1985). "This is the true flint. It can be knapped and a new edge can created easily."

The French amber flint is another quality sparker, said Bridges, although it's not as abundantly available as American flints which are supplied with most new muzzleloaders. The latter are prone to chipping and, while they provide a good shower of sparks, they require regular replacement. Extras should always be carried afield.

Mounting a flint in the lock's jaws may require some experimentation, Bridges advises. He prefers placing the flint so that the bevel is on the bottom, causing it to strike the frizzen sufficiently high to maximize contact in its swift downward

Teacher, writer and muzzleloader authority Dave Ehrig of Berks County carries "ol' Betsy" during the buck season -- often with success.

motion without "kicking" the frizzen away too soon.

The flint must be aligned parallel to the frizzen so that the full edge-contact is made between the two components for maximum spark.

The possibles bag

Most accessories — "possibles" — carried by flintlock-toters are the same as those found in any muzzleloader's possibles bag. But there are some items specifically for flintlockers.

One is a pan primer, used to add powder to the pan without spillage. The device, about the size of a 30-06 shell, holds sufficient 4F powder for many primings. Each time it's tapered spout is depressed against the pan a small amount of powder is released. An internal spring closes the primer when pressure is released.

Quick-loading devices such as the Pennsylvania-produced E-C Loader are popular with black powder hunters.

Some shooters fashion similar dispensers from eyedrop bottles, plastic 35mm film containers and spent rifle shells plugged with cork.

I also carry an old toothbrush which is used to clean the pan each time a new charge is added. A stubby, wide-edge screwdriver is also necessary for adjusting or changing a flint while afield.

And, as previously mentioned, don't forget a pick of some sort to keep the flash-hole clear.

Developing the load

Of course, developing an efficient and consistent load is also of utmost importance. Each rifle holds its own set of peculiarities.

The first decision is which projectile to use. The relatively slow twists of most flintlock barrels best serve patched roundballs, which are required by Pennsylvania law. Conical bullets or hollow-based Minie balls are illegal except in the regular deer seasons.

For a 50-caliber rifle, a good roundball "starter" load consists of 60-70 grains of FFg (2F) blackpowder (or an equivalent volume of Pyrodex) under a .490" roundball. But remember that this is only for getting started. My preferred Hawken load with a patched ball is 90 grains of FFg. This powder is considerably more granular than the 4F powder used for priming.

The ball must be seated over the load with a tight-fitting patch of cotton (commercially available), linen or pillow-ticking. A commercial muzzleloader lubricant, of which there are many, will ease the patched ball down the barrel. Some shooters opt for pre-oiled patches.

Many newcomers to muzzleloader shooting consider the patching process an incidental matter although, in truth, its tightness is often the most overlooked factor in developing an accurate load. A thin patch will allow for easy loading but permits gases to escape, thereby affecting accuracy. If the patch is loose, the ball will not attain maximum spin in its flight down the barrel and beyond.

Practice is the key to developing an efficient load and becoming familiar with a gun's idiosyncrasies.

The ball must also be tightly seated against the charge. Black powder is most efficient when compressed and a loose-fitting charge will reduce velocity by 150 feet per second or more.

Another factor affecting accuracy is fouling. When working up a load, always swab the barrel between shots.

As muzzleloading, particularly with an iron-sighted flintlock, is a short-range sport, my preference is to sight in at 75 yards. A 3-4 inch group is the goal, more than sufficient for hitting the vital zone of a deer. Of course, this is a personal matter with some flintlockers attaining surprising accuracy at 100-yard ranges and others limiting their shooting to 50 yards.

No matter, a benchrest and sandbags are a must. Consistency is the key to refining the components and shooter error cannot be a factor when balls or bullets and powder charges are tested.

Fire a three-shot group before adjusting the powder load. If you're not satisfied, change the powder charge five grains at a time until a satisfactory load is established.

Manufacturer's manuals list suggested loads for specific rifles and that's the perfect place to start.

Experimentation is the key to finding the best load for your particular rifle. Maintaining consistency is the secret to accuracy on the range and in the field.

Cleaning the frontloader

The first lesson of blackpowder shooting is to keep the firearm clean. Even a speck of corrosion or powder-caking in a touch hole, for example, can keep a gun from firing.

Most touch holes on modern muzzleloaders are housed in a removable bushing. This bushing can be removed during the cleaning process for maximum flow of hot soapy water or solvent. However, it's usually necessary to do this only a few times a year, depending on how often the gun is fired. The gun can be cleaned without removing the touch hole.

The area around the touch hole can quickly become fouled with fine powder and the salts remaining from burnt charges. Use an old toothbrush along with a blackpowder solvent to get into the crevices and other hard to reach areas on the lock and pan.

The frizzen must also be kept clean but be cautioned that any oil on the steel face must be removed before shooting. The slick surface will reduce or eliminate sparking. However, the frizzen is prone to rust and a light coat of oil should be applied when the gun is to be stored.

After determining the proper bullet and load for your muzzleloader, load the rifle and insert the ramrod into the muzzle. Then, using a penknife, mark the point where the ramrod exits the muzzle. This will help determine (1) that the gun is loaded or unloaded and (2) that you've used the proper powder charge.

The famed Kentucky Rifle should properly be called the Pennsylvania Rifle. This Revolutionary War firearm was fashioned with a grooved barrel that provided spin to the ball and better accuracy. In time the Pennsylvania-made gun became famous as Daniel Boone's "piece." His wanderings may have attributed to the name "Kentucky" instead of maintaining the tag of its proper birthplace.

Save those old socks with the worn toes and heels. A pair slipped over the stocks of your guns during storage or transportation will keep them from getting scratched. Of course, you may want to wash them first after they've last been worn, as my wife insists.

If the zipper on your hunting coat sticks, rub it lightly with paraffin or candle wax before going afield. It will lubricate the studs without adding scent or grease to your clothing.

Lost in the woods with no compass? If the sun's shining your watch can serve as an emergency compass. Point the hour hand toward the sun. South will fall in the center of the angle of the hour hand and 12. North is opposite, of course.

Chapter 9

THE CONTROVERSIAL CROSSBOW

Pennsylvania Newcomer

A law first passed in 1992 permitting the limited use of crossbows during the Pennsylvania archery seasons was liberalized a year later with passage of House Bill 718.

It was the first time these largely misunderstood hunting instruments were permitted in the Keystone State, even though they've become as popular as longbows in neighboring Ohio.

The bill provides for any hunter who cannot draw a compound or long bow, based on a physician's determination, to hunt with a crossbow during the fall and late winter archery seasons.

Rep. Robert Godshall of Montgomery County spearheaded the change, which was backed by many Keystone State sportsmen's organizations.

"The law's importance lies in the fact that it opens doors to archery hunting to every physically-disabled individual," said Godshall, who led a 197-0 House of Representatives approval of the measure. "The previous law did not address many individuals who suffer from conditions that make them physically unable to draw a bow."

As with any change, the crossbow law created a flap, particularly among diehard bowhunters. While this is not to imply that diverse opinions deserve no credibility, I have hunted with the crossbow in other states while on assignment for magazines, underscoring my belief that most of its opponents know little about this controversial bow.

"The appearance of the crossbow has a whole lot to do with people's misimpressions and misunderstandings," said Mark Bower, director of operations for Horton Manufacturing Company, an Ohio business specializing in crossbows.

One of the biggest misconceptions is that some opponents claim it shoots the same distance as a gun. Another stems from a crossbow's high poundage — 150-pounds or more. However, that doesn't mean it's three or four times more powerful than a compound bow. The short powerstroke on a crossbow must be

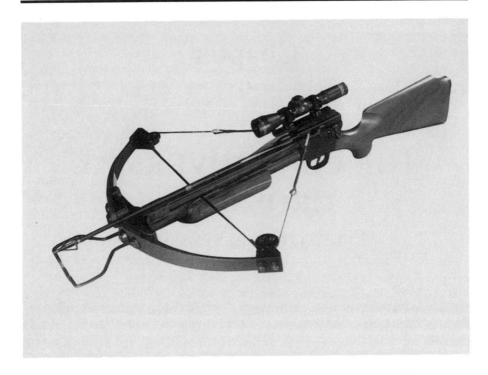

The crossbow's effective range is about the same as a compound bow.

balanced with a high poundage on the limbs to generate the equivalent power of a 65-70 pound modern compound.

Another notable difference between shooting a compound and crossbow is the length of the arrow — called a "bolt" in crossbow terminology. A bolt measures 17-20 inches and weighs 445-490 grains, including a 126-grain broadhead. Arrow speeds have been chronographed at 225-260 feet per second when triggered from a 150-pound bow.

Like compounds, crossbows utilize a variety of sighting systems — telescopic or open sights, non-telescopic crosshairs, military V-sights and illuminator pins. The challenge and necessity of getting close to game is no different than that employed by compound-users.

However, a notable difference — foremost in the arguments posed by critical bowhunters — is that a compound or recurve-equipped hunter must draw and hold the string, sometimes for long periods, without being detected. The crossbow hunter can aim and fire with little movement.

The crossbow can be quickly mastered with accuracy achieved — at the same 10-30 yard distances as preferred by longbow users — with only an hour or two of sighting and practice. Opponents criticize it as being "too accurate," a shallow argument no matter what the hunting tool.

Another widely heard criticism is that the crossbow is a "poacher's weapon" but even that has little validity, according to Buckeye State law enforcement agents.

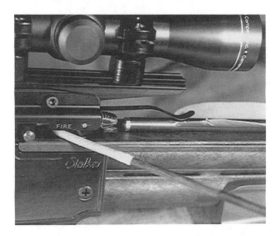

The Horton crossbow has a "no fire" safety which prevents string release if a bolt isn't nocked.

"Their use (by poachers) is way overblown," according to Jim Bunn, an Ohio Fish and Game Department wildlife officer. "A poacher wants to get in and get out fast, he's not going to want to track a deer. The crossbow has presented no problem here."

The fear among opponents of legalizing crossbows in Pennsylvania is that their use will be even further liberalized. Indeed it may. However, this writer sees little evidence it will become a part of the regular archery season.

But other seasons may benefit from its legalization. Special Regulations Areas — suburban landscapes in the Southeast and Southwest where the use of guns is limited, offer a big alternative for crossbow use. And few will argue against disabled sportsmen and women (possibly senior citizens, as well, in the years ahead) already being given the opportunity to shoulder a crossbow, even in the archery season. Or why not permit their use in seasons other than the fall bowhunt?

It remains to be seen how the controversial crossbow will weave its way into the scheme of things in seasons to come. No matter, understanding this maligned hunting tool before forming an opinion is the duty of every responsible Pennsylvania sportsman.

For the time being, disabled sportsmen and others who wouldn't be able to participate in the archery season are the benefactors.

And who deserves it more?

Not all wounded deer drop their tails when running off after a shot. Depending upon where a deer has been struck, it may bound away as if nothing's happened -- except for having been frightened by sound of a shot or loosed arrow. Check for blood and/or hair after every shot, no matter what position the buck or doe held its tail.

Annoyed by the sling on your deer gun constantly slipping off your shoulder? That's easily fixed by sewing a large button atop each shoulder of your hunting coat to keep the strap from sliding.

Chapter 10

BUCK FEVER and ONE SHOT HUNTS

"You shoulda seen the shot my kid made," said the voice on the other end of the phone. "If that buck was 10 yards off it was 200. He emptied his clip on it and got it through the neck — two outa five shots hit it."

"And it was running," he underscored. "I've never seen anything like it. It was unbelievable."

As the outdoor editor of a southeastern Pennsylvania newspaper I cover the hunting scene with editorial policies permitting a cherished free rein in covering this oft-controversial sport. Following the Pennsylvania buck season I list the names of hunters and, particularly, their sons and daughters who tied their tags to whitetail bucks — no matter what the size of their "trophies." I also do a column on unusual occurrences afield and other notable and humorous happenings at deer camp, enjoyed by over a million Pennsylvanians each December, that may be of interest to readers.

I get plenty of letters and calls, among them the one cited above. But that particular tale never made it into print. The caller phoned again a week or so later to question why it hadn't appeared. I patiently explained that I didn't consider the long-shot very ethical and would not add credibility by telling a quarter-million readers about it. The conversation ended quite abruptly when he made a few disparaging comments regarding my ancestry — and hung up.

The act of aiming and shooting at a deer takes a matter of seconds. The quick squeeze of the trigger can determine the outcome of a hunting season that encompassed hours, days, even weeks, of a sportsman's time. More important is the efficient, humane kill of a deer or any other game, for that matter.

The essence of the hunting ethic is to cleanly and quickly kill your quarry with but one shot. No matter if it's a modern high-power rifle, slug-throwing shotgun, ball-spitting muzzleloader or a well-placed arrow, the one-shot hunt should, and must, be every hunter's ultimate challenge.

With today's plethora of book, magazine and newspaper articles on deer and

Outdoor writer Kermit Henning (left) and wildlife artist Ken Hunter (right) had no time to get buck fever on the 1993 season opener. Henning bagged his Bedford County 8-pointer at 7:05 a.m. "before I could eat my Snickers" and Hunter shot his 7-pointer near his Montour County home with a 300-yard shot.

deer hunting available to the hunter, few sportsmen are without the knowledge of where to place the kill shot. The biggest problem in misplaced shots, many hunters agree, is the hunter's nemesis — buck fever. Long a joke of deer camps, buck fever is, nevertheless, a very realistic affliction.

It may strike the experienced still-hunter as well as the first-timer in a tree stand. Symptoms are much the same for both; too often accounting in a miss or an injured animal.

In the 40 years I've been hunting whitetails I've experienced buck fever many times. Any hunter who says it's never happened to him or her has never encountered a buck afield or is telling an outright fib. Early on, my buck fever resulted in the predictable missed or lost deer. Later it reared itself when some sizable buck made a surprise appearance and demanded a now-or-never decision.

What can the typical hunter do to lessen the chance of misses or crippling shots and make that "one shot" count?

Ask yourself these four basic questions:

(1) Are my firearms (bow pins, iron sights, scope) accurate? Might the sights have shifted since the last hunt when the gun fell, was jarred, banged by baggage handlers at the airport or warped from being subject to foul weather or high humidity?

(2) Have I done enough preseason shooting? Not just firing at a target 50 yards off but actually standing, kneeling or bracing myself against a support, as under field situations, and taking aim at targets of varied distances?

(3) Given the opportunity to shoot at a deer under differing situations, do

I know the proper bullet placement positions?

(4) Am I subject to "buck fever" and, if so, can I learn to control it?

The first two questions have obvious answers and the serious deer hunter will attend to them long before the season opens. Practice, and lots of it, is the key to knowing your gun shoots where it's aimed and that you are actually aiming where it is intended to strike.

The third question shouldn't, but often does, draw a response of "Well, usually!" from some hunters.

Most experienced hunters will agree the "classic" broadside pose demands a lung shot. The lungs make up the largest vital area covering the region from the brisket to a point immediately behind the shoulder. A deer's lung region is about the size of a basketball. It can be hit while the deer is in several positions other than the broadside stance and whenever I take new hunters afield I stress this aiming point.

Several years back, on hunts in Pennsylvania, New York, Alabama, Georgia and Quebec, I bagged six bucks — four of them with neck shots. Had I not been cock-sure that I could place the bullet exactly where I wanted it I'd have opted for a lower bullet placement. Long ago I was taught that under ideal circumstances neck shots are preferred over all others. I've discovered differently, however, and only take them under special circumstances.

Four of those bucks were less than 70 yards off and looking in my direction (two of them directly at me in high grass). The bullet went through the throat and broke the neck in three of the four situations. One deer was hidden nearly neck-high in a deadfall with the white of its throat exposed. I opted not to take a chance on bullet deflection and aimed high on the neck.

On broadside shots I prefer to place the crosshairs on the rear edge of the foreleg and about a third to a half way up the chest. That should deliver the bullet directly in the center of the lungs. Even a slightly misplaced shot will take out the heart (low), spine (high), esophagus or aortal vessels (front) or, if too far back, the liver. In all such cases there will be minimal meat loss, another important consideration to most sportsmen.

If the deer is facing you and its chest is visible, the recommended shot placement is immediately above the point where the neck joins the trunk. This will take the bullet directly into the center of the lung area.

On a deer quartering away the shot should be positioned through the short-ribs so that the bullet enters the lung region. This may be difficult to judge depending on the angle, which varies with each step.

I'm speaking here primarily of situations with firearms. When bowhunting never try a neck shot but always pick the lung-heart area and mentally isolate a patch of hair and aim for it. More than one deer has been within range of experienced archers but never drew an arrow as its positioning was not ideal.

Of course, there are other sure-kill zones, not all of which appeal to gun hunters for one valid reason or another. Most head shots are devastating and drop deer as if they had stepped into unseen holes. But the head is a small target and a shot may also hit the jaw or nose and result in a merciless, but eventual, death hours or days later. Don't take it.

This handsome 8-pointer offers the perfect broadside shot.

This quartering shot will strike the short-ribs and lungs.

This shot's path will deliver the bullet to the lung area.

Another shot that's said to be vital but which I prefer not to take (and have never made) is through or slightly above the anus on a deer moving directly away from the hunter. It's often dubbed the "Texas heart shot." Such a shot, well-placed to the base of the tail, will shock the spinal system and put the deer down. A second shot will be needed to dispatch the animal. Should such a shot miss the mark considerable damage will be done to the hams and severe blood loss will occur. Yet, I'm convinced most rump shots result in lost deer.

The preference of a heart shot is another subject open to question. The heart is a small target, only slightly bigger than a man's fist, and is often hit by accident when a low lung shot is taken. Then, too, few hunters know the precise location of the heart.

Hunters utilizing tree stands must adjust all shots accordingly as the path of the bullet will differ when it's taken from on high. Sometimes the spine will be penetrated on any shots from a severe overhead angle and drop the deer in its tracks. This is also true for bowhunters who typically shoot high when aiming from a tree.

Sometimes the aim is right on but the deer seems to duck out of the way in time. Slow-motion videos show what really happens. As the deer tenses and begins to run it bends its forelegs, automatically lowering its back. Many bowhunting videos show the phenomenal reaction time of the deer — and the arrow sailing cleanly over its back.

The best way to learn proper bullet or arrow placement is to study photographs of deer in varied poses and visualize kill zones when observing deer throughout the year.

Shots at fast-moving deer may require considerable leads and should only be attempted at close ranges.

Another excellent way to study the bullet's or arrow's preferred path is with a model such as the type offered by the National Bowhunter Education Foundation. It's a small (eight-inch high) plastic model of a white-tailed buck. One side of the model is a cutaway showing the major organs, in color, in their exact positions. Hard-wire probes supplied with the model can be pushed through the plastic deer in the many angles that a bullet or arrow might take. It shows which vital (or non-vital) organs are affected.

Hunter education instructors and archery clubs may want to consider purchasing such a model for use in teaching novice hunters. Get details by writing to the NBEF, Route 6, Box 199, Murray, KY 42071.

As for buck fever, that, too, can be controlled, or at least minimized.

My personal battle with the affliction was ebbed by experience, which cannot be fabricated. Most long-time hunters with racks on the wall will attest to that. I still experience it but today, given similar situations of 20-30 years back, I find myself in complete control.

Mind control and recognizing the onset of the affliction, even talking to one's self, helps accelerate the maturation process. Of course, some hunters never get over it.

One final problem that also accounts for bad hits and complete misses may only matter-of-factly be attributed to buck fever.

That's flinching.

Most hunters, caught up in the captivating prospect of aiming at a deer, will not flinch. Indeed, many hunters say they seldom recall hearing the explosion or the gun's kick when afield while being ultra-sensitive to both when on the range.

My wife, who started hunting in 1981, missed a mule deer and a whitetail her first times out because she flinched. In the case of the muley, she shot at least 30 yards in front of it (the deer was about 175 yards off) when she tensed her upper torso a mini-second before squeezing the trigger. She claimed she didn't flinch but I'd watched her do just that as I was looking over her shoulder at the time.

The next morning, on a range, I feigned loading her rifle but, instead, handed her a gun with a spent shell in the chamber. She again flinched, even though the gun didn't fire, and realized that, indeed, she'd tensed before triggering the shot. Once she understood the problem it was quickly overcome.

Taking the life of a game animal, especially one as majestic as a deer, is not without its responsibilities. The flood of emotions, from regret to pride, that command the body when a buck is at your feet are closely mapped by the method in which it was taken.

The one-shot hunt is the essence of such poignant and memorable times. As hunters we owe it to ourselves, our sport, and especially to our quarry, to abide by it and promote it as an integral part of Pennsylvania deer hunting.

Olympic Archery Gold Medalist Jay Barrs, who is also an avid deer hunter, recommends "daydreaming" as a way to help cure buck fever. Barrs frequently pictures a big buck in his sights as he mentally reviews the process of drawing, picking the kill spot and smoothly releasing the arrow. "Think about it enough and when the time comes it will seem like you've done it before." says Barrs. "I used similar mental preparation to win the Olympics."

When analyzing a blood trail, remember that pinkish fluid with small "bubbles" suggests a lung hit, bright red blood is most likely from the heart, a major artery or large muscle and dark blood probably means a liver shot. Green matter mixed with watery blood comes from the stomach or intestines.

Most hunters wear two pairs of socks -- a thin pair next to the feet and heavier socks over the top, depending on the weather. Avoid the temptation of wearing cotton dress socks against the skin. Cotton retains moisture and can cause blisters. Opt instead for orlon or orlon-wool socks like hikers wear.

An inexpensive police whistle should be a part of every hunter's gear. Not only will it alert others to trouble, should you need help, but it's also a far-ranging signal when you're lost. It has even been known to stop fleeing deer in their tracks -- for a clean shot.

Hunters typically use their binoculars only when movement or a distant deer is seen. In thick cover or high grasses, and at the edges of the day, scanning with binoculars often turns up hidden deer that would otherwise remain undetected. Establish a slow, methodical grid pattern to cover the entire area every 10-20 minutes or so.

Take a few minutes to stretch leg, back and arm muscles before climbing into a treestand. Do the same before walking after spending a long period cramped in a stand. A couple minutes of stretching exercises can prevent sprains and pulled muscles.

Chapter
11

GEAR FOR DEER

Visit your favorite sporting goods store or flip the pages in the dozens of catalogs showing up in the mailbox each fall and you'll find the widest selection of deer hunting gear ever available.

And new items are created each year.

To attempt to suggest an "ideal" outfit for hunting in Pennsylvania would be futile and we won't even attempt it here. From the October bow opener through the buck and doe seasons and into the January hunts, weather conditions, hunting styles, legalities and how much money's in the checking account influence what's worn.

The biggest differences in external clothing are found in the bow and gun seasons. Not only do temperatures vary by as much as 60 degrees or more but it's common knowledge that bowhunters don't want to be seen — by deer or by others afield. That's why they wear camouflage.

Gun hunters don't want to be seen by deer either but they do want their presence noted by others in the deer woods. Archers can have it their way the first four weeks of the season but must conform to state law (250 square inches of blaze orange on the head, front and back, visible from 360 degrees) by wearing the safety color when the bow season runs concurrent with the small game season.

The color is not required in the late bow-muzzleloader hunt although many participants wear at least an orange hat or vest.

When fluorescent orange was first mandated in Pennsylvania, grumbles were heard from old-timers accustomed to donning their dark Woolrich outfits and heading to the woods. But that's all changed as hunters today want to be seen when afield, resulting in lower accident rates.

Although it's not easy to remain hidden when dressed in the required clothing, there are a couple of factors to keep in mind when buying blaze orange.

Scientists who have studied the reactions of deer to hunters in orange garb

"Soft" orange garments, such as worn by Wilkes-Barre Times Leader outdoor writer George Smith, are more quiet and less visible to deer.

noted that some outerwear is easier for deer to see than others. They advise wearing "soft" orange clothing. The shininess of cheap, orange vests of plastic or vinyl will be brighter and more likely to draw attention. They're also be noisier. Some orange hats also produce a "shine" and should be replaced with a hat of softer fabric.

Deer see orange as white or light gray, not the way we see it. When hunting in snow, blaze orange blends in with the white countryside, as deer see it. To other hunters it stands out like a neon sign.

In darkened woods and under dull skies the fluorescent orange provides the greatest contrast and is most readily seen. Nevertheless, it's movement of the hunter that most often reveals his presence to deer.

Camouflage-orange, which never seemed to take hold among Pennsylvania hunters despite its wide availability, may be the best bet for eluding a deer's attention. The mottled orange, black and, in some patterns, green, gray or brown, breaks up the human outline and creates a blending effect with the environment. At least deer see it that way.

Camo-orange is legal in Pennsylvania as long as the total amount of visible orange meets or exceeds the legal requirement.

Full camouflage is legal in all but the buck and antlerless deer seasons. Since the early 1980s the choice of camo clothing has gone from the old Viet Nam and woodland patterns to a wide array of choices from nearly 20 manufacturers. Realtree, Trebark, ASAT, Tru-Leaf, Mossy Oak, Bushlan, Hide-N-Tree and others fill shelves and catalogs for the camo-conscious and fashion-conscious hunter.

As important as choosing a pattern is knowing what it's made of and how well it holds its colors after repeated washings. From cotton to fleece and wool to Cordura, camouflage is the dress of the day, especially in bow season.

Again, picking a pattern to match the environs in which you plan to hunt is the

Sporting goods stores stock camo for all seasons, such as the Mossy Oak Winter Treestand (left) and Realtree All-Purpose Gray (right) patterns.

key to choosing the outdoor wardrobe. Selections have never been greater.

Daypacks

Important to every hunter is wearing or carrying the proper gear for a day afield. For many years a daypack has been part of my deer hunting gear. No matter if heading only 300 yards from the cabin door or setting out on a cross-country jaunt, I cart it along. It's packed with lunch, a couple candy bars, contact lens fluid, drag rope, two sharp knives, bottled water or juice, flashlight, toilet paper, compass, a large, zip-type plastic bag (for the heart and liver), a small zip-bag with a wet cloth to clean up after field-dressing, extra socks and extra shells. Side and front pockets in the daypack hold a camera, raingear, deer calls and one or two other items.

While it sounds like a bundle, the pack weighs only 4-5 pounds and can be stashed in a treestand or hidden along a trail should I choose to hunt a patch of woods without it.

When conditions turn foul I have rain gear. If it gets warm, as Pennsylvania's fall weather often does toward mid-day, I have a place to stuff a sweater or vest.

If a cold front is forecast, I'll roll a heavier garment in the bag before heading out.

Often, if the hike to my stand is long and/or arduous, I'll shed my outer garment and stuff it in the daypack to prevent a build-up of perspiration, which later results in chilling as the body cools. Several minutes after arrival at the stand I'll "get dressed," after I've had the chance to cool and dry.

A daypack (left) or fanny pack (right) of fleece fabric comes in handy for carrying gear afield.

While my choice of daypack-stuffers may seem extreme, I find use for all the items at one time or another throughout the season. Preference is for a mini-backpack in camouflage fleece, which is quiet and rain resistant. Nylon or canvas packs may be durable and waterproof but they're also noisy when scraping brush and limbs. Choose a pack with two or three side pockets for calls and other small items. Also make sure it has wide, comfortable straps and tough zippers.

The fanny-type pack is too small for my needs on all but short jaunts from the house or camp but I prefer it when hunting near home during the bow season. The advantage of any pack is that pants and jacket pockets are kept free and don't hinder climbing and walking.

Field-dressing knives

I always chuckle when I meet a hunter in the woods carrying a "pig-sticker" on his belt. Few places I hunt lend themselves to hacking through with machetes and I can't imagine how anyone could field dress a deer with a bayonet.

I always carry two knives; one a small, 3-4 inch lockback blade and the other a gut-hook knife for slitting the belly skin prior to field dressing. The latter knife is also used as a back-up blade, which is sometimes necessary for completing the gutting process.

Most hunters use knives far to large for the job. Sharpness is much more important than size and long sheath-knives just add extra weight to the pack or belt. They're unwieldy when it comes to the precision cutting needed to peel skin

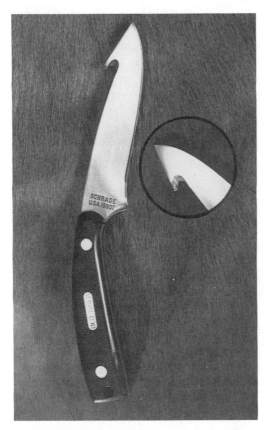

The unique feature of this Schrade knife aids in slitting the belly skin without puncturing the intestines.

or slice tough tissue.

Although I seldom carry it afield (except on western hunts), a small knife sharpener is also a handy item. At day's end, after the knife is cleaned, it's used to restore the finely-honed edge that will be needed for the next job.

When bowhunting I also add a pruning shears to my pack. It comes in handy when snipping troublesome twigs and small branches around the treestand — or from the base of the tree where you plan to sit.

Binoculars

I'm constantly amazed at the number of hunters who don't use a binocular. Mine is a constant companion. It has revealed deer I wouldn't otherwise have seen, as well as identifying whether a distant whitetail is sprouting antlers long before it becomes visible to the unaided eye. To me, a quality binocular is as important as a top-notch riflescope.

Knowing a bit about binoculars before putting down your credit card will help in making a comfortable decision, no matter if you're spending $40 or $400.

The wise shopper should be armed with basic knowledge of the three numbers shown on all binoculars, no matter what the style or make.

The first number (on a 7x35 binocular, for example) designates that the binocular will produce a 7-power magnification. A 10x50 binocular will magnify an object 10 times. An object viewed at 100 yards will appear seven times closer with a 7x and 10 times closer with a 10x binocular. It's that simple.

My personal choice is a 10x.

The second number (in this case 35 or 50) indicates the diameter of the objective (front) lens, measured in millimeters (mm). The larger the objective lens, the more light reaches the eye and the brighter the image. Large objective lenses are blessings when used under low-light conditions, such as viewing game at dusk and dawn.

The third number indicates "field of view at 1000 yards." It designates the width, in feet, that can be seen at a distance of 1000 yards. The stronger the

The Simmons Roof-Prism binocular (top) and Nikon Diplomat (below) are good choices for hunters needing both full-size and compact optics.

magnification, the less the field of view. Wide-angle lenses increase the view from 35-65 percent and are most useful when glassing for big game, as is necessary for mule deer and elk in the West. It is seldom an important factor for Pennsylvania hunters.

The biggest decision in choosing a deer hunting binocular is whether to purchase a compact or full-size model. Full-size binoculars provide the brightest viewing because they're constructed with large lenses. Compact binoculars are less cumbersome when a day's hunting means covering lots of ground. The trade-off of smaller size is smaller objective lenses. When heading out to a treestand for a morning or afternoon hunt I'll take my full-size glasses (best for dim light). When still-hunting, the compact is my choice.

When shopping for a binocular, sight on some distant object — across the showroom or out a window. Check how easily the glass can be focused, remembering you may have to do it while wearing gloves. Also be certain the eye relief is comfortable and provides the full scene. If you wear glasses, fold down the rubber eyecups before testing.

Then make sure these "second eyes" are around your neck whenever you head into whitetail country.

Useful accessories

The hunting industry has flooded the market with "must have" items that many hunters buy — but may only use once or twice. However, some of these aids serve useful purposes when hunting whitetails.

One's a spongy seat of some sort. Several types are available, including the long-popular "hot seat," which is not only noisy but soon compacts as the foam nuggets inside quickly compress.

My favorite is the Buck Bagger Handi-Seat from D&H Products in Valencia,

Pennsylvania. The 9x18 inch Cordura seat buckles across the beltline with the 2-inch foam seat riding on the lower back, out of the way and quickly detachable when sitting.

The company also makes a compact deer drag — an orange, nylon web strap which fits over the shoulders and attaches to the deer, freeing the hands and arms.

For the bowhunter, a calibrated range-finder is also an invaluable accessory. It allows hunters to take accurate distance readings of various items in the area — a rock, deadfall, stump, nearby path or some other point of interest — while posted or in a treestand. The rangefinder takes the guesswork out of deciding which sight pin to use relative to the distance of some pre-determined spot — near which a buck or doe is feeding.

Bowhunters using release aids should also carry an extra with them. Should one malfunction or be lost, the hunt won't be over.

Of course you'll find dozens of items on the shelves at the local sports shop and filling the pages of outdoor catalogs. Only you can decide whether you need another gadget, how much use it will get and whether the cost justifies its purchase.

The Ranging Rangefinder is helpful to bowhunters in determining shooting distances.

PART
III
TIPS AND TECHNIQUES
For Pennsylvania Whitetails

Bob Greenbaum with his exceptional Carbon County 14-pointer.

Chapter 12

IDENTIFYING "DEER PARTS"

The first buck I ever shot, in McKean County back in 1962, showed up broadside at 15 yards. It was plainly seen from nose to tail-tip.

I remember it well.

The last buck (as this is being written) to which I tied my tag was bedded in a thicket of black spruce in a Canadian forest. Had it not been for the attention-getting movement of its left antler, I'd probably have wandered on by.

Indeed, in my 40 years of pursuing whitetails from Maine to Mexico, most bucks on which I've centered the crosshairs wouldn't have been seen except for one or two "deer parts" that revealed their presence.

While experienced deer hunters are attuned to looking for tails, ears, legs, noses, eyes, antler segments or the horizontal line of a back or belly, newcomers to the sport often fail to "make the connection" when an entire animal isn't seen.

Novices in the deer woods (and we were all novices at one time) typically take wide-angle views of the terrain, often failing to see deer whose "parts" betray their presence. They expect that any deer in the area -- any "whole" deer -- would be seen.

Taking a newcomer afield prior to the hunting season is an oft-overlooked facet of his or her training. But it's as important as sighting in a rifle, searching for deer sign, mapping trails, judging shooting distances, locating treestands and practicing gun safety.

Many experienced hunters can also use the practice.

How do you go about teaching such a lesson?

Over the years I've undertaken the satisfying task of training my own sons, several other young relatives and friends and my wife in the art of finding "deer parts."

First, we reviewed photographs of deer in their natural habitats. Magazine photos clipped for the occasion served the purpose well.

Too elementary? Not at all.

The magazine picture lesson is a productive way to spend an evening with a future hunter. Remember, this may be old stuff to a veteran woodsman but, to a first-timer, the information's new and revealing.

Secondly, take a preseason trip to a park, wildlife preserve or research area where deer sightings are guaranteed. Actual sightings of bucks and does in their natural habitat provide the student with first-hand experience in finding "deer parts."

Another effective teaching tool involves a life-size deer target used by bowhunters. Placing the model in brush, high grasses, behind deadfalls and in other situations where only a rump, head, legs, back, belly or other body part is seen at a distance of 30-100 yards or more serves as an excellent teaching tool.

Remember that the novice hunter typically takes a panoramic view of a habitat. He or she expects to see a whole deer, not just a nose or tail.

The veteran knows it's often the small details -- like a patch of brown among the greenbriar or a smoothly-curved neck or rump that's somehow out of synch with vertical trees or grasses -- that yield sightings of deer before they see you.

Yet another lesson involves keeping a ready eye for movement -- not the motion of a running buck but rather the twitch of an ear, a swishing tail or the low sweep of feet and legs through a pine grove.

The experienced hunter will find himself or herself gazing for long minutes at stumps that look like bedded deer, windwhipped leaves that resemble deer tails or low branches shaped like trophy antlers. Sometimes they're just that.

Once a "part" is spotted, binoculars should be used to confirm your sighting -- or verify the "fat, bedded doe" is actually a stump. No hunter should go afield without good optics.

Once a hunter goes afield in the frame of mind that anything out of synch might be a whitetail, he knows he's come a long way in picking out the "deer parts" that put venison on the table.

And antlers on the wall.

Finding "deer parts" is the key to successful whitetail hunting.

Rather than allowing your extra shells to jangle about in your pocket, roll them in the toilet paper you surely carry with you. Use a large rubber band to keep the shells from falling out.

Hunters who tread off the beaten path rely on map and compass to find their ways. Topographic maps are the most useful of backcountry guides and the knowledgeable hunter will take the time to learn to read them. The U.S. Geological Survey has topo maps for the entire U.S., including your favorite hunting areas. For free information on maps and aerial photographs, call 1-800-USA-MAPS.

Ever get lost looking for your treestand in the pre-dawn darkness? We all have. An excellent "guideline" can be fashioned from a few dozen wooden clothespins, some reflective tape and orange ribbon. Staple a 6-8 inch length of fluorescent orange ribbon to the pin and wrap a piece of silver reflective tape around one of the flat ends. Clip the pins to trees and bushes at intervals of about 15-20 yards, from which a flashlight's beam will readily reflect off the tape. When stand locations are changed, simply pluck the markers from the trail as you exit the woods.

To get some idea of how heavily a deer trail is used on preseason scouting trips or in-season hunts, wet a crossing side with a couple quarts of water and smooth it with a concrete worker's trawel. Check the smooth surface 12-24 hours later to see how many deer have passed by.

Droppings can provide the best clues for deer activity in a specific area. Fresh droppings are black and soft. Within a day or two, depending on the weather, pellets will begin to lighten and become increasingly hard. By comparing droppings along a trail, the relative period of time the animals left them can be determined.

Those gritty, adhesive traction strips, sold in building supply and hardware stores for taping onto outside steps, are great for providing sure footing on ladder stands.

Chapter 13

SCOUTING
Hunter's Homework

At 5 a.m on October 1, 1988 Craig Krisher climbed into his portable treestand in northern Lehigh County's farm country.

It was a familiar spot, one in which the then-25 year old bowhunter had spent other dawns during the previous weeks. That's much of the reason he was filled with confidence that "this will be the day."

Ironically, despite the anticipation, it was no colossal surprise when a monster buck moved down a trail tramped into the nearly impenetrable thicket.

Krisher had seen the same buck nearly two dozen times and, along with his lifelong friend and hunting companion Vince Fugazzotto, had captured the velvet-antlered stag on film and video-tape six weeks earlier.

While Krisher awaited sunrise, Fugazzotto hunched in another treestand several hundred yards away, also hoping for a shot at the monster buck they'd first seen in mid-June and, later, painstakingly backtracked to its bedding area in a scrub thicket.

Its morning retreat always followed one of several well-worn trails, among them the "apple tree route."

Krisher had arrived at the apple tree, his stand already intact, well before sunrise via a small brook that flowed nearby. On other mornings he and Fugazzotto had patterned the movements of the 23-point whitetail and Krisher was confident it would be passing by to its bedding area between 6:15 and 6:45, as it had on other mornings.

But on this morning — the season opener — the buck was a bit late. At 6:50 Krisher heard something move in the nearby gully and, through a drizzly mist, recognized the magnificent buck that had dominated his thoughts for several months.

(Left) Craig Krisher's state record non-typical bow-buck scored
203-3 Pope & Young points.

**Patterning a specific buck is the
ultimate challenge.**

The kill was almost anticlimactic. At 12 yards the buck paused to sniff a curiosity scent pad Krisher had placed in the narrow path. The shot was perfect and the buck toppled after only a 30 yard sprint.

At that moment the Pennsylvania non-typical, bow-buck record also fell. Following the mandatory 60-day drying period, it scored 203-3 Pope & Young points, providing Krisher and his companion their reward for over 100 hours of pre-season scouting.

While not every hunter can spare that kind of time previewing hunting grounds, this success story proves that scouting plays a very definite role in hunting success—even when patterning a specific buck.

Scouting means different things to different hunters. Some simply want to learn where escape routes, bedding areas and favored feeding sites are located. Time and the distance from their homes to the places they hunt may dictate only cursory pre-season visits. Even a day or two of scouting, however, can reap benefits for the effort.

Others search for big bucks and a few — like Krisher and Fugazzotto — pattern specific animals.

Unless you live close by your hunting grounds and can spare mornings before work, then take advantage of daylight remaining after punching the time clock, establishing a dossier on a specific deer may be futile.

Truth is, most hunters can afford only portions of a few pre-season days to track their prey.

So what's the recipe for making the most of those scouting hours?

Here are 10 items that should be on every scouter's menu.

(1) The first is simple observation. Krisher and Fugazzotto caught first sight of the record book buck by driving back roads at the edges of the day and observing where deer were feeding and taking inventory of both buck and doe numbers.

They began their quest in mid-June, well ahead of the hunting season. At this time deer are relatively undisturbed. They build their daily schedules on filling their bellies and moving back and forth to their bedding areas.

(2) As food sources change and farm crops mature, deer will expand their feeding areas. The Lehigh County bowhunters first noted whitetail activity in

alfalfa and clover fields and later in corn and soybean fields.

Oak ridges provide meager enticement in midsummer but when acorns drop in late summer and early fall, they attract deer like magnets. Locating oak-rich tracts provides a back-up plan as the season progresses.

Krisher also spent considerable time spotlighting, which is legal in Pennsylvania (up until 11 p.m. each night except during the deer hunting seasons when spotlighting is illegal), revealing nocturnal activity. The men noted the 23-pointer frequented areas as far as 1-1/2 miles apart. But early morning and late afternoon sightings were typically made in the same place, hinting as to the proximity of the buck's bedding area.

Driving back roads through public lands prior to the season often reveals deer travel routes.

(3) "Mock hunts" also provide helpful information on deer activity. Spending time in permanent and portable treestands on back fields or woodlands enables the documentation of deer movements and numbers.

On such outings a binocular and a spotting scope are necessary. Close-up

Some rubs indicate aggressive activity such as on this scoured tree.

views reveal individual identities. The travel patterns of the same deer seen in several sectors will provide clues to their travels.

(4) Once bucks are located, the next order of business for those with sufficient time is a closer look at the "keeper" bucks observed.

Big bucks sometimes leave distinctive tracks. Krisher and Fugazzotto noted the specific spots where their buck was seen. Close study revealed it had a cleft hoof on its right front foot. The distinctive hoof-print enabled them to backtrack it to its general bedding area over a span of several weeks.

(5) While it's a time-consuming task, tracking one buck or a bachelor group from feeding areas to bedding site often reveals more than one notable trophy. On the morning Krisher made his kill, Fugazzotto spotted a big 9-pointer, one of four or five bucks that traveled together well into September and were still in one another's general company on the season opener.

As the warm days of September yield to October's chill, many of these bachelor groups break up as dominance is established.

(6) Of course, the traditional buck barometers — rubs and scrapes — are among the easiest of signs to locate. Before and during the rut (especially before) fresh scrapes are among the most reliable locaters as they indicate recent use.

Unless specific "new" rubs are seen on follow-up scouting jaunts, their ages are often hard to analyze. Early rubs and scrapes, made during September in most

Topographic maps and airphotos of your hunting grounds aid in locating deer hideaways and potential travel routes.

states, are the result of anxiousness among individuals in bachelor herds. Bucks make them but don't necessarily revisit them.

As fall progresses, sparring is common and small sumacs, pines, cedars and other scrub vegetation will take much of the brunt of such "shadow boxing." As the prime rut period nears, saplings and bigger trees will be attacked.

The adage that only big bucks rub big trees is generally true. They will also spar with small trees but the size of a strafed trunk is a reliable indicator as to the comparative size of a rub's maker.

(7) Merely finding a sizable rub or two is encouraging but locating a rub line demands focused attention.

Problem is, such "lines" may not be quickly recognizable. Field edges, stream banks, skid trails, old logging roads and readily recognized deer trails must be given special attention as that's where more than half of all rubs are often found.

Keeping track of fresh rubs and, later in the season, scrapes, on a topographic map, airphoto or a homemade map of an area may piece together prime runs and passages between feeding and bedding areas.

It's here where predictable activity occurs and where tree stands should be hitched.

(8) Scouting involves more than looking for deer, their food or their signs. On public hunting areas it doesn't take long for deer to shift into Plan B or C and abandon the runs and trails, even the bedding areas, to which they became accustomed throughout summer.

For several years I hunted, with moderate success, a Corps of Engineers tract in northeastern Pennsylvania. During the squirrel and grouse seasons I spent more time looking for deer sign as seeking bushytails and ruffs.

But on opening morning and throughout the gun season, places I'd spotted bucks and seen does casually walking trails yielded little.

That's when I bought a topographic map and airphoto of the area and discovered an alternate route into the backcountry. Using a canoe with a 3-horsepower motor, a friend and I cut an hour's walk into a 15 minute boat ride, putting us into the region where hunters pushed deer each morning.

For several years we enjoyed early season success, until others also started using the boat-in passage.

(9) Bowhunters, in particular, like to position stands on the fringes of feeding areas. Traipsing the perimeter of a cornfield or alfalfa patch will readily reveal the deers' approach to a food source. If undisturbed, they'll continue to utilize the same routes, at least up until the transition period when changing foods or rutting activity demands new and more varied wanderings.

With exception, I prefer setting up within a woodlot or forest edge rather than immediately on its rim. Big bucks tend to linger in the shadows until darkness, even though they may accompany the does that often begin feeding well before sunset.

(10) While scouting trips combine knowledge with the welcome enjoyment and anticipation of another season on the horizon, don't let your guard down by "polluting" the area.

Sight and smell, even before the first arrow is released or shot fired, is sufficient to alert wary bucks that something's amiss.

Use reliable cover scents or liquid scent "shields," wear rubber boots and be certain no foreign odors are carried in your clothing. As in an actual hunt, be aware of wind direction and keep breezes in your favor.

Prior to each of their scouting trips, Krisher and Fugazzotto washed their camo clothing in baking soda, then stored it in a plastic bag and applied a scent-block before entering the woods. They were also careful not to leave undue scent in the woods.

Scouting paid off for Keith Schuyler, Pennsylvania Game News archery columnist since 1962, with this double brow-tine buck shot near his Columbia County home.

As said, scouting and the degree to which it's performed is a personal matter among hunters. Give it as much time as you can afford, even if only for a day or two. The more knowledge gained about your hunting area in preseason, the better your chances of being in that magical "right spot" on opening morning.

A 20-foot length of strong cord with small, spring-type dog leash snaps on each end allows quick and reliable attachment of bows, guns, daypacks and other items when climbing treestands. Latch your gear on one end and snap the other to your belt. Then haul up the gear when you're safely "belted" into your stand.

Hunters using screw-in climbers should always be sure to take an extra one or two with them. Screwing one in above the stand offers a reliable grasp when making that final step up or the first step out. A second step should be fastened just above shoulder height to hold a gun sling or bow.

When removing screw-in steps from a tree you plan to use later in the season, stick small twigs or wooden matches in the holes. It will aid in quickly re-establishing your "staircase" next time around.

Foam pipe-wrap (available at hardware, plumbing and building supply stores) attached to guards, rails and rests on treestands will help muffle sounds that can alert deer.

Wing nuts used on portable treestands are easily dropped, especially when cold weather brings stiff fingers. They can be difficult to find in leaf litter and when stands are being hung or removed in darkness. Spray paint the nuts with fluorescent orange (they show up well in the beam of a flashlight) and carry a couple extras just in case one is lost.

Small alligator clips come in handy for pinching off the bladder ducts when field-dressing a deer. The ducts can also be tied before removing and discarding the bladder. It prevents urine from tainting the meat.

Chapter 14

TAKING A STAND

When I was a kid it was a treat to hunt deer from a treestand.

Then, "taking a stand" meant climbing onto a wooden platform nailed in a tree and staying there most of the day.

The wooden platforms from which I hunted in Pennsylvania's deer-rich north-country were stationed in places where deer sooner or later wandered past. If deer were seen, great. If not, I often spent a long, cold day watching squirrels and listening to distant shots.

Today the portable treestand, like grunt tubes, bow sights, modern camouflage, commercial scents and dozens of other modern whitetail hunting aids, has revolutionized the way hunters seek their prey.

In a matter of minutes a stand can be moved to a hotspot, sometimes making the difference between a dinner of venison chops or bean soup.

Of course, many stands are permanent structures, most much better built than the wooden planks hunters nailed up 20 or 30 years ago.

But it's the portables that have revolutionized the way most hunters, particularly archers, today hunt whitetails. Knowing how to read deer sign and figuring out their changing patterns determines just how successful a hunter's treestand techniques may be.

Choosing The "Right" Tree

Follow these tips for choosing the "right spot" for your treestand.

* Find well-used trails between bedding and feeding areas prior to the season. Choose stand locations at the intersections of trails or in natural funnels, such as the convergence of "fingers" along ridges or natural runs where woodlands rim feeding fields.

* In farm country, where treelines, windbreaks or grassy gullies link woodlots, deer like to travel the cover rather than the open spaces. Look for suitable trees to take a stand near the junction of the fencerows and woods.

* When seeking a specific spot to place a stand on a hillside, be aware that deer moving up the hill may see you skylined, particularly in the evening hours when a hunter's silhouette is backed by a western sky.

Deer coming over the rise may also be on eye level with a hunter who chooses a tree just under the crest. Move the stand a bit farther down the slope, as necessary.

* The edges of natural barriers to casual deer movement, such as the ends of sloughs around which deer typically pass, shallow riffle areas in streams and rivers where deer can wade rather than swim or gentle inclines along an otherwise abrupt drop-off are prime spots to set up.

*Stands of oaks, beeches and other mast-producing trees are magnets to whitetails in early season. Late summer brings the nuts to the ground and areas where deer only casually passed through earlier become hotspots as long as the nuts continue to drop.

* Also consider the ease with which you can enter and exit an area in which a treestand, portable or permanent, has been placed. Shallow streams or tractor paths where man-made odors are found year-around are good choices. Whatever you do, don't plan an approach through thickets or other habitats through which you cannot walk quietly.

* If there's the chance of being seen or heard as you approach a bedding area, plan to be in your stand at least an hour before sunrise. Deer can see better than you can in

Hanging a stand in areas with abundant mast is productive in early bow season.

the dark but the cover of darkness will provide an added advantage to remaining unseen. Then, too, if you're near a bedding area or some other travel route, arriving early can put you in position before the deer return from their night's feeding.

* One of the biggest mistakes a hunter can make is choosing a tree on which to hang a stand simply because it has a "nice view." Of course, on the opening day of buck and doe seasons, when deer are pushed, such a stand may be productive. But in bow season or the winter archery-muzzleloader hunt, getting close is the key to success.

The proper balance between cover and open shooting lanes is also an important consideration. Carry a hand clipper to clear troublesome twigs both in the tree and at varied places on the ground, particularly in the bow season.

Potent Portables

Like camo and compound bows, portable treestands have come a long way since the first Baker stands were created many years ago. Portables, whether of the bulky ladder-type or the small, light climbers, provide the hunter a way to ascend the tree of his or her choice, or move the stand to greener pastures as the seasons progress.

In the market for a portable treestand?

First recognize the four basic stand types: hanging stands, climbers, ladder stands and tripods.

I've used the latter in Texas and have seen it on a couple Pennsylvania hunting club grounds, although it's not a commonly used device as in the south. Tripods are most practical where sufficient choices of climbable trees are unavailable.

Hanging stands are by far the most portable and hold the potential for most danger, particularly while ascending and descending. Ladder stands also pose some danger during set-up as hunters often climb the steps to make strap or rope adjustments before they're secured. Most manufacturers have taken it upon themselves to include detailed instructions (some companies supply videos with their products) and safety devices for customers.

By virtue of their simplicity, hanging stands are easier to carry and can be attached to almost any tree. Their downside is the need for screw-in steps (illegal on public hunting lands in Pennsylvania, and on private lands without written permission, as they damage the tree) or a climbing pole, the latter known variously as "sky-ladder" or "climbing stick." Hangers also take longer to safely attach and ascend (or descend) than do ladder stands and climbing stands.

According to one Pennsylvania bow shop owner who sells hundreds of stands each year, archers are getting away from the screw-in steps and going to the strap-on ladders which are secured vertically against a tree with nylon rope or webbing. The ladders break down into short sections for transport.

For the more athletic hunters, bowhunters in particular, hanging stands are favored. They're lower priced than other styles and much lighter. Ultra-light hangers, such as the Loc-On Limit and Loggy Bayou Lite, are both big sellers in the state. They weigh a mere 6-7 pounds each.

Climbing stands have grown in popularity in recent years as technology catches up with the need for safety. Some climbers have devices for ascending and descending which require considerable upper body strength and a bit of athletic prowess. For the uninitiated, they may strain arm and back muscles. The

The hanging stand (above) is light and portable but the ladder stand (right) is most stable.

big advantage is they can be set up faster as there's no need to first attach stepping devices to the tree.

The disadvantage is they're heavier. A plus is they're far more adaptable to a wide variety of hunters.

Some climbers are positioned by a "stand-and-sit" technique. Several years ago I discovered Brent Hunt's Trophy Whitetail Treestand from Trophy Whitetail Products in Anderson, South Carolina. (See page 100.) I now own two of them.

Hunt manufactures three types of stands, one for gun hunters (the hunter sits facing the tree), another lighter and smaller stand for bowhunters (occupant sits with his or her back to the tree) and a combo stand on which either position can be used. The bow stand can also be readily adapted for gun-hunting. Besides being among the safest stands I've seen, they're also surprisingly comfortable with both padded seats and backrests and plenty of room.

The stand, like similar models from other manufacturers, is positioned by a simple stand-and-sit maneuver that any hunter can perform. In less than five minutes it can be attached and the hunter can be in position, safely and comfortably. A ratchet-type rope secures both parts of the stand for complete safety.

Ladder stands are by far the easiest to climb and therefore many hunters, my wife included, consider them the safest. Her Loc-On Titan consists of a fold-away padded seat, a 16x18 inch grid platform, center-lock bar for attachment to the tree for stability and flat ladder steps which break down into three 40-inch sections. When fastened, the stand reaches 12 feet with a 2-foot addition available.

A ladder stand can be moved from time to time with relative ease, although it's not one to cart around the woods each day. Hunters with access to private property or members of clubs and lodges often invest in such stands rather than build permanent platforms, which cannot be relocated without considerable work. However, a ladder stand can be easily set up for a day's hunt as it weighs only about 20 pounds, despite its size.

Of course, there are dozens more treestand manufacturers producing safe and functional stands. Names include Amacker, API Outdoors, Big Buck, Lone Wolf, Trax-America, Screaming Eagle, Strongbuilt, Summit Specialties, Trailhawk and Warren & Sweat, among others.

Expect to pay from $50 to $300 or more for a portable stand with hangers being the least expensive ($50-$75 average). Steps or take-apart climbing poles will add to the cost. A quality ladder stand averages $140-$175 with climbers in the range of $125-$175.

While treestand shopping, also pick up a reliable safety rope. My personal favorite is the Deluxe Safety Belt and Climbing Harness from Game Tracker. It's a polyester strap which fastens around the hunter's waist and a nylon rope with an easily manipulated lock-buckle circling the tree. Use it both in the treestand and while climbing.

Most hunting magazines offer addresses with their ads and manufacturers will send brochures and catalogs upon request. Or stop by your favorite archery shop and see first hand what's available for scaling new heights — safely — in the deer woods.

The Permanent-Portable Stand

Private landowners and members of sportsmen's clubs, lodges and deer camps usually construct their own treestands. Most are designed as they're being built, utilizing straight trees or mazes of heavy branches in low-crotched species. Few are built according to any blueprint.

Since the early 1980s I've spent at least a week hunting in Alabama, often stopping at White Oak Plantation near Tuskegee for a visit with the Pitman family, owners of the 25,000-acre whitetail haven.

Bo Pitman, White Oak manager, has built more than 500 safe and sturdy wooden, ladder stands which he's able to move, as necessary. I've dubbed the unique, relatively inexpensive stand as the "permanent, portable treestand."

It can be built anywhere and carted on a pick-up or ATV trailer. The Pitmans cut and nail a dozen or more at a time. Of course, on 25,000 acres there's plenty of room for stands but most hunters will only need one, and maybe a second or third as property size permits.

The entire structure is made of 2x4 treated lumber with a 3/4-inch plywood platform measuring 2x2 feet.

The next two pages show the stand in position and the dimensions of all the cuts necessary to build it. It reaches nearly 14-feet above the ground. The only attachment to the tree are two or three #20 nails which must be driven through the 21-inch long, 2x4-inch support on the tree's backside.

"It's not all that hard to take down and move," said Bo. "Two people are needed

The Permanent, Portable Treestand

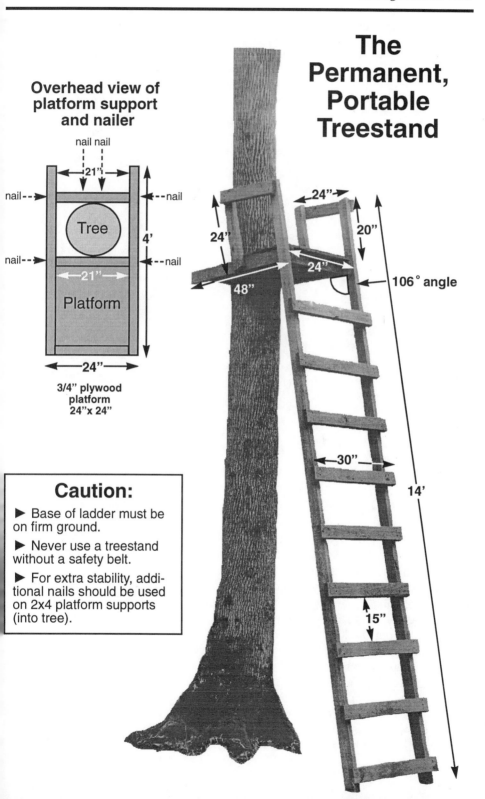

Overhead view of platform support and nailer

nail nail

21"

nail - - - - nail

Tree

4'

nail - - - - nail

21"

Platform

24"

3/4" plywood platform 24"x 24"

24"

20"

24"

24"

106° angle

48"

30"

14'

15"

Caution:

► Base of ladder must be on firm ground.

► Never use a treestand without a safety belt.

► For extra stability, additional nails should be used on 2x4 platform supports (into tree).

to shift the stand back and forth until the nails are loose, then pull them out with a claw."

An extension ladder is needed to safely attach and remove the nails.

Treestand Safety

A Georgia survey revealed that about one-fifth of all deer hunting-related injuries and fatalities include the use of treestands — both portable and stationary.

As for injuries to Pennsylvania hunters, Jim Filkosky, chief of the Hunter/ Trapper Education Bureau for the Pennsylvania Game Commission, said the state doesn't keep records on treestand accidents unless injury from bows or firearms is involved.

But the indicated treestand-related accidents are definitely on the rise in Pennsylvania. Mandatory hunter education courses now include instruction on safe treestand use.

Outdoor columnist Nick Hromiak sits in a ladder stand with a safety belt attached to the tree.

"We've had accidents where a hunter fell asleep and his gun dropped and fired, hitting him," said Filkosky. Other cases of hunters dozing off and falling from stands have also been reported.

Said Filkosky: "The earliest record of a treestand fatality while bowhunting happened 25 or 30 years ago when a hunter dropped his quiver. While he was crawling out the stand to get it he fell on an arrow that had stuck in the ground, with the point upward."

The broadhead severed a leg artery and the victim bled to death.

Today manufacturers not only make stronger, safer and easier-to-use stands than ever but are taking special efforts, including detailed instructions and videos, to assure that buyers know how to use them.

Of course, not all accidents involve portable stands. Many accidents happen on permanent stands. Hunters get into wooden platforms they haven't checked for a year or find an old stand in the woods and climb into it. Often these stands have loose nails or rotten boards — accidents waiting to happen.

According to an Associated Press report, treestand injuries and fatalities are problems nationwide. Mike Hufstetler, an outdoor recreation specialist at the Shepherd Spinal Center in Atlanta, told AP: "Each year we admit a growing number of patients with spinal cord injuries who have been injured in hunting-related accidents, mostly in falls from tree stands."

Shepherd is the country's largest hospital dedicated to the acute care and rehabilitation of people with spinal cord injury or disease. Hufstetler's job is to teach the sportsmen among them how to get back in the field — even if they're confined to a wheelchair.

The hospital completed a survey of treestand falls in Georgia over a 4-year period and found that 75 percent resulted in moderate to severe injuries. One quarter of those injured suffered permanent paralysis of arms or legs.

The study, surprising to many hunters, also revealed that factory-made treestands are much safer than home-made stands.

Hufstetler offers this advice for keeping a hunter from becoming his patient.

* Read all the instructions supplied with the stand carefully.

* Practice with the stand in daylight before you make your first hunting trip.

* Inspect the stand regularly and replace worn or broken parts with new factory parts.

* If you get sleepy, get down. Many hunters reported suffering injuries when they fell after nodding off.

* Hunt with a companion who can help if something goes wrong.

* And, of course, wear a safety harness.

He also recommends that hunters who construct their own stands should build them with new wood and not scrap material. As important is making pre-season inspections for rotting wood, broken parts, loose steps or nails and screws worked loose by tree movement.

Prevention, of course, is the best cure for ebbing the frightening prospect of falling from a tree.

Treestand bowhunters, in particular, will find plenty of use for pruning shears tucked into their daypacks. The shears will hasten the chore of clearing twigs and leaves that may hinder a shot.

Misjudging distance may be the number one reason for bowhunters' misses. Most archers spend their opening days in familiar surroundings; stand sites they've visited on pre-season scouting trips. Tying bits of orange ribbon at pre-determined distances on low branches, shrubs or stumps around your stand will help in making precise distance judgements. (Be sure to remove the ribbons when your season's over.)

Chapter
15

SCENTS and NONSENSE

Anyone who's paid his or her dues in the deer woods (interpret that as many hours outdoors and many years of mistakes) can surely relate occurrences which seem to go without explanation.

Such as deer clearly out of your scent path suddenly alerted to your presence. A buck strolling by upwind gazing directly at you perched in a treestand when you haven't twitched a muscle in 15 minutes. A doe grazing in an open field 100 yards off smelling your presence when the wind shifts.

Some whitetail phenomenons have explanations.

Having hunted with hundreds of different companions over the years it's my belief that many hunters still don't give deer sufficient respect for their abilities in detecting danger in the air.

It's been said the olfactory senses of a deer may be as much as 10,000 times more sensitive than a human's. Accurate or not, it's fact that whitetails possess "super noses." Hearing and eyesight are also used to detect other deer as well as hunters in the woods but it's the chemical lab, the nose and a portion of the roof of the mouth, that confirms what sort of molecules are drifting in the breeze.

Which brings us to scents — as well as some nonsense — about natural and commercial "deer lures" and cover-ups.

The first order of business in the deer woods is to reduce the chances that human odor will betray your presence. While I can recall squirting apple scent around my stand 35 years ago, then waiting for a buck to come charging in, it's only been in the past few years that emphasis is being given to covering your own odors.

If given only one such item to use while hunting, I'll choose a "scent-locking" liquid or powder. At first I thought the proliferation of compounds which claimed to minimize human odor — actually locking them in — was a gimmick. Later I came to respect them.

(Left) Matt Morrett of Hunter's Specialties pins a cedar cover scent wafer to his camo.

One cold night in a "deer camp" (a camping trailer) the toilet stopped up. The odor in the tight quarters was intolerable until Dr. Greg Bambenek, better known as "Dr. Juice" for his line of scent products, sprayed the waste material with his scent-locking solution.

Within minutes the odor was alleviated. And I became a believer.

Don't confuse these with cover-up scents such as cedar and pine scents or the fox, raccoon and skunk urines. I seldom use the urine cover-ups as my belief is they, skunk in particular, are far too revealing to deer. (Besides, my wife frowns on my keeping them in the house.) I opt for th fresh-earth and pine (when hunting pinewoods) cover scents.

Most scent companies today market one sort of scent-masking product or another, including sprays for carrying afield, shower soaps, shampoos, scent-free detergents and even powders. Use them on clothing and exposed skin before and during every trip to the deer woods. Clothing should be laundered in the scent-eliminating detergents.

Scent eliminating sprays, detergents, shampoos and soaps today flood the hunting marketplace.

Of course, eating an onion sandwich, flavoring your spaghetti with garlic or lacing your lunchtime pizza with spices will all work against you. As breathing tends to be a necessity with all of us, avoiding spicy and odoriferous foods for at least 24 hours prior to a hunt is suggested.

The second type of liquid (or solid) that's proven its effectiveness is the sex lure. The one caution here is that improper use can play against a hunter. Rushing the season by using rut lures in early October will do nothing but alarm deer. But used properly they're quite effective.

Rut scents, both natural and synthetic, will be most effective the last couple weeks of the Pennsylvania bow season. It's even worth a try the first few days of the gun hunt. Remember that even though does may not be ready to breed, bucks are ready to mate. Intrusion of other bucks into their "territories" arouses their ire as well as their curiosity.

Don't confuse rut-scents with pure urine scents, although they are somewhat alike. Doe urine, commonly marketed by many companies, is more a calming scent than anything else. Of course, considering the number of times does urinate in the woods, another splash of it will probably do little to bring a buck into your sights. As urine quickly breaks down to ammonia upon contact with air, it soon dissipates on the ground and opening a bottle of may reduce its effectiveness.

Estrus scents (which contain urine), however, hold the magic smell that brings bucks to attention, although does react negatively to it. This scent should not be used at any time except in the rut period. For more than 90 percent of the year the odor means absolutely nothing to bucks or does. Timing is the key to its effective use.

I use estrus lures on "drag rags" tied to my rubber boots on the way to a treestand and have watched as bucks nosed their ways up the same paths later in the day. Before climbing into a tree I'll tie the rag to a shrub 10 to 15 yards from my stand. On several occasions both bucks and does were enticed to the rag, although does always seemed uneasy. But on several notable occasions curiosity got the best of them and they had to get a closer smell. Seldom did they hang around to feed afterwards, however.

Terry Rohm hangs a tarsal scent on a "licking branch."

Among the most effective of lures is the tarsal scent of a buck. My former father-in-law, a McKean County native, made an annual collection of buck tarsal glands which he tied to his boot laces each time he went afield. He stored several of the glands, tufts of hairs from the hocks including the skin around the gland, in a mayonnaise jar in the refrigerator between hunts. He even froze fresh tarsals between seasons.

Now the combination tarsal gland and scent systems, such as offered by Wellington Outdoors (makers of the famed Tink's No. 69 estrus lure) and others, have proven their effectiveness. The glands no longer produce secretions, of course, and must be replenished. The gland is hung above an active or mock scrape to catch the wind and distract any buck enticed to check it out. The gland's oil, not buck urine, is the key element. Bucks simply use their own urine as a carrier for the oily substance produced by the darkened tarsals at rut time.

Again, the idea here is to create the illusion that another buck has moved into the area. Although I've made mock scrapes and had them attended by other deer between trips to the stand, the preference is to set up near an actual scrape. I then use a stick to add my own "trademark" so as not to pollute the area in or around it with human odor. Buck-in-rut urine is then added to the scrape and the tarsal gland hanging above it.

Tarsal glands can also be dragged behind on the way to your hunting area. Simply rig one or two to twine and tie it to your boot. Bucks moving along or across your path may follow it to your location.

A zip-type bag serves yeoman duty in keeping your clothing and hands from absorbing the smell. After all, you don't want the deer looking at you. Rather, it should be concentrating on the smell emanating from the treated scrape. Never put urine-based or glandular scents on your clothing.

Given a choice, I'll take scents made from natural sources. Flow-Rite's Deer Formula, which I've used successfully, is advertised as 100-percent tarsal glands. In Clinton County one snowy December afternoon my wife dabbed some Deer Formula on her boots, then posted about 200 yards off in the woods. Within the hour a 6-point buck came down her path with its nose to the ground. As she hadn't shot a deer at that time she acted hastily, cleanly missing the unwary buck. Minutes later we checked out the tracks in the snow and noted where the deer had picked up the scent trail (about 50 yards from and within sight of the truck) and followed it, in Betty Lou's precise footsteps. Such are the experiences which encourage confidence in a specific scent and account for favorites espoused by individual sportsmen.

For the record, I've also had luck with synthetic rut scents, such as the BucRut solid wafer from Hunter's Specialties. The oval scent wafers (available also in food and pine, cedar or earth-odor cover scents) create no mess whatsoever and their lives can be extended for several trips to the woods by keeping them in airtight containers.

Finally there's the food scents. Again, I'm sure they've been effective for some hunters but I've never had much faith in them. Acorn, apple, grape and others can be found on sporting goods store shelves. Admittedly, such scents are non-threatening to deer and curious animals may well be drawn to them. A friend from Lycoming County told me of arrowing an 8-pointer that came to his peanut butter scent three straight afternoons, the fourth evening offering a clear shot.

Of course, food scents can also double as cover scents. But don't use apple scent in a pinewoods.

One mistake most hunters make in scent use is overdoing it. If the manufacturer suggests 6 to 8 drops, human nature tells us 12 to 16 drops will be twice as effective. No necessarily. In fact, too strong an odor may be more a deterrent than an aid.

Scents are today an integral part of hunting, bowhunting and close-range muzzleloader hunting in particular. Using common sense in their use is the key to getting the most from them.

A thick-necked buck checks for strange odors at its scrape.

Pack a couple garbage bags before your next trip to deer camp, Camp odors, from tobacco to bacon, will readily penetrate hunting garments. Upon returning from the hunt, take off your clothes and hang them outdoors for an hour or so, then stuff them in a sealed garbage bag overnight. Some hunters also place cotton swabs with a few drops of their favorite cover scent in the bag with the clothing.

A friend who spends most of his deer season in farm country always makes it a point to look for fresh cow droppings on the way to his stand. He then takes a minute to "refresh" his boots with the "pies." He claims that barnyard bucks are familiar with the odor and it serves to mask both his trail and his body scent while still-hunting.

Chapter 16

CALLING ALL WHITETAILS

Remember your earliest days of deer hunting?

If your background is like mine, tagging a whitetail may have once seemed the impossible dream. But once a doe was on the ledger, scoring on a buck then became the challenge.

You studied your prey, read all you could in *Field & Stream* or *Outdoor Life*, and learned a few tricks. After the rack of a spike or forkhorn was on the wall, getting a trophy dominated your mind. That, for most hunters, becomes the impossible dream which never awakens.

But over the years you honed a few more techniques, learned a "secret" or two about whitetail hunting and took chances on techniques you'd only read about or heard about at a sport show seminar. Then, one memorable day, it all came together in the taking of a trophy. Or, at least, you developed a trick or two which provided confidence whenever you entered the deer woods.

Often the latter plateau isn't achieved because of a hunter's "rut" — the same rut many sportsmen get into because they refuse to learn about, then alter, deer hunting tactics. The hoped-for trophy is sought in the same manner as in previous seasons, often by little more than climbing into the same tree stand or posting in the same draw year after year, and hoping "this will be the day" that a trophy's path and yours cross.

To tip the scales on deer it's often necessary to try something new — to enter each year's hunt with a bit more knowledge of the prey and confidence that you're wiser and warier than ever before.

Many hunters ignore or refuse to focus their attentions on some tried and true deer hunting methods because of the attitude that "it won't work for me."

Those thoughts came to mind one winter at the Eastern Sports and Outdoor Show in Harrisburg. As I'd been host of an outdoor TV show in the region at the time, I was privileged to be recognized by viewers — many of whom had questions or stories to share about hunting and fishing.

I was especially surprised at a conversation with an older gun hunter whom I'd met previously.

"I don't bother with such things," he muttered as we stood in an aisle listening to a manufacturer of grunt tubes demonstrate his product.

"I've never even a heard a deer make a sound. I can't imagine that one could actually be called in. It may work some places but here (in Pennsylvania) it's just a gimmick," he concluded.

We shared a Coke a few minutes later and I told my tale of success on two hunts during the previous months, one in Quebec and the other in Alabama, where 8-pointers came to my calls.

"Sure, but that wasn't in Pennsylvania," the pessimist challenged. "Do you think you could call in a Pennsylvania deer?"

"I've done it," I answered. "Several times."

His eyes focused on mine as I continued, telling him of times bleats and grunts meant the difference between venison and an empty freezer.

Bear in mind that all this took place about 1985, when deer calling, at least popularly, was in its infancy.

Why should Pennsylvania bucks be oblivious to sounds that hunters make and deer respond to in other states?

Simply, they're not. More direct is the question: "Will Pennsylvania bucks respond to calling during the bow and gun seasons?"

This buck was grunting as it was being photographed by the author.

The answer is an unequivocal "Yes!"

Rut time, in which bowhunters are afield, is prime time for calling but that doesn't mean it's the only period deer are responsive. I've found that bucks and/ or does will respond to at least three types of audio lures during all the state's hunting periods — particularly the forepart of the bow season and again, although less so, in the initial days of the gun season.

Students of deer lore know these times, respectively, as the pre-rut, full-rut and post-rut periods. Pennsylvania whitetails begin gearing up for the rut during the final half of October. They do most of their breeding from about November 10-20 although does that go through their 28-day estrus cycle without conceiving will attract bucks through December or longer.

Bucks are prepared to breed considerably longer than their mid-November peak rutting time suggests — almost as long as they hold hard antlers and testosterone is produced.

Documented cases in neighboring New York show that matings have taken place between September 22 and February 22. Calling is effective during all Pennsylvania seasons, from the first day of bowhunting to the final day of muzzleloading. After all, deer talk with one another year-around, not only in the fall.

How does the archer or gun-hunter use this information?

And what sort of calls among the myriad that have hit the market in the past three years should be used?

First, don't go afield thinking you're turkey hunting and you'll get an answer. Only once in the dozen years I've been using calls have I had a deer respond vocally. That was a small Alabama 4-pointer with a "manly," baritone voice. He answered twice, probably out of the frustration of hearing me but not being able to see me.

Yet, many hunters agree the best time to call is when you actually see a deer and want to stop it, get a better look and/or bring it close enough for a precise shot.

Secondly, forget the complex information (for now) on deer vocalization that's hit the pages of deer magazines in recent years about the many voices of the whitetail. While interesting and scientifically accurate, it often serves to confuse and intimidate many hunters. Start by mastering a few basic calls, as turkey callers must, then expand your repertoire.

Following are several basic calls that may tip the odds in the Pennsylvania hunter's favor.

The Bawl Call

The "bawl" (crying) call is considered, along with the bleat and snort, as a distress sound. To the human ear it's a close mimic of a goat or sheep's nasal *maaaaa* sound. However, it's not as prolonged nor is it as loud.

One October morning, while experimenting with a Kelly Cooper call which is capable of adjustments for a variety of sounds, I used the "bawling" mode to entice a button buck to within six yards. I was squirrel hunting at the time, dressed in camo, save for an orange hat, and seated against a tree while holding a .22.

I'd seen the deer at about 75 yards and offered several subdued bawls. Its ears

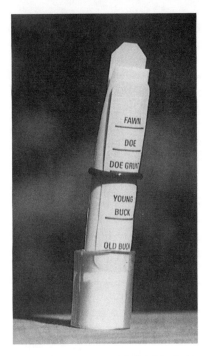

The mouth-held, Multi-Pitch Deer Call (shown actual size) from Hally Wildlife Calls in Bucks County is an excellent tool for bowhunters.

perked and it made a slow, seemingly unconcerned move in my direction. I didn't call again as it headed directly toward my position. It paused on occasion to look for the source of the sound but seemed calm and curious as it advanced. Had I been bowhunting it would have offered an easy shot.

Dave Hale, half of the Knight & Hale Game Call team, says that bawl calls, although considered mild "distress" sounds, serve as contact calls — particularly among does and young deer of both sexes.

"They have a curiosity effect," says Hale. "A deer will come to investigate the sound or maybe join up with other deer."

On occasion, a bawl call will entice a curious doe and a buck will follow. It's a good vocalization no matter which sex you're after.

Canadians and other north-country hunters have long used a simple rubber band call to simulate the bawl. Although its sound is entirely different than that produced by the Cooper call, it's similar enough to have good results.

Pennsylvanian Cooper, best known for his turkey calling skills and a new line of camouflage clothing, labels the sound as the "doe bawl."

"It's a throatier sound than the bleat," he explained while demonstrating. "It can be used to call to either a doe or a buck. Both will respond."

The bawl call is a good choice for the entire Pennsylvania archery season, not just the pre-rut period. And it can be used effectively during all gun seasons.

The Contact Grunt

Grunting is, by far, the most popular and the easiest call to master. But unlike grunts produced by bucks during the heart of the rut, "contact grunting" is a bit different but just as easy to mimic and, as Hale recommends, a good pre-rut ploy.

Hale, who studies his herd of penned whitetails throughout the year and records their vocalizations, says unbred does and pre-rut bucks are both susceptible to grunting, which he describes as "a location call."

"It's not as aggressive a grunt as you'd use in the rut," he suggests. "I won't use it unless I first see a deer. Then I might make a loud grunt or two to get its attention. After that I keep it subdued but I'll make 10 or 12 grunts a minute, always making just short grunts. Don't be aggressive."

Cooper agrees: "I refer to this as the "trail grunt." I often hear it made by the year-

Grunt calls are effective in all seasons but most productive during the fall bowhunt.

and-a-half old buck who was kicked out of the herd by its mother. She's getting ready to breed and doesn't want him around so he's out looking — trying to make contact with other deer." Cooper, like Hale, recommends using the trail (or contact) grunt in short, subdued bursts spaced by 5-10 seconds, then pausing for a minute or two.

Antler Rattling

While seldom referred to as a "call," antler-rattling is another popular, easy to master method of communicating with bucks. Indeed, it is a "call" although not done with the mouth.

Considering the period in which Pennsylvania bowhunters are afield, it's most effective during the pre-rut. That's when bucks are just getting into the swing of things and the sound of antlers clashing tells them there's probably a fight going on and does will be about.

Sparring differs from aggressive rattling in the same way the contact grunt differs from the aggressive grunt.

"I like to use rattle-bags," Hale told me during a hunt several autumns back. "It has the curiosity effect on bucks who will come to investigate. The bag is a lot

Will Primos attempts to rattle up a buck with his new "Fightin' Horns."

easier to carry, too."

The sound is similar to that made by gently striking the tips of a pair of antlers against one another. Such sparring in the wild often precedes more serious scraps during the rut period. It's also produced when bucks are entering the aggression stage but not yet in full rut.

"Sort of like checking out one another and maybe pushing and head-shaking a little bit," is the way Hale describes it. "I don't recommend doing any loud clashing early on."

Several manufacturers make rattle bags — composed of a tough, camouflaged, oblong cloth bag housing lengths of hardwoods which, when rolled between the hands, simulate the gentle sparring sounds made by bucks.

Of course, real and simulated rattling antlers can also be used. I prefer racks with at least three points each (cut off the brow tines or you'll end up with scarred fingers) and have successfully used actual antlers and simulated "rattlers".

More recent in origin are rattling antlers designed for easy carrying while duplicating the real thing. Primos Game Call's new "Fightin' Horns" are available in both natural and orange (for safety reasons) colors. The unique design, allowing a mid-point grip with tines on both sides (14 in all) for minimum movement and maximum sound production, allows their fit in a daypack.

"I'll rattle for 10 to 30 seconds at a time," advises Will Primos. "Bring them together sharply and intertwine the points, twisting and grinding them against each other, then jerk them apart."

As a curtain call, Primos strikes the ground with the antlers several times or, if in a treestand, rakes leaves or scrapes the tree trunk.

He then waits several minutes before starting the performance anew. If there's no response, Primos moves into the wind a couple hundred yards and starts all over.

As said, the pre-rut period is prime time but rattling can also be effective well into the rut. Biologists agree that in places with low buck-to-doe ratios rattling is most effective. Competition is the key. But that doesn't mean you shouldn't try them in any Pennsylvania landscape, where ratios are typically one buck to 5-6 or more does.

I've watched bucks testing one another as early as the first week of October. The encounters were always brief and never got beyond the point of a head down, antler-tickling affair. Often the accompanying bucks went back to feeding after a short stint of sparring. On occasion other bucks came in to check out the activity, although does seldom express much interest.

But it did prove that bucks, indeed, make rattling noises throughout the entire archery season. Only once have I seen a Pennsylvania buck battle in the gun season. That occurred in Lehigh County on the fourth day of the buck season and lasted a brief minute or so. It was more a sparring between a 4-pointer and a small 6-pointer than an outright fight.

Gun Season Vocalizations

By virtue of a million-plus hunters afield for every Pennsylvania buck opener, calling is largely a futile affair on that magic day. Better to find a well-used escape route than sit in your stand grunting at spooked deer. After the first couple hours of opening day most deer have encountered hunters and calling, in areas where hunters abound, is probably as useless as whistling in the wind.

But bawls and grunts can be effective during the gun season in places where hunting pressure is minimal or in subsequent days when hunters have gone back home and things start getting back to normal. Private lands and deep backwoods locations where whitetails aren't pushed will go about their daily routines relatively undisturbed.

In 1988, on opening morning, I watched a Bradford County forkhorn relentlessly chase does around my treestand. Two bucks, taken by fellow camp members, showed the swollen necks and stained metatarsals indicative of a lingering or late rut.

Make no mistake about it. Pennsylvania hunters can increase their chances of filling their tags by using calls and rattling antlers — not only in November's prime time but during fringe seasons of the rut, as well.

On rare occasions bucks come running to check the source of the sound. But usually it's a slow approach, with nose, eyes and ears probing the forest looking for the source of the sound — you.

One item of constant confusion among hunters is which way to move sights when sighting in a gun. Simply remember to move the rear sight in the same direction (left or right, up or down) you want the impact point to move. The same holds true for sight pins on bows.

Chapter
17

GO WITH A BOW
Tips From Pennsylvania's Bow-Pros

There's not been an era in Pennsylvania deer hunting history subject to as many changes to whitetail management and hunting as now.

Bonus licenses, deer damage seasons, does in buck season on some lands, special regulations areas with multi-deer limits, an August issuance of doe licenses — and much more -- are all welcome changes.

It's enough to make a camouflaged hat spin on the head of any archer who recalls, not all that long ago, a simple "one deer a year" hunt.

Some of the changes, as with any interruption of tradition, draw fire and ire. Others are welcomed. That's typical of Pennsylvania hunters; a million-plus sportsmen with a million-plus opinions.

One that brought cheers from well over a quarter-million bowhunters, however, is the two week extension of the archery season into November. It's as close to the peak of the rut as any Keystone State hunter has ever (within modern times) been permitted to seek whitetails. In many states, rut-time hunting is nothing new.

But it is in Pennsylvania. And it's given 315,000-plus Robin Hoods the thrill and challenge of hunting barrel-necked bucks. More on that later.

Of course, four weeks of hunting among October's Kodachromes precede the rut hunt. Many hunters tie their tags to bucks' ears long before the November bonus.

Bob Foulkrod of Troy, Bradford County, is a nationally known bowhunter who runs an archery school and a commercial hunting lodge from his home. I asked Foulkrod about his plan of attack at season's start.

"The first days of Pennsylvania's archery season are virgin," said Foulkrod. "But when everybody "scents up" the woods it doesn't take deer long to learn they're not out there picking blueberries."

Foulkrod's scouting plays an important role in where he spends the initial days of the season. He begins his pre-hunt studies as early as July 4. Apple orchards are prime places to set up a stand early in the bow season at which time trees are

Bob Foulkrod with a bow-buck shot near his Bradford County lodge.

still dropping the fruits they began yielding in summer and deer are habitual visitors.

"Throughout all of Pennsylvania acorns start falling about the end of August," Bob explained. "Deer will also stay in areas with lots of oaks or even beechnuts into the first weeks of October or longer,"

"Cornfields are also hit hard from August on through harvest time. When the corn's cut deer will continue to frequent the area for several days, with dominant bucks starting to feed at night."

However, Foulkrod sees annual shifts in patterns starting three to four days into the season. That may demand some relocation in heavily-hunted areas.

"I hunt deer almost the same way I might try to hunt a person," Foulkrod mused. "He'll make lots of visits to the refrigerator and the bedroom. For deer, I'll hunt the food sources but one place I stay totally away from is the bedding area."

"Once you chase a buck out of his bedroom he'll look for a new place to lay down and you'll have to start your plans all over again. You should get to know where it is then use that knowledge to set up on travel routes — just like a person traveling from the TV or kitchen to the bedroom."

In Foulkrod's seminars he tells his audience: "Deer will change their habits several times in the course of a Pennsylvania season. They'll change first after the season opens because of hunters in the woods. They'll change again when the leaves drop and the places they could stand in a hedgerow and watch traffic go by they're now being detected. When the rut starts they'll change a third time and when snow falls they'll again look for new places to find food."

The wise hunter changes with his prey.

"But if you find a good ridge that other hunters haven't found, stick to it," Foulkrod advises. "Places that attracted deer one year will attract them the next. There's nothing like being familiar with your hunting territory."

He also offers an important ethical consideration; a "golden rule" of archery.

"If you find someone else's treestand don't go near it. Someone has probably scouted the area and that's his place. I don't like strangers using my treestand and I won't use theirs. That's not what bowhunting and ethical bowhunters are all about."

Of course, the newest bowhunter's bonus is the addition of two weeks to the

The cornfield is a predictable hotspot early in the fall bow season.

season, taking the grand hunt into the November rut.

I asked four well-known bowbenders — all of whom have been hunting the rut in other states for many years — to share some advice on their rut-time tactics when hunting in Pennsylvania.

The Non-Aggressive Doe Grunt

Dr. Dave Samuel is a frequent contributor to Pennsylvania Sportsman magazine and a columnist for several bowhunting publications. He's a biology professor at the University of West Virginia, a prolific writer and a lecturer on anti-hunting activities who annually draws his bow in Pennsylvania and other states.

"If I could choose the two best weeks to bowhunt, that (the first two weeks of November) would be it. It's the time you'll get more reaction from rattling but my favorite (technique) is to use a doe grunt call. I don't know a time when it's more effective.

I use a Wood's Wise doe grunt. I've never had much luck with the aggressive, loud calls with the long tubes. Like most Pennsylvania hunters, I don't hunt many areas with big bucks. Those calls will chase away the little guys.

I've had a great deal of success in bringing in the smaller bucks that are there. I rarely use the call "blind." That is, I don't call unless I see a deer. If I don't know what it is or, preferably, if it's a buck I'll use it, especially if it's not coming in my

The doe grunt is especially effective on smaller bucks.

direction.

I don't call to does at that time. They're not ready (to mate) and won't respond. That call seldom gets much reaction from does.

I use a low volume and give two or three calls, then shut up, especially if I know he's heard it. A buck knows exactly where a call comes from. Sometimes he'll start to come in, then hang up. I'll call again and he may do the same thing. It depends on his frame of mind at the time.

One year I called to a buck and he totally ignored it. There was no reaction at all.

The next day I again saw him, called, and he came in immediately and I shot him.

My advice for the first weeks of November is to use a doe grunt. You have nothing to lose. I've never scared a buck with it.

As I said, that's one of my favorite times. Bowhunters who have never hunted that period before will find out they'll see much more deer — and they will respond to calls."

Forget "Field Days"

Jody Hugill of State College, Centre County, is a frequent lecturer on bowhunting and deer and turkey calling. He's a member of the HOYT U.S.A., Lohman Game Call and Realtree Camouflage prostaffs. He does most of his bowhunting in central Pennsylvania.

"The best advice I can give is to get away from the fields and into the woods and the edges of thickets. Deer will still go to fields to feed, usually at night, and the

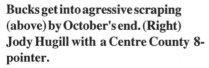

Bucks get into agressive scraping (above) by October's end. (Right) Jody Hugill with a Centre County 8-pointer.

hunter must remember that foliage is down and things have opened up — so detection of a hunter by a buck is enhanced.

After hunting during the first week or two of November in other states, I now realize that Pennsylvania bucks — maybe because of the high buck-to-doe ratio — don't scrape as intently as states where deer are more in balance. Just finding a scrape doesn't mean the buck will be back. That may not be true for all parts of the state but it holds in the mountain country where I hunt.

I prefer to first find the route to a scrape area — with several scrapes and lots of rubs — then set up on a trail. I seldom set up on a specific scrape. First you have to find the direction of travel and look for trails that indicate use by bucks. Often these trails aren't pounded down from lots of travel but they do show big prints. That's where you want to be.

Many hunters will also be rattling during the (extended season). I also rattle and call but not aggressively or loud. Too many hunters get big rattling antlers and really beat them. A big buck pretty much knows what's in his area because he stays there. No matter if you're trophy hunting or after any buck, bringing the spikes and fours and 6-pointers to you will get a big buck's attention, too. Big antlers and aggressive rattling will drive away the smaller bucks. Just light, occasional rattling is recommended.

A hunter must understand that the classic red-eyed buck charging through the woods after someone rattles seldom happens. Bucks will be on their feet more during the rut and will do things they wouldn't do earlier in the season. But they won't let their guard down every minute of the day.

Plan to stay in your stand longer that week. Deer will move all day long. It's the only time when they're up more than they're bedding and hunters must be patient enough to take advantage of it."

Scout and Scrape
Bob Kirschner of Murrysville, Westmoreland County, has taken six Pope & Young bucks. He owns his own deer scent company, has starred in several popular videos and is the author of "The Art and Appreciation of Trophy Bowhunting".

"Hunters should use the final days of the regular season to do some scouting for the (November) hunt. There will be more sign and lots of new sign. It's definitely the best time to get a buck.

Remember that this isn't the first week of the season. Deer will have been hunted for four weeks and will be much more wary than they were a month earlier. Keep your scent level at zero. I can't stress that too much.

This is a good time for an attractant lure. I produce Silver Tip, a dominant doe-based scent collected during the estrus. I've also introduced a new Buck Crystal scent — actually small crystals that have an extremely long life.

I use them on fake scrapes. The idea is to make a buck think an intruder has invaded his territory. I'll make them close to thickets, as close as I can get to bedding or feeding areas. I want a deer to be able to smell it and see it. Often I'll put the scrape on a mound or some spot where a buck can see it from 20 or 30 yards.

I also make a scent trail, usually in the shape of an inverted question mark, to my tree. Some hunters make such a trail straight to their tree but I'll walk in a circle around it before I get in my treestand.

As for rattling and calling, I simply try to intimidate. I only tickle the antlers to make a buck who hears it curious.

But no matter what else you do, keep your own body scent to a minimum. You can do everything else right but if that buck smells you, he's gone!"

Head To The Hills
Terry Rohm is a native of Blain in Perry County where his brothers and father run a turkey call business and Terry returns to hunt whenever he can. He currently lives in Georgia where he serves as public relations manager for Wellington Outdoors makers of deer and turkey hunting products.

"When you think of hunting the extended season, think about turkey hunters. They and other small game hunters will be in the woods at the same time, especially on public lands. In states where I know fall turkey hunters will be in the woods with me, I'll use them the way some gun hunters have learned to "use" other hunters during the gun season.

Deer won't be panicked but they will sooner or later move uphill if they're disturbed. That's where I'll set up -- on ridges and mountain tops. They won't be spooked badly but that week is also the first full week of the small game season and there will definitely be more hunters walking around the lowlands.

I recommend getting to your stand long before light and staying there as long as you can. Set up in the laurel and near thickets. That's where deer will go to hide. If all you see is does, remember that the prime rut is near and bucks will find them.

Also do some scouting and find out where acorns are dropping. If you can find a white oak ridge, stay on it. Acorns are only available for a short time and there's lots of competition for them — especially the white oaks which they prefer.

I'll use Tink's 69 or a tarsal gland at that time. But even more important, remember to control body odor. You can't overdo it.

Finally, don't hunt one area too much. You're presence will be seen — or even smelled, even if you're not in your stand at the time. If you hunt a place two or three times and saw deer there in the earlier part of the season but there's not much activity now, move. If you have faith in it you can always come back a few days later when you've given it a chance to rest.

I don't know of a time when Pennsylvania bowhunters have been given a better chance to harvest a buck as during this late season. It's only a few days later than the end of the regular season but a whole lot closer to the peak of the rut — the best time of all."

Bob Kirschner proved his methods work with this southwestern Pennsylvania Pope and Young trophy.

Chapter 18

OPENING DAY
Musings and Memories

Precisely one-half before sunrise on the first Monday following Thanksgiving I'll be leaning against a tree somewhere near the New York border in Bradford County. I've been there or elsewhere in this beautiful, whitetail-rich state on other openers and my presence is as predictable as tomorrow's sunrise.

Only once, in 1960, thanks to a double fracture of my leg in a college soccer game, did I miss the annual opener.

It's surprising how many of those hunts I can vividly recall. Few are cherished simply because of racks on the wall. There's plenty more to fill the memory's album.

Like the two opening days when my hunting was over minutes after legal shooting time. Once a Carbon County spike buck caused the shortened hunt and on another occasion it was a Tioga County forkhorn that prematurely ended my season. In both cases I was pleased and disappointed at the same time. The crescendo that builds with the arrival of November and Thanksgiving time is suddenly snubbed with the sound of a lone gun blast.

For that reason I've passed up opening hour bucks on several occasions (but, admittedly, never anything bigger than a forkhorn). Four years ago I passed on a three-pointer at 7 a.m. and ended the day with a spike buck. At the moment of decision, with the crosshairs on the buck's shoulder, I chose not to shoot. But eight hours later a spike with 6-inch prongs fell to my 30- 06.

Don't ask why. I don't know. What I do know is that I wasn't a bit sorry that my p.m. buck wasn't a big as my a.m. prey.

In more than three decades of deer hunting, however, I've come to realize that cherished memories don't necessarily hang on the camp meatpole. In Pennsylvania, opening day is as much ritual and tradition — maybe most a matter of just "being there" — as it is a time to bring home venison.

Ask anyone who's ever tossed in his sleep on the eve of the season opener. I did it on my first trip to camp and I still don't sleep soundly today. When I can sleep

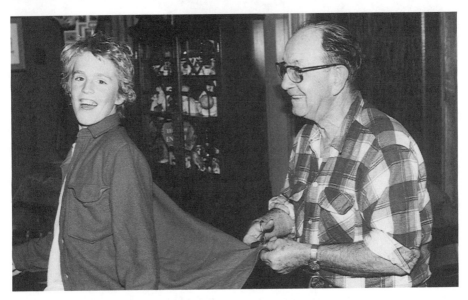

A young hunter gets his shirttails clipped -- a deer camp ritual.

deeply on the eve of the opener, perhaps it will signal a time to hang up my gun or bow.

There are always too many big-racked bucks in my dreams; bucks that usually don't materialize the next day.

Perhaps the fondest memory is a kid's first deer. Maybe it was a buck. No matter, if dad was there and the guys at camp shook your hand and patted your shoulder, it was a memory-maker.

To a deer hunter the details of downing one's first buck never dim. Don't try to explain that to a neighbor or fellow worker who doesn't hunt. They'd never understand.

My first buck was taken in McKean County in 1962, only a couple hundred yards off Barden Brook Road and less than two miles from the New York state line. I haven't been there for more than 20 years but I'll bet I could find the very tree against which I sat — if it hasn't been cut down in the meantime. I first spotted the two deer sprinting across an open valley more than 300 yards away. Then I didn't have a scoped rifle, nor could I afford binoculars (not on my annual school teacher's salary of $4,200). But my eyes were better a quarter century back and as the deer sprinted up the hillside atop which I was sitting I noted, from a considerable distance, that the lead animal had "horns." I wasted no time getting my .32 slide- action Remington to my shoulder and aiming on the buck that was still 200 yards off, a mere speck in the iron sight.

But for some reason it cut away from its appointed path and dissolved into a stand of oaks and beeches below the ridge. Foolishly, I dropped the rifle to my waist and stood, hoping to see the buck as it approached the ridgetop 100 or so yards off.

As luck had it the buck and doe turned and cut along the mountain in my direction. When they popped into view both were less than 25 yards away. They continued running, then pulled to a halt less than 20 feet away — the handsome 3-point buck in front.

Although the details up to that point are crystal clear, I've never been able to remember raising the gun to my shoulder. I think I fired from the hip, the bullet striking the buck in the neck and killing it instantly.

I do recall that I didn't move for a full minute. I just stared at the deer. My temples pounded and the thought "I finally got one" flitted through my otherwise blank mind.

I still have that stunted rack. It seems to get smaller each time I look at it. Since then I've been blessed with some true wall-hangers. But they loom no larger than the trophy 3-pointer I killed on that cloudy afternoon in '62.

There have been other opening day deer that are just as vivid. One that comes to mind is the biggest deer I ever "passed up" — which is a gentle way of admitting that I "froze up."

That one was encountered in a shotgun-only zone in the southern tier of New York, where I enjoyed my first two years of teaching. I hadn't seen a deer all morning and had agreed to meet a friend at a pre-appointed spot at 11 a.m. - under an apple tree in an overgrown pasture no bigger than a couple acres and surrounded on three sides by trees.

I arrived first, set my gun on the ground, nestled against the stocky tree and unwrapped a sandwich. Casually I glanced to my right, for whatever reason compelled me to do so at the time, and saw a 10-point buck staring at me from about 50 yards, blended against the laurel.

I know he was a 10-pointer as I counted each tine - twice!

I've counted them hundreds of times since.

A doe moved up behind

The pileated woodpecker is a regular companion in the deer woods.

the buck, paused for a second, then sprinted past me at 30 yards, leaped a wire fence, and disappeared among the trees. The buck was close behind.

I didn't even reach for my Ithaca. After the deer had disappeared I noted that the ham and cheese sandwich in my hand was crushed to the size of a golf ball. I didn't tell my friend that when he showed up 10 minutes later. Nor did I tell him that I'd just experienced a classic case of buck fever.

After all, I was 22 years old then and had deer hunted for nearly a decade. "Oldtimers" like me just don't get buck fever.

Right?

On yet another buck opener, more than 15 years back in Carbon County, near Francis Walter Dam, I'd canoed across the darkened waters of the reservoir long before first light and was seated against a charred oak tree when the first snowflakes began falling before sunup.

It was the sort of morning of which deer hunters dream; fresh tracking snow, quiet walking conditions and good visibility. Hunters moving in via the land route would be a long while in coming, allowing me the comfortable feeling of being alone in the backwoods, knowing that the orange army would be pushing deer my way in a couple hours.

It wasn't long after I heard the first shot ring out near the road, more than a mile away, that I detected a noise — like a deer pawing in the leaves for acorns — just over a rolling ridge off to my right. I readied myself for a shot, assuming that a buck would soon poke its head over the rise, some 40 yards away.

I waited five minutes. The rustling noise continued but nothing showed. Carefully I pushed away from the tree and crawled toward the rim of the hill, beyond which I fancied the big-racked buck was feeding.

It was a quiet approach, my shuffling muffled by the cottony snow. As I neared the rim I poked the gun, then my head, over the mound of snow.

But nothing was there but the blackened stumps and trunks of trees killed in a fire the previous summer. I dropped back behind the cover of the ridge to regain some composure and again listened for the scratchings. The sounds continued but the source was a mystery. Again I carefully peered over the edge. This time I was on the receiving end of a stare.

One of the stumps, it seems, was actually the backside of a bear — no more than 30 yards downhill. We locked eyes for what was surely seconds but seemed like minutes. The last I saw of him he was sprinting up the far hill, his fat buttocks quaking like a vat of Jello.

The 5-pointer that walked up to me an hour later capped my morning's hunt. But it will always be the memory of the first black bear I'd ever seen in the deer woods that's etched in greatest detail.

Of course, there are dozens, maybe hundreds, of other opening day happenings not soon forgotten — the first deer hunts with my sons, their first bucks, my 6-pointer dropped at 250 yards, the wolf-like coyote that eyed me at 30 steps, then danced off down the ridge, chickadees perched on my gun barrel, the porcupine sniffing my boots, the long-bearded gobbler roosting in the tree above, the white-footed mouse sharing a sandwich - and many other memories - not the least of which are friends to share tales at day's end.

Sure, there are tactics that work on opening day. Like using pre-season scouting knowledge to find escape routes. Or taking advantage of others' presence in the woods to push deer.

But most kills are made simply by finding a good spot and sitting tight. The magic in the air, the shots echoing off hills near and far and the anticipation around the fire still glowing from the night before are plenty.

I take opening days seriously, but not too seriously. It's a time thought about since the close of last year's season and each opener adds a new page to the memory bank. That's guaranteed.

On this year's opener, exactly 30 minutes before dawn, I'll be back. My album of memories will be opened as I await the first shot.

Like everyone else I'll hope for a fat buck. But over the years I've discovered that opening day memories aren't ranked according to whether or not a deer was killed or a shot was taken.

The best trophies, someday my sons will understand, come from the hunting of memories.

That's what opening days are for.

Some hunters only dream of close encounters with big bucks.

Chapter 19

SECOND WEEK BUCKS
When The Chips Are Down

I heard the rocks tumbling down the steep cliff a full minute before the narrow, high-racked 4-pointer poked through the rhododendron thicket.

It paused near the edge of the Lehigh River, looking back, then across the swift flow as if trying to decide what to do.

It opted to return to the safety of the tangled vegetation rather than become vulnerable while swimming the 60 or so yards to the other side. In so doing it moved to within 30 yards of the stunted hemlock that somehow managed to maintain a root hold in the infirm riverbed, now at its low-water stage.

I'd backed against the hemlock 30 minutes earlier; the only substantial cover between the rhododendron and the stony, open shoreline.

The deer's attention was focused on the rocky, wooded ridgetop from which it had just been pushed by my hunting companion. I centered the crosshairs on its neck, not yet having decided if I wanted the small buck.

For a change, that year I had the entire second week to hunt and the two-week Pennsylvania season still held four more days to seek a trophy.

Confusion reined for a few seconds when the buck disappeared from my sights. Seconds later, as the echoes rolled across the far mountain, I realized that Bob Greenbaum, my hunting partner, had made up my mind for me. His 75-yard shot from above had been true. As he inched down the stony slope on elbows and knees, south end first, I straddled the buck.

"I got him," I said. "Good drive."

Bob stopped in his descent to gather his thoughts, then caught the grin on my face.

The scenario took place more than 20 years in Carbon County. The previous evening the four of us, including two other camp members, pored over topographic maps and airphotos of our leased hunting area. Several bucks had been taken during week, one nearly a mile away, closer to the road. Dozens of others had been shot on the adjacent gameland which was being hunted each day.

Late season bucks are notoriously alert and spooky.

As we toasted the evening's planning session, we jokingly agreed to go "where no hunter has gone before."

The point of it all was to find spots that were either unhunted or difficult to access. We figured bucks that encountered orange coats at every turn and scented human intrusion on the breezes for the past week and a half had headed for quieter pastures.

Although not a "pasture," the rocky rhododendron thicket became a safe haven for the wary bucks and does as they could linger away the daylight hours relatively undisturbed.

Bucks don't become voluntarily reclusive during the second half of the hunting season. They're forced into new patterns, untrodden escape routes, night-feeding and days spent scanning their bedding areas.

Unlike some southern states, such as Alabama, where the gun season stretches across more than two months, north-country hunting is of shorter duration and considerably more hectic.

On Pennsylvania's opening day, for instance, about 60 percent of the total harvest is taken with another 25 to 30 percent or more of all bucks tagged the following day and on two subsequent Saturdays. The sheer numbers of hunters in the woods accounts for unnatural activity as deer are pushed here and there.

The quietest time in the woods is the Monday through Friday of the final week when hunters must work for their venison. The smart hunter must hit new turf and shift gears as time to fill a tag draws to a close.

Here are some suggestions for doing just that.

Scout New Country

Late season provides little time for scouting although searching out-of-the-way reaches while hunting can pay dividends. This must come at a sacrifice, however. With limited hunting time, it's hard to pass a prime location in which you may have bagged bucks on previous openers to set foot in unfamiliar territory, even though the locations may only be a half-mile apart.

Deer gathering in a sanctuary atmosphere over a relatively short period will leave obvious fresh sign. Tracks, droppings, upturned leaves, nipped brush and twigs and even recently-scoured scrapes will alert a hunter as to whitetail activity.

Scouting with rifle at ready, perhaps still-hunting from dawn to dusk, might as readily yield a shot at a buck as perching in a familiar treestand.

Think Post-Rut

The peak rut in the Keystone State falls in mid-November. Does which are not bred during that period come into estrus 28 days later when the rifle seasons are approaching their ends or special muzzleloader or archery hunts are about to start.

Where does gather, so will thick-necked bucks. While a fresh scrape may not guarantee a buck's return visit, mere sighting of fresh, urine-stained clearings indicate a buck is in the area and is active.

Older dominant bucks may be literally worn out by this time. In one Michigan study a mature buck whose previous 3-4 weeks were spent chasing and breeding does and driving off lesser rivals was observed in a near room-size area for a full 52 hours. It neither drank, fed or bred, only rising from his bed in a dense thicket to urinate and stretch.

The chosen recuperation site for such animals is almost always dense cover in which they can't be seen and where intruders cannot enter readily, at least without making sufficient noise to alert the buck.

The Thicket Is The Ticket

Thickets come in a variety of sizes and densities. Hemlock and laurel swamps, fields overgrown in briars, sumac and grasses, old orchards and 3-4 year-old clearcuts are all prime havens for deer that don't want to be bothered.

Just because overgrown acreage isn't remote doesn't mean it won't be holding deer. Some of the least likely spots, particularly in suburbs and farm country, hold appeal. Their proximity to homes and roads is often the reason few hunters tread through them, thereby making them especially enticing as daytime bedding areas.

The Mini-Drive

High-tailing whitetails were the rule when, during my early hunting years, my dad and as many as a dozen other hunters would get together and perform concerts of sorts as they pushed deer toward standers. Whistles, shouts, smacking sticks against trees and even beating pots and pans alerted every whitetail within earshot that something was amiss.

As that 4-pointer described earlier was pushed slowly by a pair of drivers and two "posters," so, too, mini-drives are often more productive than all-out warfare.

One hunter zig-zagging through a thicket with one or two standers at ready is more likely to draw a clean shot at a buck slipping away. Unlike early season drives, standers and drivers have the same chance of getting shots on mini-drives with few participants.

Don't ignore those seemingly inconsequential plots, sometimes only an acre or two in size. Often deer will be as close as 50 yards from a feeding area and will stay there throughout the day if not pushed.

When bucks become nocturnal, particularly older and wiser bucks, it takes effort to move them. Those pushed from one security area will slip into another.

No Business Like Snow Business

A fresh snowfall always brightens the gleam in a deer hunter's eyes. It also reveals the business end of a deer's travels and the relative abundance (or lack of) whitetails in the area. Add to that easy-to-decipher escape routes and movement patterns.

New snows offer the most important clues in that recent passages can be traced. Getting out the morning after a fresh covering provides the first clue in solving the mystery of disappearing whitetails.

As an option, rather than following tracks leaving a feeding area, try backtracking. Look for prints indicating where deer enter a field late in the day. Setting up a treestand in the vicinity may prove to be a prime evening spot.

Deer also leave obvious signs when forced to bed in snow, revealing their presence to even the novice hunter.

Shift Gears

Most hunters will agree that the opening day or two of deer season and subsequent Saturdays seldom offer the chance for effective still-hunting. Even painstakingly slow-hunting through a woods does little more than push whitetails to someone else. The exception, of course, is private lands where hunter access is barred or limited.

By week two, deer may continue to linger in untread pockets but, if they've not been spooked in a day or two, won't be as edgy as they were the previous week.

Still-hunting requires concentration and self-discipline to which many sportsmen and women are not accustomed. Those who have practiced the technique and respect the visual, auditory and olfactory abilities of whitetails can score on late bucks by covering lots of ground — slowly.

Carry Your Lunch

The final week's hunting hours quickly diminish to a precious few. Cutting out to visit a local diner or heading back home or to camp for lunch may provide a pleasant break but it can also cost a buck.

The "last day buck" Charlie Burchfield and brother Mark bagged in Potter County lacked a right antler. (Left) Ben Moyer, and his father Bud, with a 1993 late season Greene County buck pushed from a thicket.

By virtue of their natural instincts, deer cut short their dawn and dusk feeding hours. By noon many are up and around, not traveling far but feeding within or near their sanctuary hideouts.

My preference is to spend the noon hours — from about 11 a.m. through 2 p.m. — in a treestand. Feeding deer move cautiously with their noses to the wind, their eyes constantly scanning the terrain. A moving hunter is more readily detected than one a dozen or more feet above ground in a treestand.

When a scouting trip reveals a deer retreat, set up the stand and leave. Any stand placement will be noisy and it's best to put it in place, then use it the next day and thereafter. Then, climbing into it before dawn, at noon or an hour or so before dark can be done with minimal disturbance.

To Call Or Not To Call

The grunt tube has become a standard item among most deer hunters, even the dyed-in-the-Woolrich old-timers who have read enough articles or seen enough videos in recent years proving the instrument's effectiveness.

Unlike pre and peak rut-time hunting, when I prefer aggressive calling. I'll opt for more subdued, low volume calls in late season. Bucks are both physically and psychologically fatigued then and won't come charging out of a thicket to see who's making the sounds.

Patience cannot be emphasized enough in late season. Each hunter has his or her own philosophies on deer calling and some won't grunt unless deer are in sight. Others are content to offer 4-5 short grunts every 15-20 minutes or more.

Following the rut and opening week of buck season, big bucks become reclusive and inactive.

I lean toward the latter technique when in a treestand with only a couple days remaining in a season.

Think Creatively
The New York hunters lining the state border not far behind our Bradford County hunting camp each opening day always take a buck or two thanks to our efforts. By the time the Pennsylvania season opens, Empire Staters have already been afield for more than a week. Deer living on the edge of both states soon learn that things are quiet on the Keystone State side.

But that changes on opening day. Hunters have learned that deer return when flushed from the brush on the Pennsylvania opener.

If my tag's still unfilled on the last day of the season and nothing else has proven productive, I'll spend the finale — dawn to dusk — up a tree, having located a security area or two and with a treestand already in place. Other hunters will also be giving the season a final shot and the bucks that detect them may be pushed back into the "refuge" I've located.

I'll be there, quietly and steadfastly awaiting closing hour, satisfied that my late season fieldwork will pay off before the day slips away.

And if not, there's always next year.

The Longhunter Society is an organization providing muzzleloader hunters a record book status like the Boone & Crockett and Pope & Young clubs. Already 600 members have joined the society which has formulated its own big game records program under the auspices of the National Muzzleloading Rifle Association. Any of 28 species of N.A. big game taken with blackpowder guns may be entered.

Typical whitetails measuring 130 typical B&C points are eligible. For non-typical bucks the score must be 160 minimum.

For details write: The Longhunter Society, P.O. Box 67, Friendship, IN 47021.

When it's necessary to drag a buck and you don't have a rope, grasp the antler closest to the ground. This keeps the deer's head and neck up, offering less resistance from the ground, and prevents the antler from hitting your calf on each step.

When beginning your summer practice for the fall season, first check for subtle bow noises that may spook deer. Have a companion stand a few feet away in an ultra-quiet room. Draw the bowstring several times to determine if any annoying sounds -- like the scrape of the arrow across the rest, cables rubbing or wheels squeaking -- need attention.

Never follow a blood trail by walking atop the deer's escape path. Should you lose the trail and have to retrace your steps, it will be harder to pick it up because you may have obliterated the sign by overturning leaves or kicking dirt and pebbles over it. Always work to one side of the blood trail.

Chapter 20

LAST SHOT
Winter's Black Powder and Bow Hunt

When deer hunting days dwindle to a precious few, as the hunter's December song goes, thousands of hunters with unfilled tags get one more shot at providing some venison for the table.

For archers and flintlockers it's just that — a one-shot affair.

That's why it's important to take time before venturing into the deer woods under cold-weather conditions to make adjustments to bows and front-stuffing guns.

For bowhunters it's not a matter of unfamiliarity with the "firearm," as most archers were afield for the fall archery season and, in general, tend to spend more time on the 3-D or paper target range than do gunners.

Of course, avid blackpowder aficionados also spend the 12 months in recreational or competition shooting. But they may be the exception. Others won't draw their Hawkens from the rack until a few days prior to the post-Christmas hunt. At least one trip to the range is necessary.

Cold, wind and snow affect not only the hunter but his or her hunting tools, as well.

Cold Weather Bow Tuning

For bowhunters, the October season can be a spoiler. Sitting in a treestand for three or four hours doesn't cramp the muscles nearly as much as in winter when temperatures may dip below freezing in the morning hours and often linger throughout the day. Trying to draw the same 50- or 60-pound bow with cold hands and cramped biceps can be a problem.

Deano Farkas of Easton, one of the state's most consistent archers, recommends that bowmen reduce the weights on their compound bows for cold-weather hunting.

"I shoot with a 60 or 65 pound pull in the fall but drop six or eight pounds in the winter season," said Farkas. "I have several bows and I'll use a lighter one when it's cold."

Compound bows are adjustable between varied draw weights with room for

Mike Fegely wears his Realtree snow camo during snowy post-Christmas hunts.

adjustment within the 30-45, 45-60 and 60-70 pounds or more ranges. With a minimum of difficulty, and by referring to the instruction book accompanying every new bow, every compound's draw can be reduced. If this presents a problem, take it to a pro shop or the sporting goods store where the bow was purchased and seek help.

"I know a lot of guys who fouled up shots at deer because they found they couldn't draw the bow after they sat on stand for several hours in the cold," said Farkas.

He also stresses that bowhunters should take some time on the range before setting out for a cold weather hunt. The reduced pull not only changes the course of the arrow but also requires sight adjustment. The only way to find out what changes are necessary is to shoot paper targets and make those important tune-ups before heading afield.

Freeze-time Flintlocking

Some adjustment may also be necessary for hunters who try for late-season whitetails with muzzleloaders. The number one reason for missing a deer is that the gun simply doesn't go off.

"Misfires are the most common problems with flintlocks," says Dave Ehrig of Mertztown, Berks County, who's written a book on the making of these primitive firearms and has taken flintlock-bucks in front of video cameras. "There are a variety of reasons why a flintlock won't shoot and most common is that there are problems somewhere in the ignition system."

One snowtime dilemma is wet pan-powder pan. The spark from the flint won't ignite it. Ehrig recommends changing the fine-grain black powder in the pan several times a day, no matter what the weather conditions.

Then, too, shoving a ball down the barrel is always harder (as is everything else done outdoors) when temperatures dip. Forget using a spit patch for second shots. That's like putting your tongue on a frozen pump handle. It will freeze fast.

Winter conditions set the stage for the frustrating "flash in the pan."

Clearing the lock mechanism of any grease and lubricating it with a fine oil is suggested before any winter hunt. From personal experience, I also leave the wooden ramrod at home. Instead I'll carry a fiberglass ball-stuffer which won't as readily break, especially when stiffened, cold-penetrated muscles impede normal movements.

More than one Pennsylvania muzzleloader hunter has sent an errant shot past a doe because he nudged the trigger too quickly with a glove-covered finger. I've done it myself.

It's much more difficult to gauge pressure on the trigger with a gloved hand. In the excitement of the moment, I've also known hunters to squeeze the set trigger (on some guns) when they thought they were touching the fore-trigger. Of course, by the time they discovered the mistake their white-tailed target was off and running.

One of my more useful purchases is a pair of heavy hunting gloves with a slit aside the trigger-finger. Without removing the glove the bare finger can be pushed through, providing the delicate feel necessary for timing a shot.

Late Season Tactics
While one can romanticize the winter hunt as the most challenging of seasons, it's far from a prime time quest. If one opportunity presents itself over the course of the December-January season, consider yourself fortunate.

Altering techniques and taking some chances may be necessary to tip the scales your way. The forkhorn that wandered by your treestand at 15 yards a half-dozen times in October and November you'd now trade your best binoculars to see at 30 paces. In short, it's a new woods out there.

I do most of my late season stalking in the same Lehigh County and Bradford County woodlands in which I stash my treestand in October's bow time or the post-Thanksgiving buck season. But the view from a tree in the depth of winter is notably different than it was under October's Kodachrome setting. Where I could gaze 80 yards one direction, 50 another and maybe no more than 30 yards to yet another trail three months previous, the lack of leaves now makes it possible to watch a band of does slip onto the edge of a pasture 200 yards off. It's a pleasant way to break the monotony but not necessarily productive.

While relatively easy pickings for a rifle, muzzleloader shots of 50 yards or less are preferred with my iron-sighted flintlock and patched ball. I feel confident out to another 20-25 yards with a steady rest. With bow in hand that limit drops to 20-25 yards. No matter what the "weapon," it demands precise set-up. Positioning is the

Doyle Dietz, outdoor writer, with a flintlock button buck taken during an annual authentic hunt with other buckskinners in Schuylkill County.

key to filling a vacant tag, not simply "seeing deer."

Groves of hemlocks, pines and spruces gain new attention, particularly during cold and windy days and when snow is falling. If there's a conifer stand on your hunting grounds, give it special scrutiny.

The best place to start a winter hunt is with food sources. In my part of the country harvested corn and soybean fields continue to lure some deer well into winter, even though pickings are often minimal. Bucks which ended their rutting rituals weeks before are now resting and feeding, although no longer having the appetite of three months earlier when ripening corn and acorns dropping like jellybeans made their appearances more predictable and more visible.

Now they bed in thickets and eat more browse. Studies at Penn State show deer undergo a biological slow-down in winter. Not only do they rest more but they feed less, requiring less nutrition than at any other time of the year, although common sense analysis might dictate otherwise. Restoring lost fat and protein must wait until spring and summer. That cuts down on their home territory as the season progresses, a sure advantage to a hunter.

My late season scouting trips are focused more on bedding grounds than feeding fields, although the latter often leads the way to whitetail bedrooms. On especially frigid days I'll try to be afield as deer often move throughout the day, although they don't venture far from their sleeping quarters.

If cold is the hunter's curse, snow is the late season blessing. The white cover reveals gouged runs and the recent meanderings of small bands of whitetails. Treestand or ground set-ups are no different for late hunts than they were in October. In each, closing the distance from your position to where you predict a deer will pass, based on evidence in the snow, is vital.

Stalking in the wide open woods is often futile although, in ridge-and-valley country, the skilled bow or blackpowder hunter can do just that after a fresh snowfall when steps are muffled. If the snow is crusted, forget about still-hunting.

The changing season dictates new strategies and the acceptance of adversities inherent in cold weather hunts. Deer have been pursued for three months, their numbers have been reduced, conditions are tough and the woods are leafless and open.

That's what makes any late season bow or blackpowder deer a trophy.

The use of 35mm film containers as "scent bombs" is nothing new. Cottonballs are placed inside the film holders, then saturated with cover or attractant scents. The tight fitting caps enable hunters to use and reuse the "bombs," carrying them along when they change locations. With electrical or plastic tape, attach a clothespin to the container. Then clip it to a limb or shrub several feet above ground where the scent can more readily catch the wind.

Chapter 21

KIDS AND WOMEN IN THE DEER WOODS

Kids have always been intrigued by the deer woods. Some women, too.

Unfortunately, the number of kids being recruited is today dropping, due largely to urban and suburban upbringing and no one to guide them along the outdoor path that makes a hunter.

The good news is more and more women are taking to the woods today. A survey by the National Shooting Sports Foundation showed a jump of from four to eight percent more women hunters today than in 1980.

Some, such as outdoor writer Shirley Grenoble of Altoona, whose seminars on deer and turkey hunting attract both men and women, took up the sport on their own or via interest from a fiancee or spouse. My wife hadn't done anything but shoot a .22 once or twice when we met in 1981. Now she has several trophy whitetails on the wall and spends many fall mornings and evenings on her treestand, with bow or gun in hand.

In her seminars she's frequently approached by girlfriends and wives who want to get started in the sport. They ask predictable questions such as which gun or what clothing and footwear to choose along with personal questions (how to cope in men's deer camp, fear of darkness when traveling to a stand and how to handle "potty" duties in the woods).

This isn't to say that all women need men's assistance but a husband's, son's or boyfriend's interest is reason many distaff hunters decide to become involved. Most kids are taken hunting by parents, favorite uncles or friends and neighbors willing to share their time and experience.

No matter what their roots in deer hunting, the presence of women and kids in the deer woods is undeniably positive. Welcoming youngsters and wives or fiancees to deer camps reinforces whitetail hunting as the family sport it's always been.

Andy Fegely proudly poses with his first buck -- and a smile to match.

Kids Afield

Sometimes it pays to look back, despite Satchel Page's sage advice to the contrary.

I vividly recall my first morning in the whitetail woods; my dad an acorn's toss away beneath a towering oak. It was an exciting time following a sleepless night in which I'd rehearsed exactly what I'd do when a hat-racked buck strolled along the trail 60 yards down the ridge.

It never happened. Save for several does that sprinted by in mid-morning, the action on that inaugural deer hunting morning was minimal.

But the memory is crystal clear.

Taking kids — even a friend or relative — hunting for the first time is a colossal responsibility. With years of experience under my belt I served as mentor to my two sons, several neighborhood kids and, later, a 12-year-old step-daughter. My approach was to recall my first days — first years, actually — in the field along with the naivete and the occasional fears and unknowns with which a youthful mind approaches any new challenge.

Youngsters are not permitted to hunt in Pennsylvania until they reach age 12, although they may accompany an adult afield prior to that. Such pre-hunt training sessions are invaluable. Add to that a few other activities which will help set a kid on the right path.

If there will a young hunter at your side this year, consider these suggestions leading up to the "first time out."

* Pennsylvania requires the completion of a hunter education course before a junior license (for those under age 16) can be purchased. After the course, review the lessons and reinforce the safety aspects with the young hunter. Stress the responsibility of carrying a firearm and the importance of a clean, humane harvest.

* Spend time on the range familiarizing the newcomer with his or her firearm's operation and its safe handling. Firmly and promptly inform the rookie whenever he or she makes a mistake, such as waving the muzzle about or, innocently,

Father and son with the results of a buck hunt -- and the making of a memory.

pointing it at someone or in an unsafe direction.

A rifle or shotgun can be intimidating, with a natural fear inherent in firing it the first few times. Flinching is a common affliction. Problem is, the shooter often doesn't realize he's flinching and therefore shooting inaccurately. Sneak a spent shell into the chamber if you believe your student is flinching, then watch his or her reaction when the trigger is squeezed. The lesson is quite revealing.

* Take your new partner to the hunting grounds where you'll be on the opening day of the season. For deer season, visit the specific tree or treestand where opening morning will be spent. In Pennsylvania it's law that 12 and 13 year olds "must be close enough that verbal guidance can be easily understood."

On your pre-season trip, point out trails, escape routes, rubs and scrapes and specify distances to various landmarks. Indicate "out of range" shots and unsafe targets (deer on a horizon, for example). The scouting trip will alleviate many fears for the new hunter.

* After that memorable "first time out," discuss the day's activities and encourage questions the new hunter may have. Continue your teachings on subsequent trips including hunter ethics, game laws, safety and responsibility.

Woods-Women

Having a wife as a hunting partner has its rewards, as one might imagine. If your spouse (or girlfriend, mother or sister) has expressed a desire to join you in the field, first establish a game plan based on her desire to participate. Nothing succeeds like success when it comes to training and teaching a new partner, no matter if it's a wife, child or friend.

I'd already logged 30 years of hunting experience by the time Betty Lou came along. Frigid mornings trying to remain still on deer stands were second nature. But I knew better than to expect a her to enjoy the same sort of discomforts.

This isn't meant to sound sexist but, truth is, for every women afield there are about 14 men. The presumption that hunting is a "man's sport" may not be entirely true but it has basis in fact and it's the way most non-hunters view it.

But numbers of women hunters continue to grow .

My wife and I began her introduction to the sport by studying hunting gear catalogs and taking inventory of the cedar closet where varied clothing items ranging from brilliant orange jackets to camouflage suits hung from racks. While she admits to not being a fashion plate while traipsing the woodlands, she does

Betty Lou Fegely approaches her first flintlock whitetail in Bradford County.

appreciate a neat-looking and functional outfit. As most of the major hunting clothing manufacturers have yet to institute a satisfactory line of women's togs, she adopted some suitable small-size men's items, snipping and sewing here and there for a comfortable fit.

Footwear was less of a problem as she was able to find comfortable leather and insulated pac-boots in sporting goods stores. Whether females inherently get colder than men under similar conditions is beyond the scope of my research. But Betty Lou claims the distaff side needs additional insulation on chilly mornings and will typically appear overdressed when I'm outfitted in the basics. She's most comfortable with the pac-boots for cold weather hunts, opting for the extra warmth while walking or on stand.

The second item of business, once it was established that hunting, especially big game hunting, was more than a whim, was the purchase of a suitable gun. Her first rifle was my Model 760 Remington. On the shooting bench (we fired several boxes on the range prior to the trip) she did great for a woman who had only plinked with a .22 once or twice in her life. But afield the combination of heavy clothes, pumping adrenalin, and difficulty in finding the target through the scope at moment's notice conspired to assure the deer's clean getaway.

Following a trip in which she missed a buck, we visited a gun shop and picked out a Remington Model 7 chambered in 7mm-08. The 6-pound, 2-ounce rifle topped with a 2-7x Simmons scope was to her liking and has become her favorite firearm.

In the meantime she's also had Ernie Lambrecht of Quakertown, our gunsmith, shorten the stock on one of my Remington 700s chambered in 30-06. Gun fit is a key to building confidence afield. A woman's proportions typically demand a short-stocked firearm, one fitting smoothly against the cheek and allowing a quick sight-picture through a scope. Special care in choosing such a gun is of utmost importance in the proper introduction of your potential hunting partner (man, woman or youngster) and every bit as important as proper dress and footwear.

Those of us who vividly recall our inaugural trips to the deer woods know the excitement and subtle fear inherent in awaiting first light surrounded only by the sound of our deep breathing and the outstretched arms of barren oaks reaching for the sky. It matters little that one is age 12 or 50 when the experience occurs. Whenever I place my wife on a deer stand, pre-season scouting trips have already been taken and a few scenarios of what may occur are provided. It helps alleviate fears and bolsters confidence and independence.

Of course, just because a woman hunts doesn't mean femininity is left behind. In the years we've been traveling afield together, Betty Lou has discovered a few simple, inexpensive items that help make hunting excursions more tolerable. Pre-moistened hand and face towelettes are blessings in the deer woods and at camps lacking running water or modern lavatory facilities. Lipstick is carried in her daypack along with compass and skinning knife. Under her orange or camo cap she always wears ear rings. The only items not used are perfume and scented powder.

In the course of our travels, and through a weekly television show I hosted in southern Pennsylvania on which Betty Lou was an occasional co-host, she

For a growing number of couples, hunting and the outdoors have become a lifestyle.

received many queries from mothers, wives and girlfriends. Most letters were from women who were being encouraged to join their men on hunting trips — but hadn't tried it because of a natural fear of the unknown.

She advised them to approach it as she did — with detailed planning and a sense of adventure. The shared experience is one that partners will enjoy, and relive, each time they flash their slides on the screen or page through the family scrapbook.

Another side benefit of women afield is the confusion it brings to animal rights fanatics who love nothing more than to brand male hunters as macho jerks, killers and sexual perverts. Betty Lou has gone one-to-one with some females in the animal "righteous" crowd and left them babbling in mid-sentence.

For us, hunting is a lifestyle. The more women and kids I encounter afield, the more confident I feel about the future of our sport.

While every target shooter should wear ear protection, donning a muff or using sponge ear plugs is particularly helpful to new shooters for another reason. When practicing or sighting in, the inexperienced shooter will relax a bit more prior to squeezing the trigger if he or she isn't anticipating the loud blast from the muzzle.

A 35mm film container partially filled with old fashioned petroleum jelly (gel) can be a lifesaver when hunting. It serves as a gun lubricant, leather treatment, first aid for a cut, skin cream for chafes and burns and dozens of other uses.

When crossing barbed wire fences, take the low road. Climbing the wire may pull staples from the posts and a slip will tear your clothing or, worse, your flesh. It's best to find a spot where you can crawl under the wire, keeping both the landowner and your seamstress happy.

When wind direction cooperates, plan your still-hunts and stalks with the sun at your back. Deer show up better when sun and shadows are present and they won't note your movement as readily if they are looking toward the sun.

Heat from a fireplace or radiator, direct sunlight and cigarette smoke concentration are major enemies of game mounts. Ultraviolet rays and smoke will change hair color and constant dry air will crack the nose and hide. Choose the display area for your trophies with discretion.

Hairline cracks in your head mounts can be repaired with black model airplane paint. Use a small, artist's brush to touch up the nostril and eyelid areas where cracks often occur.

Lemon oil polish, the type used to dust furniture, restores a faint shine to the antlers on your wall mounts while removing accumulated dust.

PART
IV
WHERE TO GO

Chapter 22

BIG BUCKS OR ABUNDANT BUCKS?
Have It Your Way

Where to hunt?
For most of Pennsylvania's 1.1 million whitetail aficionados it will be the same place as last year and the year before and.......

No matter, by November most hunters aren't thinking about where they plan to hunt. They know, although each season some hunters seek new deer country and first-timers are open to suggestion.

Most back-fence and taproom or sporting club conversations instead focus on the potential offered in "traditional" hunting grounds. For some that's only a few minute's drive beyond their back doors. For others it's a trek of one or two hundred or more miles to their big-woods deer camps.

"The potential for a trophy deer is there in every county," said Bill Palmer, a Pennsylvania Game Commission biologist specializing in whitetails and whose field research takes him throughout the commonwealth. "But surely it's best in counties with better nutrition and where bucks have the chance to grow older."

Are chances for scoring on a buck better on private lands?
Surprisingly not!

A study begun in 1993 by Game Commission biologists via report cards from successful hunters revealed the harvest rate on public lands averages 8.7 bucks per square mile of forest as compared to only 5.4 per square wooded mile on private grounds.

"This tells us that there are many deer on public lands," said Palmer. "It's something that we will continue to monitor in the years ahead."

Studies show about 80 percent of each year's buck harvest is of 1-1/2 year-old deer, accounting for the dearth of mature bucks in most places. The exception is in counties with high human populations and private farms, where open hunting lands are at a minimum and deer numbers approach their maximum. It wasn't always that way but in recent years deer have been thriving in suburbia, posing problems and controversies as to how to control them.

"You're never going to grow a yearling into a trophy in Potter County as you will in Bucks County," said Palmer. "Those (Potter) deer just don't have the nutrition a farm country deer will get."

Where will you find Pennsylvania's biggest bucks?

Look for places with lots of posted land and an abundance of crops, woodlands and humans.

Not surprisingly, Chester County (west of Philadelphia) in the Southeast Special Regulations Area and Allegheny County (surrounding Pittsburgh) making up the Southwest "special doe hunt" region, hold some of the state's biggest bucks and are arguably the best places to score on a record book trophy (with a score of 140 B&C points or better in Pennsylvania's version of "the book").

In addition to good nutrition, large acreages of posted properties, many which allow limited or no hunting, provide refuge in which bucks grow old. Learning to avoid cars and trucks, of course, is a prerequisite to making it to 3-1/2 years or more.

The same counties that traditionally held big bucks continue to be cherished by hunters today, Palmer believes. Things haven't changed all that much save for the fact that many "big bucks" counties also hold the highest densities of deer. That may seem like the best of both worlds. Problem is, it's difficult finding public lands on which to hunt.

Counties in the big woods landscape — the land of "bountiful" bucks — offer the best chance for filling a tag. Here, however, trophies compose only a small percentage of the annual harvest. But deer are plentiful and public hunting grounds abound.

Regions with limited hunting opportunities hold some of the state's biggest bucks.

Free-lance outdoor writer Mike Bleech took this Warren County 8-pointer in bow season, following a late October snowstorm.

Following is a brief round-up of the state's six regions and their comparative reputations as places to find "big bucks" or "bountiful bucks."

Northwest Region

Look to Crawford, Erie and Mercer counties in this region for holding trophy whitetails. Game Commission trophy records over the years show Crawford and its farmlands, woodlots and marshes as an excellent choice.

In terms of deer numbers, a look at 1993's buck harvest as compared to the amount of forested acreage within a county provides a valid analysis. The Northwest's most notable harvest was in Crawford County with nine bucks tagged per square forested mile. It was followed by Mercer and Jefferson where hunters bagged 8.8 bucks per square wooded mile.

In terms of abundance, Warren's yield of 4,626 antlered deer led the region and ranked third in the state in 1993.

Southwest Region

When it comes to big deer, Allegheny County is the "cherished" hunting grounds here although only one state gameland tract is available and most of the Pittsburgh-region county is urban or suburban. Nearly all hunting is done on private lands. Historically, Allegheny has produced more trophies than any of the state's other 66 counties.

Also with a respectable number of record book entries are Beaver, Armstrong,

Westmoreland and Washington counties.

In 1993, the biggest buck harvest (4,193) in the region came from Somerset County. The highest harvest per square forested mile was in Greene County (10.2).

Northcentral Region

"This is the poorest region for big bucks," said Palmer. Although it's balanced by producing the most bucks each year.

He rates portions of Tioga and Lycoming counties with their "good soil" as holding potential trophies, although not in abundance. "Some of those deer living on remote ridges may get to be 3-1/2 or 4-1/2 years old," Palmer believes.

In terms of whitetail numbers, the Northcentral's big woods country goes unchallenged. Clearfield County ranked tops in the state in 1993 with 5,783 bucks harvested. Tioga was fourth with 4,454 and Potter, fifth, yielding 4,405 bucks.

Measured by buck kills per square mile of forest, Clearfield led the region at 6.8.

Southcentral Region

Bedford's farmland and "mountain refuge" country is among the best when it comes to finding big-racked bucks as is Adams County, which has grown some 140-150 Boone & Crockett class bucks. The region, as a whole, is not known for spectacular bucks although deer numbers are high.

The biggest buck harvests of 1993 were recorded in Huntingdon (4,221), Bedford (4,193) and Perry (2,638). In buck harvest per square mile of woodland, honors went to Adams County with 9.2, where the region's biggest acreages of agricultural crops are found.

TV show host Jack Hubley's 13-pointer was taken in Lebanon County.

Northeast Region

Bradford is not only the top "big bucks" county in the Northeast but it doubles as the best "abundant bucks" county, as well. Its mountains and rich, dairyland pastures and croplands provide for both honors. Bradford hunters harvested 5,044 bucks, second highest in the state, in the most recent year (1993) for which figures were available.

Palmer's picks for finding other big bucks in this region center on the ridge and valley sectors of Montour, Columbia and Northumberland counties. The Poconos (Pike and Monroe counties, in particular) offer plenty of public hunting lands but rank low in terms of deer numbers and buck harvests per square mile.

Tiny Montour, with only 131 square miles and minimal public hunting lands, scored the biggest buck kill per square woodland mile in 1993 with 9.6.

Southeast Region

Farm country and rolling hills along with scattered suburbia characterize the southern portions of this region, which holds both big deer and many deer. However, it's not all houses and shopping malls hereabouts. There's abundant farm and forestland and thousands of scattered woodlots from two to 50 or more acres.

The state record book lists bucks from all 13 counties, save for Philadelphia. Berks County boasts the most entries in the record book over the past two decades with Chester, Bucks, Montgomery and Delaware (the latter four all considerably smaller than Berks and largely within suburbia) also ranked high.

A 3-1/2 year old buck here will be as big or bigger than a 4-1/2 or 5-1/2 year old in most other parts of the state," said Palmer. "They have the nutrition they need."

In 1993, the leading harvest county was Berks (3,162) followed closely by Schuylkill (more a "hill and mountain" county) with 3,098. But on the square woodland mile list, tiny Delaware County, where open hunting grounds are difficult to find, topped the state at a phenomenal 14.2. Notably, Lancaster (11.7), York and Berks (both 10.5) also had high harvests.

Trophy hunters often "take it on the chin" from animal rights crusaders and others who think seeking the biggest and best is contrary to natural selection. Remind them that trophy bucks are older animals who have already distributed their genes throughout the herd's pool. Not only are they passed on by the bucks he's sired but his female offspring will also contribute to the genetic quality in a region. All hunters are "trophy hunters" of sorts, as opportunities warrant. But surely more sportsmen come home with average deer than wall-hangers. It's simply a case of the big ones getting more attention in the press and at the local sporting goods store.

Hunters pose at the camp "meat pole" at Wolf Run Camp in Centre County. It's a scene duplicated by the thousands each fall across The Golden Triangle.

Chapter 23

LURE OF THE GOLDEN TRIANGLE

Pennsylvania hunters have long agreed the best chances for scoring on a buck or doe, no matter what the season, lies in a triangular sector of the northcentral mountains. It's an ill-defined area including all or portions of 13 counties, with vertexes in Warren County on the west, Bradford County to the east and Centre County on the south.

Deer hunters have dubbed it the "Golden Triangle." It holds some of the state's most remote wilderness and an abundance of public hunting lands. Thousands of hunters migrate here for buck season, as their parents and grandparents did. The region has always held high whitetail populations and is rich in whitetail lore and legend.

But does the "Golden Triangle" still hold the luster of days long gone when Woolrich-clad deer-stalkers shouldered 30-30s on their winter forays into the big woods country?

As a comparison, I researched harvest figures of a third-century back, comparing buck kills made in a sampling of the counties within the triangle to harvest figures of recent years.

In 1960, Potter was the leading deer county in the state with 3,252 buck kills. Following closely were Elk (3,090), Centre (2,645), Clearfield (2,409), Warren (2,404) and Lycoming (2,095).

(Other counties in the general region include all or parts of Forest, Cameron, Clinton, Bradford, Tioga, McKean and Sullivan.)

In the most recent year for which figures were available as this is written, Potter again yielded a high buck harvest (4,405) although not the best in the state. Clearfield County led the state's harvest tallies with 5,783. Other notable northcentral numbers included Bradford (5,044), Tioga (4,454), Centre (4,001), McKean (4,082) and Warren (4,626) — again all members of the northcentral block.

In terms of deer numbers and hunter success, there's no denying things may

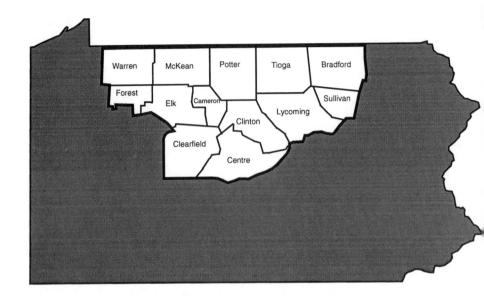

Pennsylvania's "Golden Triangle" attracts more hunters than any other sector of the state.

have improved in this part of Penn's Woods, although many critics believe otherwise. Each year from 24-28 per cent of the state harvest is taken from the contiguous counties within the "triangle" — the remaining 72-76 per cent from the remaining 56 counties.

One variable that has definitely changed is the Game Commission's desire to lower deer numbers throughout the region. It's caused a big stir in some quarters as doe license allocations continue to grow.

"There was a time, up until 1979, when we made our management decisions based on the physical conditions of the deer," a game commission information agent explained. "Today we do it based on how many deer we know a particular forest type (mature trees, pole timber, clearcuts, etc.) can support."

"There are some counties in the Northcentral Region that definitely don't have as many deer as they had 10 or 20 years ago," he said. "But in other areas the deer population is greater."

The places where hunters hunt for antlerless deer is somewhat controlled by county license allocations. The issuance of county doe tags permits biologists to gain a handle on hunter numbers and determine where they hunt in order to control the densities of the post-winter herds. Problem is, some of these counties are large and remote. Places that need population culls may not get enough hunters to make a discernible difference.

Much of the reason for the annual invasion of resident and non-resident hunters to the "Golden Triangle" is that the 13-county area can accommodate them. Check an official state highway map and it`s obvious the concrete and blacktop mazes slicing through the rest of the commonwealth are at a minimum here. State forests and gamelands abound.

There are also more than a million acres of State Forest Lands within or bordering this vast wilderness region plus a sizable portion of Allegheny National Forest to the west.

As most of the federal and state-owned lands are managed for timber and pulpwood sales, hunters can find many tracts with recent clearings. Deer are the number one enemies of regenerating forests and the animals will forage in the cut-over areas. Wise hunters will seek places with 1-5 year old clearcuts where food availability and cover hold deer.

Of course, there aren't maps to lead hunters directly to these hotspots, which are often accessible via logging roads. A call to the District Forester's office prior to the season may be a good investment.

Arguably, deer numbers are fewer in many northcentral counties than they were only 10 years ago, as the Game Commission continues to press for serious reductions in most county "management units." Timber and farming interests have played a big role in encouraging the wildlife management agency to approve larger doe license allocations. On the other side of the ledger, several local and state hunting organizations have been taking the commission to task for "killing too many does."

Bill Haldaman, proprietor of Big Moore's Run Lodge in Potter County, manages his lands for whitetails and has noted higher average deer weights and antler sizes since the late 1980s.

"I've definitely seen an improvement in the number of quality bucks in the past few years," said Haldaman. "It's not only here on my property but at other places we hunt in Potter."

In the past, Potter, which is the state's best known deer hunting county, had a reputation for many, but small, deer. That may be changing, albeit slowly, as doe numbers are reduced.

I've been fortunate to have hunted in eight of the 13 Golden Triangle counties over the past 30 years and have taken a few bucks and does, plus wild turkeys.

No matter which of the "big 13" counties you may choose, it's a good bet you'll see whitetails. They may not be big as in some other regions but they are abundant.

The Golden Triangle continues to demand attention from non-residents and Pennsylvanians seeking places to establish deer camps. No where else in the state, possibly in the entire northeastern U.S., will your chances of tying a tag to a whitetail be better.

When hunting hilly terrain, morning stands should be on high ground where natural air currents carry scent upwards. Conversely, stick to low country stands in the afternoon when scent will shift downhill.

Chapter
24

HUNTING FARMS
AND
SUBURBS

According to a Penn State study, three-fourths of the land hunted in Pennsylvania is privately owned.

Game Commission surveys have shown that more than 60 percent of the state's 1.1 million deer hunters pursue their quarry on private lands. That's good news for hunters prowling the four million-plus acres of public lands scattered about the state.

Many of these private holdings are farmlands and orchards, ranging from a few dozen acres to vast spreads with cattle and corn or apples and soybeans. Forested hills and checkered woodlots provide haven for farmland deer, providing the best of both worlds — trees and a healthy diet of crops.

Deer have always been present on Pennsylvania farms, but not in their current numbers. Here deer populations have exploded in the past quarter-century, costing farmers big bucks as the insatiable animals take bites of their money crops and profits.

The newest boom areas stretch beyond forest and farm. The suburbs and city fringes of Pittsburgh and Philadelphia are now being burdened by too many deer which gain little favor by eating yews and backyard flowers. People who once welcomed these "cute" brown-eyed animals now curse them, demanding that municipal managers and the Pennsylvania Game Commission "do something about it."

The most recent analysis from Game Commission biologists show deer densities ranging from 25-52 deer per square mile of woodland in these areas. In parts of the Southeast and Southwest, deer densities jump upwards of 150 per forested square mile.

Residents of suburbia are beginning to lose their love affair with whitetails, which not only devour their shrubs but have caused numerous accidents and deaths in recent years. In the summer of 1994 a Montgomery County woman was killed when her bicycle collided with a deer. Other human fatalities have also occurred.

Deer are often welcome "pets" in the suburbs until they begin devouring shrubbery and gardens.

The change of attitude has animal rightists searching for new arguments as even their own neighbors are becoming weary of protectionist attitudes. However, it must be noted that even though suburban residents are leaning to "our side" (hunting), their simplified reasoning of what it takes to control whitetails isn't always rational. At a recent Game Commission meeting, one Southeast Pennsylvania woman took the same attitude many of her neighbors surely hold — that the Game Commission is somehow responsible for the population explosion of "city deer."

Another woman drew snickers from the audience at a commission session when she insisted the agency "facilitate the removal of an additional one million deer this hunting season." (For the record, the entire deer population of the state is estimated at about a million.)

A representative of Fox Chapel, north of Pittsburgh, told the commissioners: "We have lost millions of dollars worth of shrubbery in our community of 2,000 residents". The Fox Chapel borough manager added that a trial bowhunting program, which links property owners to archers, hasn't done much to solve the problem. Bowhunters took only 128 deer in the 1993-1994 season and vehicles killed another 84 in the community.

Nevertheless, the paradox is that the places deer numbers are highest and bucks are biggest are the same spots where open hunting lands are most difficult to find (the cause of the problem in the first place). It's a vicious and problematic circle.

So how does a hunter go about finding private lands — in farm or suburb — on which to hunt?

There's no guaranteed recipe, of course, but Tom Tatum, a Chester County school teacher, part-time outdoor writer and avid bowhunter has some encouraging advice which applies to both country farmlands and city-fringe woodlots.

"It's not easy to get permission to hunt from landowners but it can be done," Tatum, whose treestand is set up within sight of houses, advises. "It's my experience that landowners are much more inclined to grant permission to a bowhunter than a gun hunter."

Some landowners who want deer culled are willing to allow the use of shotguns or muzzleloaders, however, barring municipal regulations to the contrary.

Tatum recommends approaching landowners early in summer (a cardinal sin is waiting until the day before a season opens or, worse yet, minutes before you plan to hunt.) Dress and act like a gentleman or lady and you'll stand a better chance of getting an O.K. Tatum also takes his young daughter with him when rapping on doors. Should you gain the privilege, Tatum suggests following up with a Christmas gift — maybe some smoked venison sausage or some other creative gesture as a sincere way of saying "thanks" and keeping the doors open for next season.

The pair of farmers who allow my wife and me to set our treestands in lower Lehigh County are annually thanked with a gift certificate to a local restaurant.

Of course, you must also treat the hunting rights "like the precious treasures they are," says Tatum, who's freezer and office wall annually show the benefits of attaining rights to several suburban woodlots.

More than 45,000 deer are killed annually on state highways, many in the suburbs.

Techniques For Suburban Whitetails

Once hunting grounds are found, what techniques are necessary for getting close to bucks and does among houses and shopping centers?

Like hunting remote areas, scouting is the key to filling a tag, says Tatum. He suggests looking for small, secluded, semi-accessible pieces of private ground (he hunts a 25-acre woodlot on a small estate) bordering larger, undeveloped tracts or adjacent to county parks. If hunting is permitted on the larger tracts, deer will soon seek cover in the smaller, posted refuges. Patterning whitetail movements prior to and during the season will often narrow the ideal spot for a portable treestand.

Tatum has discovered one big advantage to suburban whitetail hunting (besides deer numbers): their travels are predictably restricted. Deer negotiate backyards, skirt the edges of woodlots, move within feet of kenneled dogs, trace treeline "funnels" between woodlots and generally stay close to houses. The deer are acclimated to human activity although encountering a hunter brings them back to their inherent cautiousness.

"They can sense when bowhunting predators invade their haunts and, if an archer is careless,, suburban bucks can make themselves as scarce as an honest politician," Tatum's learned.

Despite the scent of barbecues and exhaust in the air, the smell of a human in a woodland setting still perks their noses. Using scent-locking solutions and cover scents is as necessary as when hunting big woods country.

Of course, no one looks forward to following a deer trail downtown, so setting up as close as possible to where deer make their trails is important. Only sure-shots should be taken to avoid the prospect of a long tracking session through suburban backyards.

But Tatum warns there's no guarantee that conditions will stay the same and you'll have a place to hunt "forever." One year he discovered a travel route from a woodlot to a cornfield, then patterned and eventually bagged an 8-point bow-buck. The next year the cornfield was gone — and so were the deer's travel lanes.

"Last season's hotspot could turn out to be this year's fast-

Teacher and outdoor writer Tom Tatum with a Chester County 8-pointer.

A pair of bookend bucks pause in a Northampton County farmfield.

food parking lot," he cautions. "And it often does."

Surprisingly, Tatum's learned deer here may change their patterns faster than those in forest country. Hunting pressure on properties which permit hunting urges the deer to move on, specifically to posted parcels (of which there are many) where they linger as long as necessary.

In many ways deer here "are like deer everywhere," Tatum's learned. "They respond to grunting and will go through all the same rituals and routines during the rut."

Another observation he's made over the years is the first couple days of the buck season are relatively quiet in suburban haunts. The first and second Saturdays, however, "are like opening day is everywhere else," says Tatum. "That's when the guys are back from deer camp and they're hunting locally."

Despite the burgeoning popularity of hunting the suburbs, deer overpopulation continues. To the dismay of the animal rights crowd, suburbanites are getting a costly lesson on the subject of whitetail management and many are welcoming ethical and responsible hunters in the process.

Hunting Farmland Whitetails

I was weaned on farm-country deer, although it came late in my hunting career when buck and doe numbers began to grow in my "neck of the woods" in the heart of Pennsylvania Dutch farm country.

Places I hunted pheasants as a kid have now turned into whitetail havens (although pheasants can no longer be found). I've come to the conclusion that patterning farm-country whitetails is easier than gathering a dossier on big-woods deer. Maybe that's because I grew up hauling milk and tossing hay bales with the scent of cattle and wheatfields in my nose. As a kid I spent untold hours in the woods and cropfields. Although I've read nothing to support or deny my belief, I believe farmland whitetails wander larger ranges than their forest-dwelling cousins. They also travel more specific travel routes, which provides patterning ease.

As the deer make their rounds they revisit food sources and other familiar territory, often hanging in one place for several days before moving on. My pre-season bow scouting may turn up an identifiable buck or two which I often don't see for another few days after which they magically reappear. At times I've seen bucks (one a piebald 6-pointer) as far as six miles from previous sightings in a matter of two or three days.

The biggest advantage of farmland hunting is that food sources can be pinpointed. My farmer-friend's corn always starts taking a hit in mid-August. His apple trees lure them by mid-September (along with the unharvested corn) and winter wheat brings predictable visits later in the season. Alfalfa and clover add to the menu selections.

Knowing what's growing on neighboring properties is also important. During the snowy winter of 1993-1994 an unharvested soybean field in northern Lehigh County drew more than 100 deer, like kids to free ice cream. As the farm was posted, hunters were present on adjacent lands and snow-sign readily revealed the animals' travel routes.

Red and white oaks along with beech stands are prime places to set treestands anywhere in whitetail country. On farms, however, a cornfield often rims an oakwoods, serving as double enticement for deer, especially during bow season.

In their daylight travels or when pushed out of a feeding or bedding area, deer will take advantage of treelines rimming open fields. One spot I hunt annually shows beaten paths leading into the 50-acre woodlot wherever it joins windbreaks and treelines. They're perfect spots for starting the season as acorns are always abundant and funnels are heavily used.

Nearly 30 percent of Pennsylvania is covered in agricultural lands with broad diversity from one farm to another. My homeland farms are rolling and hilly with some large, relatively flat tracts. In the Appalachian and Allegheny highlands, however, farmlands are often rimmed by mountains.

In either, deer will take advantage of land breaks forming natural funnels. The cuts and shallow valleys offer deer seclusion while traveling from one salad bar to another. They double as escape routes and often provide bedding areas nearby where a spooked buck can quickly leave without detection.

Funnels linking two or three food sources or adjoining bedding areas are the most productive. One spot I visit each year is a grassy swamp, next to a secondary road, with numerous stunted birch trees. Next to it is a small grove of wild cedars, a three-acre woodlot and a cornfield. It doesn't take a Sherlock Holmes to wander the area prior to the bow season and find rutted paths and pressed grasses in the thicket where the deer have bedded.

Opening days in farm-country are little different than in forest country. Hunters spook deer from one place to another and, by late November, leaves have fallen and visibility is 10 times better than it was at the start of the archery season. The hunter who can sit still for the day will likely see deer and often bucks within reasonable range.

As the season progresses, however, driving deer may be necessary. I can recall my first days as a deer hunter when I joined my father and his friends on local deer drives. Then, permission to hunt was easier to find than today. We'd spend the morning traveling from one woodlot to another, alternating between standing and posting. When one woods was worked, we'd drive on to another.

Small, 10-75 acre woods dotting farmland can be more easily covered. Deer pushed from small woodlots often break into open pastures or wheatfields as they flee to yet another woodlot or overgrown thicket, offering clear shots to standers.

Then, too, for the early a.m./late p.m. hunter who must work from 8 to 4, a treestand on the edge of an open field (especially the three or four days following the harvest of corn) can make the most of limited hunting time. I can park my car and be in my treestand less than 10 minutes, another farm-hunt advantage.

The rims of fields are also good spots to set stands during the last couple weeks of bow season, when rutting bucks are more likely to show themselves in daylight. Learning their favorite entry points is necessary for close shots with a bow. For that reason I'll set my stand at least 20-25 yards inside the treeline along their likely entry and exit routes, not directly on the field edge.

Getting back to basics, farm-country whitetails are no smarter or dumber than their suburban or big-woods counterparts. The advantage to hunting them is finding their food, which is usually the cash crop of the farmer-landowner.

Come the first few days of October you'll find my treestand within sight of a cornfield. I'll be somewhere just inside a woodline, waiting for that buck to enter or exit the maze of standing maize which often doubles as a feeding and bedding area.

The bonus is that some of the state's biggest bucks are farm products; like the 10-point, 130-class B & C deer that outwitted my wife and me in the fall of 1993.

But that's a story for my next book.

Special doe seasons are held on farms plagued by crop damage.

RALPH STOLTENBERG, ~

FIRST PLACE
TYPICAL WHITE-TAILED DEER
ARCHERY
SCORE 174-2

Chapter
25

TROPHY COUNTRY

Where The Biggest Bucks Have Been Taken

Looking for a trophy buck?

Head toward town. Or at least its fringes.

That's what a study of big buck harvests over a 20-year period indicates. Big woods country, like the popular "Golden Triangle" of northcentral Pennsylvania, yields lots of deer but chances of finding a trophy are slim.

The same holds true for most of Pennsylvania's northeast.

Conversely, the counties bounding city and suburbs in the southeast, northwest and southwest have been providing haven for some wall-hangers in the past couple decades.

Places like my "backyard" in southeastern Pennsylvania, where even a deer track drew comment when I was a teenager in the late-1950s, now produce some of the heftiest, corn-fed whitetails in the state.

Take, for example, the 23-point, non-typical, Lehigh County stag Craig Krisher of Allentown shot on the opening day of bow season in 1988. It scored a whopping 203-3 Pope & Young points, qualifying it for both state and national record books.

Krisher's trophy stole the number one spot in the non-typical bow category from a 187-2 P&Y buck shot by David Krempasky three years earlier. As the proverbial crow flies, both deer fell less than 40 miles from one another. Krempasky's kill was made on a farm in the heart of Montgomery County's suburbia, less than a half-hour drive north of Philadelphia.

Then there's Ralph Stoltenberg's Butler County record typical bow-buck, scoring 174-2. It's followed by second and third place bucks shot in Allegheny County, where Pittsburgh is the county seat.

Of course, farm-country and private-land suburbs don't exclusively hold the state's top trophies. Lycoming, Sullivan, Tioga, Clearfield, Bradford and over

(Left) Ralf Stoltenberg, Jr.'s 174-2 Pope & Young typical ranks number one in the state. It was taken during the 1986 bow season in Butler County.

three dozen other forest counties sporadically provide bucks in excess of 140 B&C points. But places that held legendary, deep-woods whitetails a half-century ago now produce quantity rather than quality. The areas in proximity to highest human population today yield the biggest racks.

In many parts of the commonwealth, a half-hour drive from the center of town yields excellent habitat, along with fields of corn or soybeans and acorn-studded woodlots. Places where ringnecks and rabbits were once king have become whitetail country.

One popular video shot in southwestern Pennsylvania shows a respectable whitetail bow-buck shot within a short walk of a major highway. The archer parked in a Kmart lot.

Surely buck hunting has taken on a new look in the Keystone State since I was a Woolrich-decked kid only dreaming of deer with racks bigger than forks.

Anyone who studies whitetails knows the key ingredients to the growth of big bucks — genetics, food and age. Even deer with genetic potential for trophy-size antlers will not achieve their maximum growth without the other two ingredients. Many well-fed deer are culled before they reach age three (about 80 per cent of the Pennsylvania bucks shot each year are only 1-1/2 years old).

In high (human) population counties, the greater proportion of lands are under private ownership. On many of these acres, such as those bordering Pittsburgh and Philadelphia, whitetails that learn to avoid cars and trucks on the numerous

Fritz Janowsky's 1943 Bradford County buck, scoring 189-0, continues to rank as Pennsylvania's best-ever typical gun buck.

roadways live to ripe old ages. Many of them dwell behind "No Hunting" signs and limit their travels to nocturnal wanderings, especially during the hunting seasons.

It's these bucks, which eat well and develop their full genetic potential, that occasionally make fatal errors and end up immortalized in the record book.

Of course, there are exceptions.

The reference in my quest for finding where, in recent history, Pennsylvania's biggest bucks have been tagged is *Pennsylvania Big Game Records: 1965-1986,"* published by the Pennsylvania Game Commission. Also referenced were more recent records from the commission's tri-annual measuring sessions in 1986, 1989 and 1992.

While earlier data is available, I limited my figures to the 1971-1991 hunting seasons as conditions have changed throughout most of whitetail country since previous decades. Of course, not all trophy bucks have been measured but the commission's figures provide a good basis for determining just where the "Keystone kings" dwell.

Only typical bucks measuring 140 Boone & Crockett points and non-typicals with minimum scores of 160 were considered.

Statistics show three "corners" of the state provide the best chances for taking a Pennsylvania "book buck." Many of the locales are within farm-country and suburbia — or a short drive away.

Allegheny County, encompassing Pittsburgh, stands alone in producing monster bucks. Over the 20-year period, 50 bucks exceeding 140 typical or 160 non-typical B&C ratings have been measured — more than any other county.

"There's a lot of private land throughout this section of the state," said Dennis Jones, a Game Commission land management supervisor. "The deer have the chance to get older because they're largely inaccessible to most hunters and, of course, they get bigger."

Allegheny holds only one state gameland tract within its borders. The majority of big bucks are taken on private acreage. The counties surrounding Allegheny add to the reputation of the region. Beaver, Butler, Armstrong, Westmoreland and Washington counties have all yielded 73 state record-book trophies since 1971 with Butler at the top of the list.

Head directly north of Allegheny for the number two trophy terrain. Crawford County's 27 state record book entries, 19 from Erie County and 13 in Mercer County, underscore the Northwest's big buck potential.

Bob MacWilliams, information agent for the commission's Northwest Region office until his death from cancer in March, 1994, verified the presence of big bucks in the marshes, woodlots and farmlands of Crawford, Erie and Mercer.

"Diet and refuge," MacWilliams told me, are key ingredients in allowing the Northwest's well-fed deer to reach their growth potential.

Look to the far Southeast as another trophy producer. The "bedroom" counties rimming Philadelphia rate high on the list as well as the rolling woodland/farmfield environs to the immediate west and north.

Berks County has placed 16 bucks in "the book" during the two decades researched. Add to that Lancaster's 14 trophies with Bucks, Montgomery, Delaware and Chester counties combining for another 59 entries. The majority

(Left) Paul Weisser's 15-point bow-buck came from Columbia County. (Right) Jeff McConeghy's 161-3 P & Y buck is from Allegheny County.

David Krempasky's Montgomery County non-typical bow-buck ranks third all-time.

Sal Pitera owns Chester Allison's 182-5 B &C Huntingdon County gun-buck from 1951.

Dan Van Houdt's Bucks County trophy 189-0 B&C non-typical.

Jodi Korff's Allegheny County bow-buck is seventh all-time.

(Left) Wayne Edwards, 153-0 P&Y typical, Lawrence County.
(Center) Lewis Black, 174-1 B&C typical, Beaver County.
(Right) Richard Carl, 197-0 B&C non-typical, Northumberland County.

of these suburban deer came from Chester County which, alone, entered a dozen bucks in the book during the most recent measuring program in 1992.

According to Jim Williams, former supervisor of the Game Commission's Southeast Region, "genetics and age account for those big bucks."

"There seems to be a very exceptional gene pool here and because the deer live in places where they're not heavily hunted, or seldom hunted at all, they get old enough to grow big racks," he explained.

The northern rim of the Southeast Region offers more public lands than are available near the metropolitan sectors. Berks County, for example, holds nearly 20,000 acres of state gamelands.

As for the traditional deer-rich mountain counties, where quantity typically yields to quantity, Lycoming and Columbia hunters put five bucks each in the record book (in the last measuring session) followed by Bradford with four bucks exceeding 140 B&C points.

While most hunters will settle for smaller bucks, few go afield without at least fantasizing about that buck of a lifetime showing up in their sights.

Every year the whitetailer's dream comes true for a few select hunters, either by design or sheer luck. Statistics show one's chances for "making the book" are highest in three of the state's four corners where bucks feed well, grow older and remain off-limits behind posted signs.

Recent Book-Buck Entries And How They Did It

A Big Game Awards Program has been sponsored by the Pennsylvania Game Commission and the Pennsylvania Outdoor Writers Association for more than 25 years. Scoring sessions, based on Boone & Crockett standards, are held every three years (with sessions in 1995 and 1998) at the commission's six regional offices. Dates and times hunters may bring in their racks and mounts for free scoring, no matter what the size, are announced in most newspapers and in *Pennsylvania Game News*.

Four behemoth bucks highlighted the last Pennsylvania Game Commission Big Game Awards Program held in Carlisle.

Game Commission Executive Director Pete Duncan awarded the Pennsylvania hunters plaques for their record-setting entries in the agency's tri-annual measuring program, which will again be held in 1995 and 1998.

Here's how the new record book entrants did it.

A 17-year-old hunter took top spot for his 1991 buck in the non-typical gun category. Daniel Van Houdt of Quakertown bagged the 15-point, drop-tined whitetail near his upper Bucks County home on opening day. The buck scored 189 B&C points, ranking it thirteenth on Pennsylvania's all-time list. The rack held four drop-tines, a fact not unnoticed by VanHoudt and his father in earlier sightings.

"We watched it all summer long," said Van Houdt. "We even have it on video."

But opening morning the big deer was elusive as ever. At 4 p.m the youngster decided to leave his stand and stalk through a marshy area into which an 8-pointer he'd fired at earlier that day had run and where he'd seen an abundance of rubs several weeks before.

"All of a sudden he just stood up — about 30 yards way," said Van Houdt. "I shot and he went right down."

Van Houdt and his father, Dan, Sr., had seen the deer the past two bow seasons but it became elusive once hunting seasons arrived. Dan used a slug-loaded 12-gauge Ithaca Deerslayer to make the one-shot kill.

Jeff McConeghy, 27, of Clairton was honored for an Allegheny County 10-pointer, the largest typical bow-buck (161-3) measured in the 1992 session and the third biggest in the commission's all-time record book.

Making the trophy even more unusual, McConeghy shot the deer on December 28 during the winter archery-flintlock season while hunting from the ground "a few miles south of Pittsburgh."

"I saw it 10 or 12 times in the first season but couldn't get close enough," he explained. "I hunted three days straight (in the late season) and about 7:30 I was walking along the edge of a field when I spooked it."

McConeghy couldn't get off a shot so he and a friend wandered across a hillside field to the opposite end of the knoll on which they'd scouted several heavily-used trails.

At 11:20 the massive, symmetrical stag appeared on the trail and was shot at by Jeff's hunting partner, who was also set up against a tree about 50 yards away. The deer fled toward McConeghy and paused long enough for him to place the arrow in the shoulder area at 20 yards.

The two waited a half hour, then followed the blood trail off the knoll where they easily found the monster deer. McConeghy used a Bear Whitetail II bow, an Easton Gamegetter arrow and Satellite Broadhead.

Paul Weisser, 48, of Numedia received a plaque for the largest non-typical whitetail entered in the 1992 measuring program. The 15-pointer scored 161-1, ranking it sixth in the Keystone State's all-time list. The deer was taken on the third Saturday of the 1989 bow season.

"He was with another big buck when I saw him the week before," a smiling Weisser explained. "I was in a treestand and he came down a trail and just stopped broadside about 20 yards away."

"He was looking straight ahead," Weisser recalls. "He never knew I was there."

Weisser said he passed up a 12-pointer earlier in the season in anticipation of a chance at the 15-pointer. After the shot he waited an hour before blood-trailing the book-buck. During that time he watched six other bucks pass by his treestand, set only 400 yards from his Columbia County home.

Weisser used a PSE Laser Mag bow, Easton arrows and a 160 grain Thunderhead broadhead.

Robert Hoffman, 65, of Mt. Pleasant received an award for a Westmoreland County buck he shot in 1949. The deer now holds the tenth spot on the Pennsylvania "typical gun" all-time roll with a score of 174-6.

He bagged the 12-point trophy with a 50 yard shot from his 8mm Mauser late in the day, as he was returning to his car.

Hoffman has hunted each year since he returned from serving in World War II in 1946. He said he thought about having the rack scored in years past but "never got around to it". His nephew, who accepted the award, talked him into taking it to a scoring session.

"I'm happy we did," said Hoffman, "it scored a lot more than the 165 I thought it was."

Surely the next measuring sessions will reveal more record book entries -- including a monster buck from south-central Pennsylvania and others shot in the past three years.

PENNSYLVANIA'S RECORD BOOK BUCKS
TYPICAL / GUN

NAME	HOMETOWN	COUNTY TAKEN	YEAR	SCORE
Fritz Janowsky	Wellsburg, NY	Bradford	1943	189-0
Ivan Parry	Graysville	Greene	1974	184-6
Chester Allison	Harleysville	Blair	1951	182-5
Floyd Reibson	N/A	Sullivan	1931	180-4
R. E. Miller	Bedford	Bedford	1957	177-5
Perry Kinley	N/A	Jefferson	1920	177-0
John Zerbe	N/A	Mifflin	1936	176-5
Clyde Rinehuls	Sayre	Bradford	1944	176-0
Arthur Young	N/A	McKean	1930	175-4
Robert Hoffman	Mt. Pleasant	Westmoreland	1949	174-6

NON-TYPICAL / GUN

NAME	HOMETOWN	COUNTY TAKEN	YEAR	SCORE
Edward Dodge	Knox	Erie	1942	238-6
A.L. Prouty	Tampa, FL	Lycoming	1949	214-0
Ralph Landis	N/A	Juniata	1951	207-7
R. W. Rozetar	Pottsville	Schuylkill	1948	207-4
R.K. Mellon	Ligonier	Westmoreland	1966	200-1
Richard Carl	Shamokin	Unknown	1982	197-0
Kenneth Resinger	Ickesburg	Perry	1949	196-6
Edward G. Ligus	Greensburg	Westmoreland	1956	196-0
C.K. Bero	Hopwood	Fayette	1949	195-4
Ernest Smalley	N/A	Potter	1937	193-6

TYPICAL/BOW

R. Stoltenberg, Jr.	Butler	Butler	1986	174-2
C. Joyce	Pittsburgh	Allegheny	1985	167-6
Jeff McConeghy	Clairton	Allegheny	1991	161-3
Gregory Sarvey	Alliquippa	Beaver	1990	155-2
Andrew Getsy	Patton	Cambria	1965	155-1
Brian Jones	N/A	Somerset	1988	153-7
Jodi Korff	Gibsonia	Allegheny	1985	153-0
Wayne Edwards	New Castle	Lawrence	1981	153-0
Steve Metzger	Germansville	Lehigh	1989	151-4
Robert Bonser	W. Pittston	Wyoming	1960	151-4

NON-TYPICAL/BOW

Craig Krisher	Allentown	Lehigh	1988	203-3
Robert Mertiff	Tyrone	Unknown	N/A	192-5
David Krempasky	Ambler	Montgomery	1985	187-2
Timothy Hunyady	Roncoe	Fayette	1988	178-0
Willis s. Kuhns	Ligonier	Westmoreland	1970	161-2
Paul Weisser Jr.	Numedia	Westmoreland	1989	161-1
T. Cammarota	Media	Delaware	1986	158-7
George Hendricks	Ligonier	Westmoreland	1977	152-5
Thomas Griffith	Apollo	Westmoreland	1990	143-2
David Penn	Natrona	Heights Butler	1990	139-4

One of the heaviest (documented) whitetail bucks ever reported was killed in Maine in 1955. Shot by Harry Hinkley, the deer weighed 355 pounds, field-dressed, three days after it was killed. It was weighed on official scales. Biologists estimated its live weight at 461 pounds. For the record, the buck held a 16-point rack but didn't have the mass of many of Maine's smaller-bodied deer. A 1926 Minnesota deer is said to have field-dressed at 402 pounds; its live weight calculated at 511 pounds.

Chapter
26

COUNTY PROFILES:
Introduction

Public hunting lands scattered across Pennsylvania total more than four million acres, ranging from gamelands, Game Commission cooperative programs and state forests to massive federal acreage and local watershed and municipal lands.

Few, if any, states in the East offer the range and variety found in Pennsylvania. Public hunting lands can be found in almost every county with the widest choices in the more remote areas of the state.

Detailed in the following pages are the most extensive listings of deer hunting information ever published under one cover. Information was gathered from a variety of private and government agencies with updates (such as additions to gamelands) included. Figures are as precise as possible, considering that public recreation lands are under the jurisdictions of more than a half-dozen government agencies.

Profiles of Pennsylvania's 67 counties are given as a guide to choosing the best hunting lands based on deer numbers and public hunting opportunities. The most recent harvest and doe license allocation figures have been included for comparison.

Maps show the relative locations of gamelands, state forests, state parks and roads in each county. Precise locations and major and secondary roads leading to the hunting lands are shown on official Pennsylvania Dept. of Transportation highway maps.

Information on properties and their acreages was accumulated from a variety of sources, both public and private. Figures included on the following pages were as up-to-date as possible at the time of printing.

However, co-op agreements and other private land-use programs change annually. Lands may be shifted in and out of the program for varied reasons or acreages will be reduced or expanded from time to time.

Anyone wanting updated information on specific tracts should contact the Game Commission, forest and parks departments, federal agencies or individual cooperators for details. Sources of information are provided along with addresses and telephone numbers.

Information included in the "In Brief" listings under each county profile include the following:

State Game Lands

More than 1.4 million acres of gamelands are owned and managed by the Pennsylvania Game Commission. These properties were purchased at $450 per acre or less, beginning in 1920 when the first gameland was purchased in Elk County (at $2.75 per acre). Most of the funds for setting aside these properties, open to the general public, were funded through hunting license dollars.

Detailed maps of individual gamelands are available through the Pennsylvania Game Commission's regional offices and the Harrisburg headquarters. The 9x15-inch Sportsmen's Recreation Maps cost 50-cents each and show streams, roads and towns in the surrounding area plus trails, roads, parking lots and prominent natural land features within each gameland.

Of value to every hunter seeking open lands is the set of six Outdoor Recreation Maps, one for each of the commission's half-dozen regions, depicting public and leased lands open for hunting. In addition, each map shows municipalities, roads, drainage areas, contour intervals and other physical features to help the user become familiar with the region. Each 24x36-inch map costs $4 and can be picked up at or ordered through commission offices (see addresses in regional listings).

Each map folds to a convenient 6x9-inch size. The maps are printed on spun-bonded stock which resists fraying and tearing.

State Parks and Forests

The Dept. of Environmental Resources owns and manages Pennsylvania's state forests and parklands. The Bureau of State Parks is in charge of the latter; the Bureau of Forestry handles the former. They are not the same entity although some parks are located within or adjacent to state forests.

Pennsylvania has 114 state parks, most offering camping, fishing, hiking and hunting, although hunting is not available at all parks. In the larger parklands, however, hunting land is available with Safety Zone areas strictly enforced. In some suburban parks, special, controlled deer hunts are conducted every year or two.

The parks also offer camping and several have modern cabins for rent throughout the four seasons. Maps and information on specific state parks are available by writing: Pennsylvania Dept. of Environmental Resources, Bureau of State Parks, P.O. Box 8551, Harrisburg, PA 17105-8551. Or call 1-800-63-PARKS.

More than two million acres of state forests in 44 counties are under the auspices of 20 offices across the state. The lands are managed to provide sustained yields of timber, protect watersheds, conserve water and afford recreational opportunities. More than 2,600 miles of roads and 2,500 miles of hiking trails penetrate these lands.

In most regions, forest lands are not contiguous, rather they're scattered across a region in specific tracts. Highway maps clearly show access and borders of all public forest lands.

For specific information on hunting state forest lands, contact the following offices.

FOREST DISTRICT OFFICES
Forest District   **Address**   **Telephone**

Forest District	Address	Telephone
Michaux S.F.	10099 Lincoln Way East Fayetteville, PA 17222	(717) 352-2211
Buchanan S.F.	RD2, Box 3, McConnellsburg, PA 17233	(717) 485-3148
Tuscarora S.F.	RD1, Box 42A, Blain, PA 17006	(717) 536-3191
Forbes S.F.	POB 519, Laughlintown, PA 15655	(412) 238-9533
Rothrock S.F.	Box 403, Rothrock Lane, Smithfield, Huntingdon, PA 16652	(814) 643-2340
Gallitzin S.F.	131 Hillcrest Dr., Ebensburg, PA 15031	(814) 472-8320
Bald Eagle S.F.	POB 147, Laurelton, PA 17835	(717) 922-3344
Kittanning S.F.	RD3, Box 705, Clarion, PA 16214	(814) 226-1901
Moshannon S.F.	Box 952, Clearfield, PA 16830	(814) 765-3741
Sproul S.F.	HCR 62, Box 90, Renovo, PA 17764	(717) 923-1450
Lackawanna S.F.	Rm. 401, 100 Lackawanna Ave., Scranton, PA 18503	(717) 9634561
Tiadaghton S.F.	423 E. Central Ave., S. Williamsport, PA 17701	(717) 327-3450
Elk S.F.	RD 1, Route 155, Box 327, Emporium, PA 15834	(814) 486-3353
Cornplanter S.F.	323 N. State St., North Warren, PA 16365	(814) 723-6951
Susquehannock S.F.	P.O. Box 673, Coudersport, PA 16915	(814) 274-8474
Tioga S.F.	Box 94, Route 287 S Wellsboro, PA 16901	(717) 724-2868
Valley Forge S.F.	RD 2, Route 23, Pottstown, PA 19464	(610) 469-6217
Weiser S.F.	Box 99, Cressona, PA 17929	(717) 385-2545
Delaware S.F.	POB 150, 474 Clearview Lane, Stroudsburg, PA 18360	(717) 424-3001
Wyoming S.F.	POB 439, Bloomsburg, PA 17815	(717) 387-4255

Farm-Game and Safety Zone Co-ops

Thousands of acres of Farm-Game and Safety Zone Cooperatives are available to hunters. The lands are privately owned with certain landowner benefits afforded participants. Through these programs more than four million acres are available for small and big game hunting. The Game Commission does not publish specific listings of these properties although cruising back roads or querying regional offices will bring information as to what may be available in a specific area. Most co-ops have special signs on the property borders.

General location of co-op lands are shown on the Regional Outdoor Recreation Maps listed previously.

Forest-Game Co-ops

Over 600,000 Forest-Game Co-ops are scattered across the state, courtesy of more than 50 owners of large tracts of private woodlands. They're most abundant in big-woods and mountain country where timber and pulpwood, oil, gas, coal, water authority and other companies and individuals open all or portions of their holdings for public hunting. However, some of them are close to larger towns and cities.

Again, the properties are not detailed on Game Commission maps as they're in a near-constant state of change. However, the Outdoor Recreation Maps do show general areas where such properties are located.

As of late 1994, the following list of Forest-Game Cooperators offered open recreation lands.

Forest-Game Cooperatives
* Adobe Mining Co., Grove City: 1,434 acres; Butler and Venango counties.
* Bailey Estates, Clearfield: 1,276 acres; Clearfield County.
* Blythe Twp. Municipal Authority, New Philadelphia: 2,757 acres; Schuylkill County.
* Bradford City Water Authority, Bradford; 12,000 acres; McKean County.
* E.M. Brown Inc., Clearfield: 5,625 acres; Clearfield County.
* James & Shirley Burke, Weedville: 1,000 acres; Elk County.
* Camp Mack Boy Scout Camp, Lancaster: 1,600 acres; Lancaster and Lebanon counties.
* Chatham Water Co., Woolrich: 5,200 acres; Clinton and Lycoming counties.
* Matson Lumber, Inc., Brookville: 20,000 acres; Clarion, Crawford, Forest, Indiana, Venango and Warren counties.
* Minersville Borough Municipal Authority, Minersville: 4,500 acres; Schuylkill County.
* National Fuel Gas Supply Corp, Erie: 1,709 acres; Elk, Forest, McKean and Warren counties.
* Nesquehoning Borough Water Auth., Nesquehoning: 2,553 acres; Carbon County.
* New Holland Borough, New Holland: 2,500 acres; Lancaster County.
* Northern Forests Co., Smethport: 5,000 acres; Cameron and Elk counties.
* P&N Coal Co., Punxsutawney: 1,807 acres; Armstrong, Clearfield, Elk, Indiana and Jefferson counties.
* Pennsylvania Electric Co., Johnstown: 1,350 acres; Wyoming County.
* Collins Pine Co., Kane: 104,108 acres; Cameron, Clarion, Elk, Forest, Jefferson, McKean, Potter and Warren counties.
* Cooney Bros. Coal Co., Cresson: 9,321 acres; Blair and Cambria counties.
* Curtin Real Estate, Bellefonte: 6,455 acres; Centre County.
* City of Dubois, Dubois: 4,684 acres; Clearfield County.
* East Broadtop Railroad, Rockhill Furnace: 5,000 acres; Huntingdon County.
* Elk Lick Reserve, Smethport: 1,500 acres; McKean County.
* Girard Estate, Girardville: 1,367 acres; Schuylkill County.
* Glatfelter Pulp Wood Co., Spring Grove: 24,385 acres; Bedford,

Cumberland, Franklin, Fulton, Huntingdon, Juniata, Mifflin, Perry and Snyder counties.

* Borough of Hamburg, Hamburg: 4,300 acres; Berks County.
* Hauto Estates, Nesquehoning: 3,258 acres; Carbon County.
* HEJ Corp., Mt. Pocono: 1,763 acres; Clinton County.
* International Paper Co., Erie: 22,500 acres; Cameron, Forest, McKean, Potter, Venango and Warren Counties.
* Larimer & Norton Inc., Warren: 1,078 acres; Warren county.
* M.A. Lawson, Warren: 1,200 acres; Warren County.
* City of Lock Haven, Lock Haven: 5,200 acres; Clinton County.
* Mahanoy Township Authority, Mahanoy City: 1,784 acres; Schuylkill County.
* Mallery Lumber Corp., Emporium: 59,220 acres; Cameron, Elk, Jefferson and McKean counties.
* Mansfield Water Co., Mansfield: 1,100 acres; Tioga County.
* Pine Grove Borough, Pine Grove: 2,036 acres; Schuylkill County.
* Quaker State Oil Refining Corp., Titusville: 12,546 acres; Crawford, Forest, McKean, Warren and Venango counties.
* Ram Forest Products Inc., Shinglehouse: 11,823 acres; Elk, McKean and Potter counties.
* Roaring Spring Borough, Roaring Springs: 1,400 acres; Blair County.
* Rochester & Pittsburgh Coal Co., Indiana: 30,285 acres; Armstrong, Clearfield, Clinton, Indiana and Jefferson counties.
* Schuylkill County Commissioners, Pottsville: 3,292 acres; Schuylkill County.
* Schuylkill Haven Borough, Schuylkill: 4,500 acres; Schuylkill County.
* Seneca Resources Corp., Erie: 75,591 acres; Armstrong, Cameron, Clarion, Elk, Forest, Jefferson, McKean, Mercer and Venango counties.
* S.F. Properties Inc., Coudersport: 26,210 acres; Potter and Tioga counties.
* St. Mary's Area Joint Water Auth. St. Marys: 1,860 in Elk County.
* Stone Valley Exp. Forest, University Park: 6,182 acres; Huntingdon County.
* Borough of Tyrone, Tyrone: 3,634 acres; Blair County.
* West Penn Power Co., Greensburg: 2,300 acres; Armstrong County.
* West Penn Power/Allegheny-Pittsburgh Coal Co., Greensburg: 4,235 acres; Washington County.
* Westmoreland Co., Greensburg: 4,182 acres; Westmoreland and Fayette counties.

Harvest/Density Information

In addition to available hunting lands, information provided under each county's In Brief listing includes the most recent (1993) buck and doe harvests, doe permit allocations, current deer densities, density goals and buck harvests based on the amount of forested square miles (designated as FSM). Of course, these figures change each year but remain proportionately similar.

The information is provided as ready reference for the reader to make comparisons of deer hunting opportunities in each of the 67 "management units".

Food, Lodging and Services

An address and telephone number for requesting information on food, lodging and services is included in each county profile.

Federal Lands

In addition to state and co-op lands, many federal lands are also open to hunters. National forest, military, Corps of Engineers, National Wildlife Refuge and National Recreation Area lands are detailed at the end of the county information section.

County Treasurers

In Pennsylvania, County Treasurers handle all doe license applications and sales. Each year hunters apply to counties for regular, bonus and second bonus permits. Bonus tags, actually left-over "regular" doe tags, are often available. Hunters applying for bonus permits via mail are advised to call the fiscal offices to check on license availability prior to sending their applications.

Potter and Philadelphia counties' doe tag sales are handled through the respective regional offices of the Game Commission.

The county seat for each county is indicated on the maps. County treasurers' telephone numbers are as follows.

COUNTY TREASURERS OFFICES

Adams (717) 334-6781	Dauphin (717) 255-2677
Allegheny (412) 355-4111	Delaware (610) 891-4271
Armstrong (412) 548-3260	Elk (814) 776-5323
Beaver (412) 728-5700	Erie (814) 451-6203
Bedford (814) 623-4846	Fayette (412) 430-1256
Berks (610) 378-8837	Forest (814) 755-3536
Blair (814) 695-5541	Franklin (717) 261-3119
Bradford (717) 265-1700	Fulton (717) 485-4454
Bucks (215) 348-6245	Greene (412) 852-5225
Butler (412) 284-5151	Huntingdon (814) 643-3523
Cambria (814) 472-5440	Indiana (412) 465-3845
Cameron (814) 486-3348	Jefferson (814) 849-1609
Carbon (717) 325-2251	Juniata (717) 436-8991
Centre (814) 355-6810	Lackawanna (717) 963-6731
Chester (610) 344-6370	Lancaster (717) 299-8222
Clarion (814) 226-4000	Lawrence (412) 658-2541
Clearfield (814) 765-2641	Lebanon (717) 274-2801
Clinton (717) 893-4004	Lehigh (610) 820-3112
Columbia (717) 389-5626	Luzerne (717) 825-1764
Crawford (814) 336-1151	Lycoming (717) 327-2249
Cumberland (717) 240-6380	McKean (814) 887-5571

Mercer (412) 662-4440
Mifflin (717) 248-8439
Monroe (717) 424-5100
Montgomery (610) 278-3070
Montour (717) 271-3016
Northampton (610) 559-3167
Northumberland (717) 988-4161
Perry (717) 582-2131
Philadelphia (610) 926-3136
Pike (717) 296-3442
Potter (717) 398-4744
Schuylkill (717) 628-1434

Snyder (717) 837-4221
Somerset (814) 445-2071
Sullivan (717) 946-7331
Susquehanna (717) 278-4600
Tioga (717) 724-1906
Union (717) 524-8781
Vernango (814) 437-6871
Warren (814) 723-7550
Washington (412) 228-6780
Wayne (717) 253-5970
Westmoreland (412) 830-3167
Wyoming (717) 836-3200
York (717) 771-9603

Some bowhunters refuse to use brightly colored nocks and fletchings because they believe deer will see them more readily than dark colors. That's probably true. But consider that fluorescent yellow, green or orange fletching is more readily detected on the arrows in the quiver, not the arrow nocked for the initial shot. Bright fletchings will enable you to better detect the area of the hit -- and find your arrow among the vegetation.

On cold days, grunt tubes and other deer calls can freeze up after a few breaths are blown through them. Carry the calls in an inside pocket to keep them warm between uses. Also consider packing an extra call in case one fails to perform.

A small, shallow "pocket" sewn on your hunting trousers just above the knee provides a welcome rest for your bow. Not only will it ease the eventual strain of holding the bow but it will be in a convenient position should a quick shot present itself.

Wound areas in venison tend to become contaminated or start to rot at a surprisingly fast rate, especially in mild weather. After skinning and before hanging, cut away the gelatinous bloody areas. The undamaged parts will "glaze" over and become dry to the touch, serving as a protective barrier for the carcass.

NORTHWEST REGION

"The Northwest is comprised of two geographic areas. The line representing the southern extent of the Wisconsin Glacier, here some 70,000 years ago, runs diagonally from the northeast to the southwest, cutting the region in half. Land in the glacial zone, north of the line, is characterized by small ponds, swampy depressions and knob-like mounds of sand and gravel. The glaciated part tends to be damper, flatter and more suited to agriculture than the more hilly and forested land to the south. The land not affected by the glacier is characterized by the 'big woods' of Warren, Forest, Jefferson and Clarion counties. The terrain is marked by deep river valleys and steep hills and mountains. For big game hunters, deer, turkey and bear are getting more plentiful and widespread with each passing year."

Bob MacWilliams, Pennsylvania Game Commission

Pennsylvania Game Commission
Northwest Region
P.O. Box 31, Franklin, PA 16323
Phone: (800) 533-6764 and (814) 432-3187
Butler, Clarion, Crawford, Erie, Forest, Jefferson, Lawrence,
Mercer, Venango and Warren counties.

BUTLER COUNTY

Situated north of Pittsburgh, Butler County ranks high on the list of counties with trophy whitetail potential. Covering 789 square miles, Butler's landscape is largely hills and broad sandstone and shale ridges along with mountainous country composing the Allegheny Plateau. Elevations range from 740 to 1,580 feet.

Fifty-one percent of the county is forested with another 30 percent in farmland (half in harvested cropland). The primary crops are oats and corn.

Butler holds two state gamelands tracts, the largest SGL No. 95 near Old Annandale with 8,536 acres. Much of the 13,600-acre Moraine State Park is also open to deer hunters. A scattering of mature oak woodlots bordering crop farms make this a prime whitetail spot.

Food, lodging and services, contact: The Magic Forests of West Central PA Tourism & Travel Bureau, c/o Brookville Office, R.R. #5, Box 47, Brookville, PA 15825. Phone: (800)348-9393, (814) 849-5197.

IN BRIEF

State Gamelands: 8,935 acres

State Parks & Forests: 13,640 acres

Farm-Game Co-op: 13,500 acres (126 farms)

Safety Zone Lands: 59,000 acres (500 tracts)

Forest-Game Co-op: 77 acres

1993 Buck/Doe Harvest: 3,308 / 5,181

1994 Doe Permit Allocation: 15,100

Deer Density/FSM: 32

Deer Density Goal/FSM: 23

Average Buck Harvest/FSM: 8.3

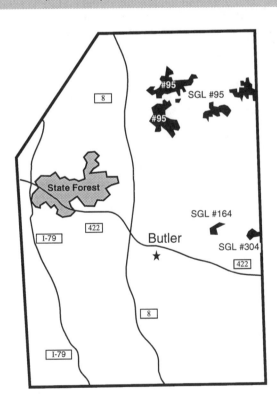

CLARION COUNTY

Farmland makes up one-fourth of Clarion's 607 square miles of landscape, about three-fourths of that in livestock production. Hay, corn, oats and wheat are its primarily crops.

Mountainous with rolling hills and steep ridges, the plentiful second and third growth hardwood forests are home to numerous whitetails. About 60 percent of the county is forested with elevations ranging from 740 to 1,580 feet. Reclaimed strip-mines have also improved wildlife habitat here.

Three large gamelands tracts hold deer: SGL No. 63 near Shippenville (3,413 acres); SGL No. 72 near Clarion (2,025 acres); and SGL No. 74 near Strattanville (6,320 acres).

Cook Forest State Park near Cooksburg has 4,000 acres open to hunters.

Food, lodging and services, contact: The Magic Forests of West Central PA Tourism & Travel Bureau, c/o Brookville Office, R.R. #5, Box 47, Brookville, PA 15825. Phone: (800) 348-9393, (814) 849-5197.

IN BRIEF

State Gamelands: 11,758 acres

State Parks & Forests: 4,000 acres

Farm-Game Co-op: 40,000 acres (337 farms)

Safety Zone Lands: 20,424 acres (140 tracts)

Forest-Game Co-op: 4,884 acres

1993 Buck/Doe Harvest: 2,969 / 4,752

1994 Doe Permit Allocation: 12,000

Deer Density/FSM: 31

Deer Density Goal/FSM: 26

Average Buck Harvest/FSM: 8.0

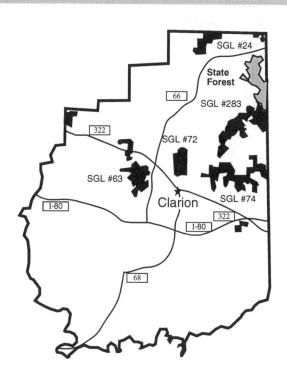

CRAWFORD COUNTY

South of Lake Erie on the Ohio border, Crawford may be best known for its great fishing potential and its attraction for waterfowl but it's also one of the state's top trophy whitetail counties.

Its 1,011 square miles are hilly and mountainous in some places with an abundance of low wetland and riparian areas. Woodlots and forests make up 48 percent of county.

A dozen separate gamelands tracts are scattered across Crawford, many in wetlands and all with woodlands. Gamelands acreages range from 154 to 5,555, with some new additions in the early 1990s. Erie National Wildlife Refuge, one of two such federal refuges in Pennsylvania and the only one on which hunting is permitted, is located at Guys Mills.

Most of Pymatuning State Park's 18,275 acres are open to hunters. It's here and in other farmland-wetland areas where hunters stand the chance of encountering big bucks, for which Crawford is known. The sector from Meadville north for a couple dozen miles or more into neighboring Erie County draws considerable hunter attention.

Food, lodging and services, contact: Crawford County Tourist Association, 211 Chestnut St., Meadville, PA 16335. Phone: (800) 332-2338, (814) 333-1258.

IN BRIEF

State Gamelands: 22,380 acres

State Parks & Forests: 18,275 acres

Farm-Game Co-op: 72,000 acres (725 farms)

Safety Zone Lands: 43,000 acres (319 tracts)

Forest-Game Co-op: 3,585 acres

1993 Buck/Doe Harvest: 4,342 / 7,858

1994 Doe Permit Allocation: 17,250

Deer Density/FSM: 33

Deer Density Goal/FSM: 18

Average Buck Harvest/FSM: 9.0

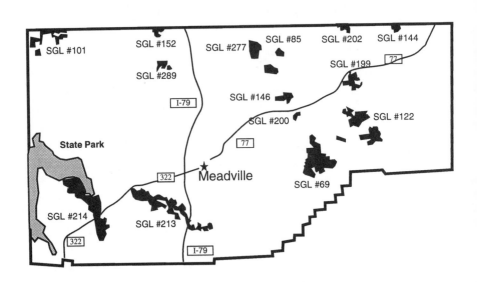

ERIE COUNTY

The only county touching a Great Lake, Erie County's deer hunting takes a back seat to its fishing potential. However, Erie regularly produces trophy-class bucks on its 804 square miles of terrain.

As part of the glaciated region, its rich soils support 47 percent of the county that's forested. The terrain is rolling with swampy valley floors and occasional wet uplands. Elevations span 573 to 1,900 feet.

Farms occupy 39 percent of the county, providing potatoes, oats, corn and apples, all to the liking of hungry deer.

Erie has more gamelands (13) than any other Northwest Region county, with nearly 14,000 acres. Similar to neighboring Crawford County, many gamelands tracts are composed of wetland and woodland habitat. It's in this mix of marshlands and farmlands that the biggest deer make their homes.

Food, lodging and services, contact: Tourist and Convention Bureau of Erie, 1006 State St., Erie, PA 16501. Phone: (814) 454-7191.

IN BRIEF

State Gamelands: 13,885 acres
State Parks & Forests: None
Farm-Game Co-op: 31,000 acres (295 farms)
Safety Zone Lands: 46,000 acres (338 tracts)

Forest-Game Co-op: None
1993 Buck/Doe Harvest: 2,563 / 2,839
1994 Doe Permit Allocation: 12,400
Deer Density/FSM: 30
Deer Density Goal/FSM: 29
Average Buck Harvest/FSM: 6.9

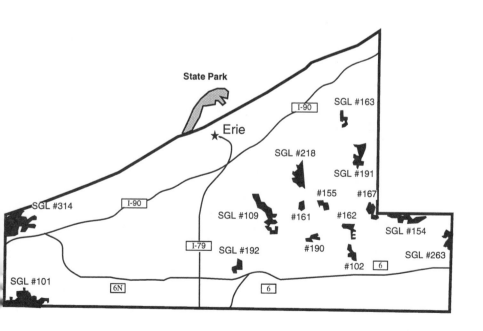

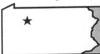

FOREST COUNTY

Covering only 428 square miles, Forest County lies within the Allegheny Plateau region with elevations from 1,040 to 1,944 feet. As with most other northwestern counties, its topography is hilly and mountainous in some regions, with deep stream valleys.

However, as its name implies, 93 percent of the county is covered in woodland. Farms here occupy only three percent of the land, placing it in the bottom four in the state in agricultural importance. The county is also the least populous in the state with only a dozen people per square mile.

Two sizable public hunting tracts are available including 2,247acres of Kittanning State Forest and SGL No. 24 near Newmanville with 8,390 wooded acres.

Flavoring the entire county's scenery and recreational opportunities is Allegheny National Forest, composing more wildlands than a hunter could cover in a lifetime. All national forest land, save for inholdings and safety zone areas, is open to hunting.

Food, lodging and services, contact: Forest County Tourist Promotion Agency, P.O. Box 608, Tionesta, PA 16353. Phone: (800) 222-1706, (814) 927-8818.

IN BRIEF

State Gamelands: 8,390 acres

State Parks & Forests: 2,247 acres

Farm-Game Co-op: None

Safety Zone Lands: 16,236 acres (80 tracts)

Forest-Game Co-op: 53,081 acres

1993 Buck/Doe Harvest: 2,368 / 4,034

1994 Doe Permit Allocation: 10,550

Deer Density/FSM: 29

Deer Density Goal/FSM: 23

Average Buck Harvest/FSM: 6.0

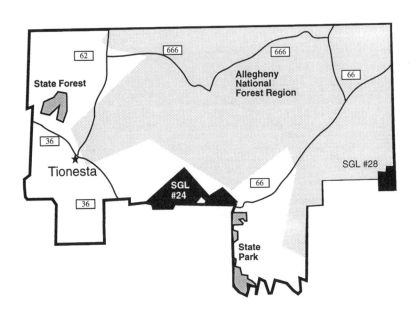

★ JEFFERSON COUNTY

Like most counties in this region, the hilly countryside ranges in elevation from 1,100 to 2,220 feet with some steep mountains and broad ridges. Some 61 percent of Jefferson's 657 square miles is forested.

Topography is rugged and reclaimed strip mines now covered with grass and planted trees are obvious, and beneficial to deer. Cattle pastures and croplands cover 21 percent of the county, the latter producing alfalfa, corn and grains.

Kittanning State Forest, northeast of Munderf, offers 9,380 acres of public hunting lands with five gamelands providing another 39,723 acres. The biggest is mountainous SGL No. 54 near Brockway with 22,049 acres followed by 6,564acre SGL No. 283 near Cooksburg's oil well country and hilly SGL No. 31 (5,176 acres) near Punxsutawney.

Food, lodging and services, contact: The Magic Forests of West Central PA Tourism & Travel Bureau, c/o Brookville Office, R.R. #5, Box 47, Brookville, PA 15825. Phone: (800) 348-9393, (814) 849-5197.

IN BRIEF

State Gamelands: 39,951 acres

State Parks & Forests: 9,590 acres

Farm-Game Co-op: 67,145 acres (401 farms)

Safety Zone Lands: 24,196 acres (162 tracts)

Forest-Game Co-op: 11,315 acres

1993 Buck/Doe Harvest: 3,562 / 6,744

1994 Doe Permit Allocation: 13,000

Deer Density/FSM: 31

Deer Density Goal/FSM: 19

Average Buck Harvest/FSM: 8.8

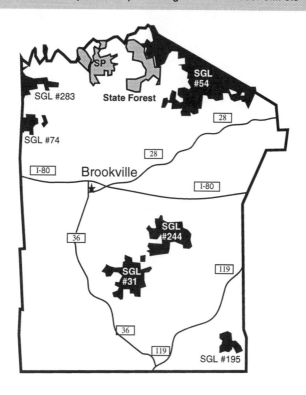

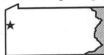

LAWRENCE COUNTY

Typical of most of the Allegheny Plateau, Lawrence County's landscape is characterized by hills and mountains ranging in elevation from 760 to 1,440 feet. Swampy valleys and moist uplands are typical of the region, which borders Ohio on the west.

Forty-two percent of the county is wooded with an equal amount of acreage in farmland. Livestock farming exceeds crop production, the latter primarily alfalfa, corn, oats and wheat.

Six gamelands tracts are open to hunters, all except one under 1,000 acres. SGL No. 151 near Harlansburg contains 1,039 acres. McConnells Mill State Park west of Portersville offers another 2,000 acres.

The average deer harvest numbers slightly over 2,000.

Food, lodging and services, contact: Lawrence County Tourist Promotion, Shenango Street Station, 138 West Washington St., New Castle, PA 16101. Phone: (412) 654-5593.

IN BRIEF

State Gamelands: 2,574 acres

State Parks & Forests: 2,000 acres

Farm-Game Co-op: 74,000 acres (770 farms)

Safety Zone Lands: 4,900 acres (56 tracts)

Forest-Game Co-op: None

1993 Buck/Doe Harvest: 730 / 1,377

1994 Doe Permit Allocation: 3,500

Deer Density/FSM: 19

Deer Density Goal/FSM: 22

Average Buck Harvest/FSM: 4.8

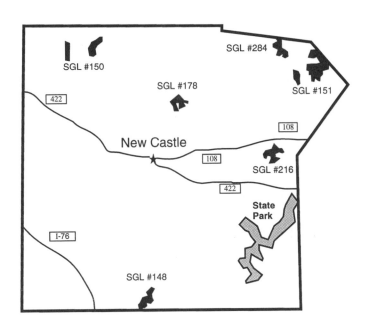

MERCER COUNTY

Set on the Ohio border, 672-square mile Mercer County is covered in hardwoods on 39 percent of the county's landscape.

Hills and mountains ranging from elevations of 822 to 1,620 feet and farms, composing 41 percent of the county, offer varied game habitat. Dairy farming dominates although oats, corn, hay and wheat also benefit whitetails throughout the county.

Mercer's three gamelands all hold deer, the biggest being SGL No. 130 at Sandy Lake with 2,356 acres. Close by, Maurice Goddard State Park offers another 1,316 acres. Add to that 84,000 acres on farm-game holdings and 43,000 acres under Safety Zone projects.

Like Erie and Crawford, Mercer County boasts an abundance of marshlands rich in game. The buck harvest here averages between 8-9 per square forested mile.

Food, lodging and services, contact: Mercer County Tourist Promotion, One West State Street, Sharon, PA 16146. Phone: (800) 637-2370, (412) 981-5880.

IN BRIEF

State Gamelands: 4,196 acres

State Parks & Forests: 1,316 acres

Farm-Game Co-op: 84,000 acres (947 farms)

Safety Zone Lands: 43,000 acres (371 tracts)

Forest-Game Co-op: 199 acres

1993 Buck/Doe Harvest: 2,319 / 4,272

1994 Doe Permit Allocation: 7,900

Deer Density/FSM: 32

Deer Density Goal/FSM: 22

Average Buck Harvest/FSM: 8.8

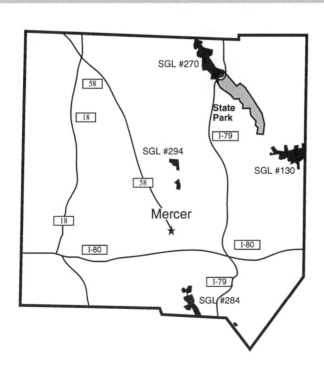

VENANGO COUNTY

Mixed hardwoods characterize this 679 square mile county of hills and steep mountains. Topography consists of irregular woodlands sliced by steep stream valleys.

Fully 72 percent of Venango is forest land with only 15 percent farmland, the latter primarily cattle country with the remainder yielding corn, oats and wheat. Elevations span 860 to 1,725 feet.

Venango's Oil Creek State Park near Oil City offers hunters access to 6,500 acres with five gamelands tracts providing more than 22,000 public acres. The largest is SGL No. 39 near Franklin (9,635 acres) followed by SGL No. 45 at Van (5,170 acres) and SGL No. 96 near Dempseytown (4,973 acres).

Of special note is the pending sale and transfer to gamelands of the 11,116-acre President Oil Tract costing $3.3 million.

Food, lodging and services, contact: Venango County Area Tourist Agency, Box 147, 501 Main St., Emlenton, PA 16373. Phone: (800) 776-4526, (412) 867-2472.

IN BRIEF

State Gamelands: 22,659 acres

State Parks & Forests: 6,500 acres

Farm-Game Co-op: 54,000 acres (571 farms)

Safety Zone Lands: 24,711 acres (203 tracts)

Forest-Game Co-op: 13,127 acres

1993 Buck/Doe Harvest: 3,431 / 4,940

1994 Doe Permit Allocation: 14,850

Deer Density/FSM: 28

Deer Density Goal/FSM: 19

Average Buck Harvest/FSM: 7.1

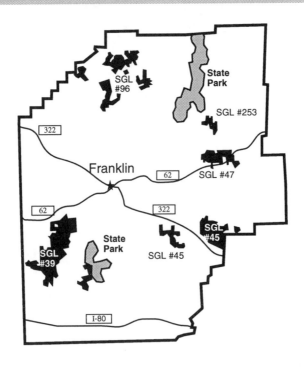

WARREN COUNTY

On the state's northern border, Warren County is well-known as a whitetail haven with an abundance of public hunting grounds. Best known is the 512,000-acre Allegheny National Forest which is shared with McKean, Forest and Elk counties.

Most of the county (79 percent) is in forest. Topography varies from 1,080 to 2,220 feet across the rugged mountains and steep riverine valleys.

Only 15 percent of Warren is farmland, primarily cattle raising land. Hay, corn and oats grow on the five percent of the county devoted to cropfarms.

In addition to national forest land, Warren also holds six gamelands, three exceeding 8,000 acres. SGL No. 86 at Tidioute is 14,227 acres, SGL No. 29 near Warren has 9,363 acres and SGL No. 143 near Garland, 8,177 acres.

Some hunters use boats to access their deer hunting grounds on the shores of 12,000-acre Allegheny Reservoir (Kinzua Dam) which separates Warren and McKean counties.

Food, lodging and services, contact: Travel Northern Alleghenies, 315 Second Ave., P.O. Box 804, Warren, PA 16365. Phone: (800) 624-7802, (814) 726-1222.

IN BRIEF

State Gamelands: 33,768 acres

State Parks & Forests: 360 acres

Farm-Game Co-op: 31,578 acres (239 farms)

Safety Zone Lands: 44,329 acres (275 tracts)

Forest-Game Co-op: 18,125 acres

1993 Buck/Doe Harvest: 4,626 / 10,164

1994 Doe Permit Allocation: 17,700

Deer Density/FSM: 27

Deer Density Goal/FSM: 21

Average Buck Harvest/FSM: 6.6

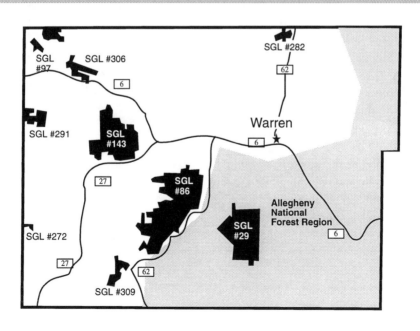

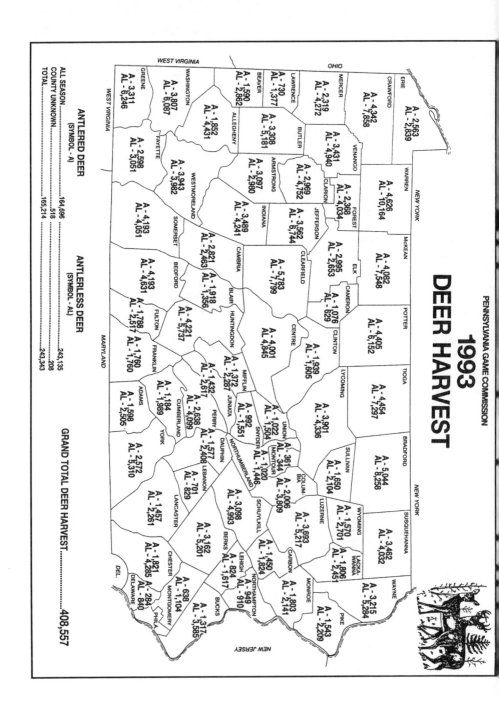

PENNSYLVANIA GAME COMMISSION

1993
DEER HARVEST

ANTLERED DEER
(SYMBOL - A)

ANTLERLESS DEER
(SYMBOL - AL)

ALL SEASON 164,696
COUNTY UNKNOWN 518
TOTAL 165,214

.... 243,135
.... 208
.... 243,343

GRAND TOTAL DEER HARVEST 408,557

SOUTHWEST REGION

"Grouse and squirrel are thriving in the reverting farmlands and woodlands in this corner of the state. The small timber operations typifying this area further enhance the abundance of many desirable game species. The same habitat diversity and an abundance of foods also mean many deer. Deer hunting is excellent, particularly in certain areas of Armstrong, Beaver, Cambria, Greene, Indiana, Somerset, Washington and Westmoreland counties. Deer in these counties are often heavier and produce larger racks than those found in the highly publicized, more mountainous regions."

**Barry Moore,
Pennsylvania Game Commission**

Pennsylvania Game Commission
Southwest Region
P.O. Box A, Ligonier, PA 15658
Phone: (800) 243-8519 and (412) 238-9523
Allegheny, Armstrong, Beaver, Cambria, Fayette, Greene, Indiana, Somerset,
Washington and Westmoreland counties.

ALLEGHENY COUNTY

Despite its urban-suburban personality, the rugged rolling hills and valleys surrounding Pittsburgh annually yield some of the state's biggest bucks.

Woodlands rise 400-500 feet from valley floor to summit, in places quite abruptly. Forests comprise 37 percent of the county. Farmland composes only eight percent of the county's 728 square miles with apples, corn and grains the chief crops.

As in much of Pennsylvania's suburbia, finding public hunting lands here is a problem — which accounts for the higher age structure of whitetails which find haven on private lands and other 'no hunting' areas. Only one gameland — SGL No. 203 near Armitage with 1,245 acres — is available and no state park or forest lands are present.

Deer density here in the mid-1990s approach about five times the carrying capacity — and many more times beyond the tolerance levels of most suburban homeowners. Some of the bucks found in Allegheny are monsters, serving well its reputation as a trophy producer.

Allegheny County composes the Southwest's Special Regulations Area with liberal doe hunting opportunities.

Food, lodging and services, contact: Greater Pittsburgh Convention and Visitors Bureau, Inc., Four Gateway Center, Suite 514, Pittsburgh, PA 15222. Phone: (800) 366-0093 and (412) 281-7711.

IN BRIEF

State Gamelands: 1,245 acres

State Parks & Forests: None

Farm-Game Co-op: 16,333 acres (118 farms)

Safety Zone Lands: 5,597 acres (62 tracts)

Forest-Game Co-op: None

1993 Buck/Doe Harvest: 1,852 / 4,431

1994 Doe Permit Allocation: 24,600

Deer Density/FSM: 25

Deer Density Goal/FSM: 5

Average Buck Harvest/FSM: 7.1

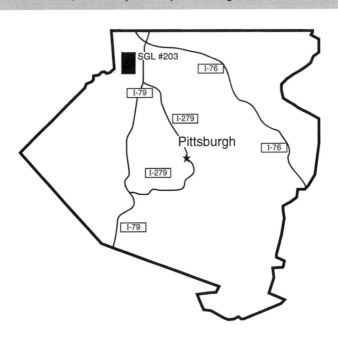

★ ARMSTRONG COUNTY

Covering 646 square miles, Armstrong is hill-country interspersed with high mountainous plateaus. Its rolling terrain is flat in few places with hilltops rising several hundred feet above floodplains. Elevations span 740 to 1,720 feet.

Thirty-one percent of the county is in farmland, primarily in crop production. Corn, cabbage and grains are the chief harvest products. Well over 100,000 acres of Game Commission co-op and Safety Zone lands are available to sportsmen exploring access opportunities, mostly on these farms. Look to the region in Armstrong's northwest, on the Butler border, as holding good bucks.

The county offers five gamelands tracts, the largest SGL No.105 with 2,613 acres near East Brady. A portion of the 3,300-acre Mahoning Flood Control Area, shared with Indiana County, is also open for hunting.

Food, lodging and services, contact: Armstrong County Tourist Bureau, 402 East Market St., Kittanning, PA 16201. Phone: (412) 548-3226.

IN BRIEF

State Gamelands: 5,217 acres
State Parks & Forests: None
Farm-Game Co-op: 76,129 acres (589 farms)
Safety Zone Lands: 27,799 acres (196 tracts)

Forest-Game Co-op: 5,981 acres
1993 Buck/Doe Harvest: 3,097 / 2,980
1994 Doe Permit Allocation: 15,150
Deer Density/FSM: 39
Deer Density Goal/FSM: 29
Average Buck Harvest/FSM: 8.7

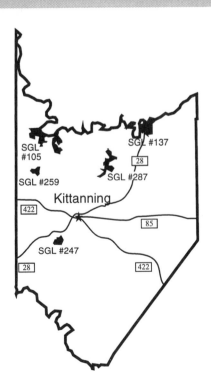

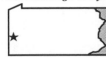

BEAVER COUNTY

Bordering Ohio, Beaver County's share of the Allegheny Plateau is 48 percent forested with 21 percent of the county in farmland, mainly used for cattle raising. Less than half is croplands of corn, grains, beans and apples.

Topography is hilly with spacious plateaus. Elevations vary from 660 to 1,380 feet throughout its 436 square miles. Glacial soils cover the county's northwest region.

Like many counties, most deer hunting here takes place on private lands. Hunting pressure on public lands is relatively light.

Three gamelands are available to Beaver County hunters, the biggest SGL No. 285 near Darlington with 2,169 acres. Raccoon Creek State Park offers 3,647 acres of hunting grounds. Each year the Raccoon Creek region in the southern part of the county yields some hefty bucks.

Food, lodging and services, contact: Beaver County Tourist Promotion Agency, 215B Ninth St., Monaca, PA 15061. Phone: (800) 564-5009 (in area code 412) and (800) 342-8192 and (412) 728-0212.

IN BRIEF

State Gamelands: 1,478 acres

State Parks & Forests: 8,663 acres

Farm-Game Co-op: 50,362 acres (590 farms)

Safety Zone Lands: 364 acres (5 tracts)

Forest-Game Co-op: None

1993 Buck/Doe Harvest: 1,590 / 2,862

1994 Doe Permit Allocation: 11,050

Deer Density/FSM: 31

Deer Density Goal/FSM: 22

Average Buck Harvest/FSM: 7.6

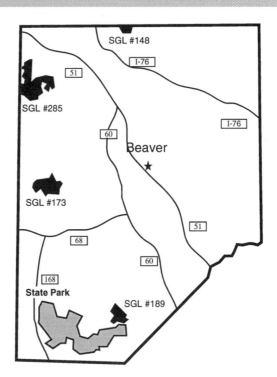

CAMBRIA COUNTY

Covering 691 square miles, Cambria's land is hilly, mountainous in some areas, with 64 percent of the county in forest habitat. Elevations run from 1,120 to 2,880 feet.

Farms cover another 19 percent of the county with just over half attributed to livestock and the rest in potatoes, oats, hay and apples.

Cambria's seven gamelands all hold whitetails. The largest tracts include 20,443-acre SGL No. 108 near Frugality and 15,632-acre SGL No. 158 near Blandburg.

Add to that Prince Gallitzin State Park with 3,440 acres and Gallitzin State Forest in White, Jackson and Reade townships, totaling 1,470 acres. A portion of 13,625-acre Gallitzin State Forest is also a popular Cambria hunting area.

Food, lodging and services, contact: Cambria County Tourist Council, Inc., 111 Market St., Johnston, PA 15901. Phone: (800) 237-8590 and (814) 536-7993.

IN BRIEF

State Gamelands: 51,399 acres
State Parks & Forests: 4,910 acres
Farm-Game Co-op: 64,517 acres (471 farms)
Safety Zone Lands: 14,626 acres (117 tracts)

Forest-Game Co-op: None
1993 Buck/Doe Harvest: 2,821 / 2.463
1994 Doe Permit Allocation: 13,350
Deer Density/FSM: 31
Deer Density Goal/FSM: 21
Average Buck Harvest/FSM: 6.4

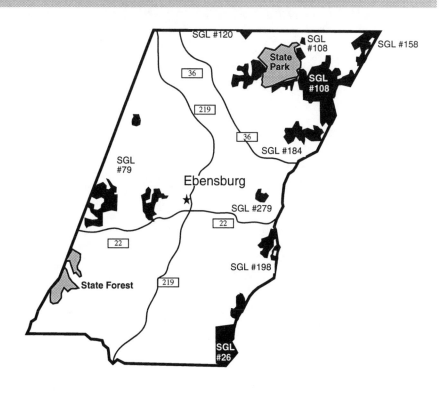

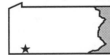

FAYETTE COUNTY

Sixty-one percent of the county's 794 square miles are composed of woodlands. Topography ranges from elevations as low as 740 feet to 3,000 feet.

Cattle, poultry and field crops share the farmland regions across 24 percent of the county. Corn, grains and apples are raised on about a quarter of the agricultural acreage with livestock dominating the remainder.

Five gamelands are scattered across Fayette, the largest SGL No. 51 near Uniontown with 15,498 acres. South of Uniontown is the Braddock Unit of Forbes State Forest providing another 15,792 acres. Included on the public hunting grounds list is 18,719-acre Ohiopyle State Park, overlapping into Somerset County.

Most of the little coal towns provide good hunting little more than a short walk away. The Laurel Mountains offer plenty of public and private (permission needed) deer country.

Food, lodging and services, contact: Laurel Highlands, Inc., Town Hall, 120 East Main St., Ligonier, PA 15658. Phone: (800) 925-7669 and (412) 238-5661.

IN BRIEF

State Gamelands: 21,464 acres

State Parks & Forests: 34,792 acres

Farm-Game Co-op: 27,597 acres (243 farms)

Safety Zone Lands: 21,618 acres (123 tracts)

Forest-Game Co-op: 2,036 acres

1993 Buck/Doe Harvest: 2,598 / 3,051

1994 Doe Permit Allocation: 7,850

Deer Density/FSM: 24

Deer Density Goal/FSM: 23

Average Buck Harvest/FSM: 5.4

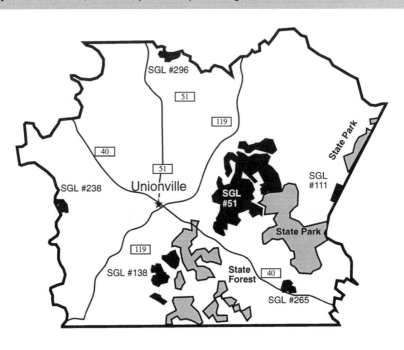

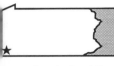

GREENE COUNTY

Bordering West Virginia on its western and southern borders (the county is set squarely in the far southeast corner of the state), Greene County's 577 square miles meander over hill and valley landscape with elevations from 760 to 1,660 feet.

Forests cover 56 percent of the county with farms on another 40 percent of the landscape. Cattle and sheep occupy nearly three-fourths of the farmland with hay, corn, wheat and oats raised on the remainder.

Greene's two gamelands are sizable. SGL No. 223 near Dunkard and Daviston is 6,972 acres while SGL No. 179 near Aleppo and Nettle Hill covers 5,329 acres.

Ryerson Station State Park west of Waynesburg offers another 900 acres of hunting grounds.

This county ranks among Pennsylvania's highest in terms of buck harvests per square mile of forest. Thanks to farmland vegetation and abandoned farms, Greene's deer are typically heavier than those dwelling in the more mountainous portions of the region.

Greene lays claim to the second biggest typical Pennsylvania record book buck.

Food, lodging and services, contact: Laurel Highlands, Inc., Town Hall, 120 East Main St., Ligonier, PA 15658. Phone: (800) 925-7669 and (412) 238-5661.

IN BRIEF

State Gamelands: 12,301 acres

State Parks & Forests: 900 acres

Farm-Game Co-op: 63,672 acres (471 farms)

Safety Zone Lands: 6,316 acres (48 tracts)

Forest-Game Co-op: None

1993 Buck/Doe Harvest: 3,311 / 6,246

1994 Doe Permit Allocation: 14,050

Deer Density/FSM: 37

Deer Density Goal/FSM: 20

Average Buck Harvest/FSM: 10.2

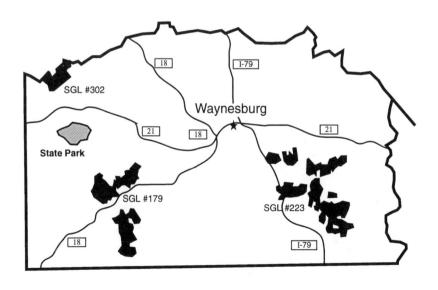

INDIANA COUNTY

Hilly, mountainous and with broad ridges and plateaus, Indiana's elevations range from 830 to 2,160 feet across its 829 square miles.

Forests compose 61 percent of the land with 32 percent in cattle, poultry and crops. Oats, corn, alfalfa and apples can be found in the latter areas.

The larger of Indiana's seven gamelands are SGL No. 276 near Coral (3,942 acres), SGL No. 174 near McGees Mills (3,125 acres) and SGL No. 153 near Bolivar and Robinson (2,812 acres).

Other state hunting lands can be found at 2,000-acre Yellow Creek State Park, east of Indiana.

Conemaugh Flood Control Reservoir, shared with Westmoreland County, accounts for another 6,000 wild acres.

An average of about 7,500-7,800 whitetails are harvested here annually.

Food, lodging and services, contact: Indiana County Visitors & Convention Bureau, Courthouse Annex, 827 Water St., Indiana, PA 15701. Phone: (412) 463-7505.

IN BRIEF

State Gamelands: 12,743 acres

State Parks & Forests: 2,384 acres

Farm-Game Co-op: 69,949 acres (586 farms)

Safety Zone Lands: 50,635 acres (203 tracts)

Forest-Game Co-op: 21,039 acres

1993 Buck/Doe Harvest: 3,489 / 4,241

1994 Doe Permit Allocation: 14,350

Deer Density/FSM: 30

Deer Density Goal/FSM: 23

Average Buck Harvest/FSM: 6.9

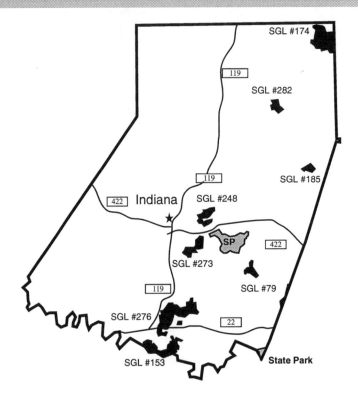

SOMERSET COUNTY

Bordering Maryland, 64 percent of Somerset County is wooded. Another 34 percent is in farmland characterized largely by livestock with just under half in farm crops, including oats, corn, potatoes and apples.

It's hilly and, in some places, mountainous landscape covers 1,073 square miles with elevations running 1,040 to 3,213 feet.

Six gamelands set aside more than 12,000 acres specifically for hunters, all with notable deer populations. The biggest include SGL No. 111 near Confluence with 10,520 acres, SGL No. 82 at Wittenberg with 6,708 acres, 3,158-acre SGL No. 50 near Somerset and 3,029-acre SGL No. 228 near Central City.

State holdings on Forbes State Forest tracts (Babcock, Blue Hole and Negro Mountain) total 26,231 acres with nearly 25,000 additional acres shared with Westmoreland County. Portions of Laurel Ridge and Kooser state parks are also within the county.

Pennsylvania's highest point, Mount Davis, is located in southern Somerset. It peaks at 3,213 feet.

Food, lodging and services, contact: Laurel Highlands, Inc., Town Hall, 120 East Main St., Ligonier, PA 15658. Phone: (800) 925-7669 and (412) 238-5661.

IN BRIEF

State Gamelands: 25,699 acres

State Parks & Forests: 37,668 acres

Farm-Game Co-op: 138,431 acres (749 farms)

Safety Zone Lands: 45,881 acres (257 tracts)

Forest-Game Co-op: None

1993 Buck/Doe Harvest: 4,193 / 4,051

1994 Doe Permit Allocation: 12,150

Deer Density/FSM: 29

Deer Density Goal/FSM: 24

Average Buck Harvest/FSM: 6.1

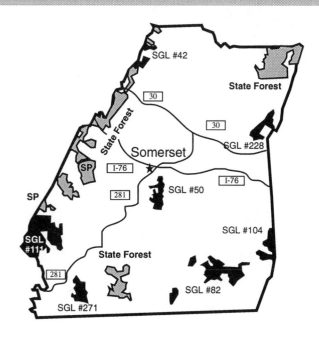

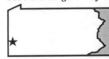

WASHINGTON COUNTY

Bordered by Ohio on its west, Washington County's woodland covers one-half of its 858 square miles. Elevations range from 720 to 1,540 feet across the hilly and often mountainous terrain.

Farms occupy 40 percent of the county with just over one-third planted in alfalfa, hay, corn and other crops. Cattle and sheep graze throughout the region.

A half-dozen gameland tracts offer hunters more than 11,000 acres. The biggest is SGL No. 245 near Prosperity (3,653 acres) seconded by SGL No. 117 at Burgettstown with 2,932 acres.

The undeveloped Hillman State Park in the far northern sector of Washington holds 3,654 acres. In 1992, West Penn Power Company opened some 4,000 acres to hunters in the Buffalo Creek area.

In terms of buck harvests per square woodland mile, averaging 10-12, Washington annually ranks in the state's top 10.

Food, lodging and services, contact: Washington County Tourism, 59 North Main St., Washington, PA 15301. Phone: (800) 531-4114 and (412) 222-8130.

IN BRIEF

State Gamelands: 9,250 acres

State Parks & Forests: 3,654 acres

Farm-Game Co-op: 57,848 acres (312 farms)

Safety Zone Lands: 26,663 acres (205 tracts)

Forest-Game Co-op: 4,235 acres

1993 Buck/Doe Harvest: 3,807 / 6,087

1994 Doe Permit Allocation: 20,650

Deer Density/FSM: 35

Deer Density Goal/FSM: 28

Average Buck Harvest/FSM: 8.9

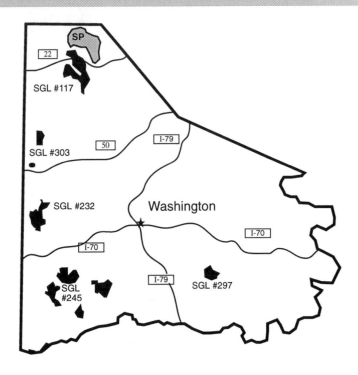

WESTMORELAND COUNTY

★

Fifty-one percent of this 1,033 square mile county is forested. As is typical of the vast, hilly, mountainous region, elevations span 740 to 2,960 feet.

Farms cover one-quarter of the total acreage with about 46 percent in crops and the remainder dedicated to sheep, cattle and poultry production. Alfalfa, corn, oats and wheat are the main money-crops.

SGL No. 42 spans 12,745 acres near Johnstown with 2,004 acre SGL No. 296 shared with Fayette County.

Also open to hunters is 656 acres of Keystone State Park, north of Latrobe, and 350-acres of Linn State Park near Rector.

The county shares two units of Forbes State Forest with neighboring Somerset, totaling nearly 25,000 acres, along with a portion of 13,625-acre Laurel Ridge State Parka lapping into Cambria, Somerset and Fayette.

The Conemaugh and Loyalhanna flood control areas add another several thousand acres to Westmoreland's public deer hunting options.

Food, lodging and services, contact: Laurel Highlands, Inc., Town Hall, 120 East Main St., Ligonier, PA 15658. Phone: (800) 925-7669 and (412) 238-5661.

IN BRIEF

State Gamelands: 13,900 acres

State Parks & Forests: 20,141 acres

Farm-Game Co-op: 59,645 acres (625 farms)

Safety Zone Lands: 11,468 acres (100 tracts)

Forest-Game Co-op: 2,146 acres

1993 Buck/Doe Harvest: 3,943 / 3,982

1994 Doe Permit Allocation: 19,950

Deer Density/FSM: 34

Deer Density Goal/FSM: 28

Average Buck Harvest/FSM: 7.6

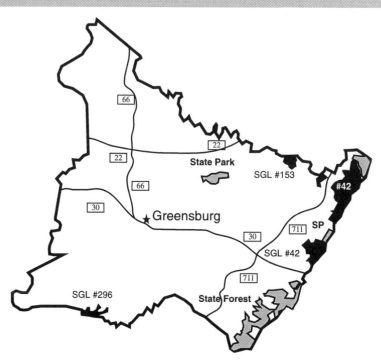

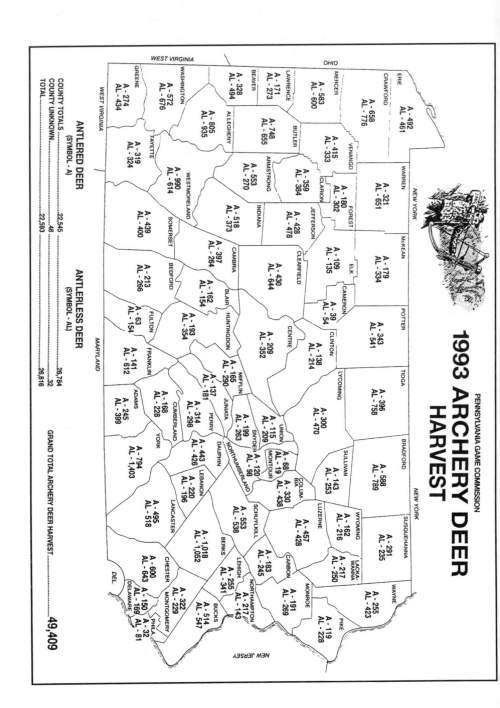

NORTHCENTRAL REGION

"Steep mountains, deep canyons, sycamores reaching ghostly from meandering stream bottoms, secluded wooded valleys and ice cold streams characterize northcentral Pennsylvania. Nowhere else in the commonwealth can one find so much wild land. The changes that occur in many of the towns when deer season arrives are almost unbelievable. At that time of the year one subject is on everybody's tongue — deer hunting. Ten top-notch big game counties make up the Northcentral Region. These counties annually account for 25 to 30 percent of our state's deer harvest (with) Potter, Tioga and Clearfield recording exceptionally large harvests."

Harry Merz,
Pennsylvania Game Commission

Pennsylvania Game Commission
Northcentral Region
P.O. Box 5038 Jersey Shore, PA 17740
Phone: (800) 442-7551 and (717) 398-4744

Cameron, Centre, Clearfield, Clinton, Elk, Lycoming, McKean, Potter, Tioga and Union counties.

CAMERON COUNTY

Ninety-four percent of the land is forested within Cameron's 398 square miles. As suggested by the vast mount of woodland, Cameron is one of the state's most sparsely populated counties. Deep, narrow v-shaped valleys and steep slopes make accessing the backcountry a challenge. Cameron is reputed by some to be the 'roughest' county anywhere in the northern tier.

In spite of, or, perhaps, because of its wild landscape, numerous deer camps are located along most every backwoods road and hunters can gain access to whitetails throughout the region.

Hay, wheat and corn can be found although most farms raise cattle and poultry. Timbering is important throughout the region with numerous clearcuts and second growth areas offering prime deer habitat.

Despite its vast woodlands, Cameron holds only two gameland tracts. The biggest spans 12,963 acres on SGL No. 14 near Emporium.

Elk State Forest's 118,466 acres offer unlimited hunting opportunities. Add to that 1,150 acres at Sizerville State Park, northeast of Emporium.

The large amount of forest land, in part, accounts for one of the lowest buck harvest rates per wooded square mile in Cameron.

Food, lodging and services, contact: Cameron County Tourist Promotion Agency, P.O. Box 118, Driftwood, PA 15832. Phone: (814) 546-2665.

IN BRIEF

State Gamelands: 12,693 acres

State Parks & Forests: 119,616 acres

Farm-Game Co-op: None

Safety Zone Lands: 7,154 acres (48 tracts)

Forest-Game Co-op: 27,592 acres

1993 Buck/Doe Harvest: 1,076 / 629

1994 Doe Permit Allocation: 2,100

Deer Density/FSM: 21

Deer Density Goal/FSM: 19

Average Buck Harvest/FSM: 2.9

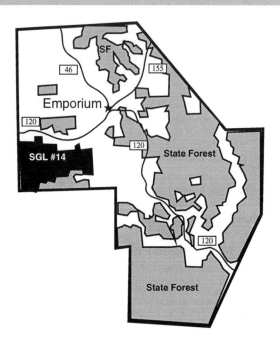

CENTRE COUNTY

As its name implies, this is the central-most county in the state, covering 1,106 square miles. Forests compose 76 percent of the landscape with farms supported on 22 percent.

Just over half of the farms grow alfalfa, corn, oats and wheat, the remainder in apple orchards or cattle. Long, narrow, mountain ridges dominate the southeast with hilly, broad-ridged topography to the northwest.

Hunters can choose from a plethora of state parks and forests or six gamelands. Of the former, 47,000 acres of Sproul State Forest, north of Snow Shoe, 38,000 acres in Bald Eagle State Forest, east of Potters Mills, 34,900 acres in Moshannon State Forest, east of Philipsburg, and Rothrock State Forest's 20,645 acres southeast of State College offer unlimited choices.

The largest gamelands can be found on SGL No. 100 at Pine Glen (17,019 acres), SGL No. 33 near Philipsburg (16,585 acres) and SGL No. 103 near Snow Shoe (8,993).

Food, lodging and services, contact: Centre County Lion Country Visitors & Convention Bureau, 1402 South Atherton St., State College, PA 16801. Phone: (800) 358-5466, (814) 231-1400.

IN BRIEF

State Gamelands: 64,277 acres

State Parks & Forests: 142,935 acres

Farm-Game Co-op: 32,783 acres (202 farms)

Safety Zone Lands: 28,522 acres (170 tracts)

Forest-Game Co-op: 6,455 acres

1993 Buck/Doe Harvest: 4,001 / 4,845

1994 Doe Permit Allocation: 14,850

Deer Density/FSM: 26

Deer Density Goal/FSM: 20

Average Buck Harvest/FSM: 4.8

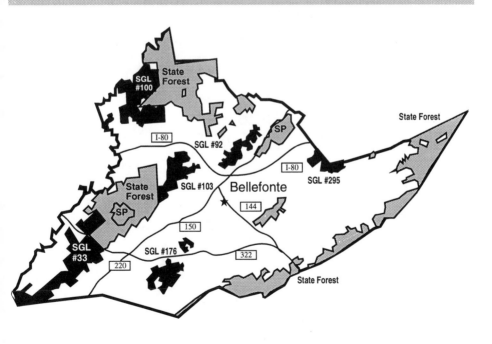

CLEARFIELD COUNTY

Clearfield always ranks near the top in annual whitetail harvests with 74 percent of its 1,149 square miles in forest. Elevations range from 780 to 2,380 feet.

Less than 10 percent of the county is farmland, primarily cattle operations with some corn, grains and apple orchards. Stripmines, mostly reclaimed and of benefit to deer and other game, are abundant. Steep hills and mountains of second and third growth woodlands rising from valleys characterize this popular deer hunting county.

Clearfield's hunters take more than 13,000 whitetails each year.

Eight gamelands areas are scattered across the county. The larger tracts include 4,876-acre SGL No. 93 near Sabula and SGL No. 90 with 3,957 acres near Goshen.

Clearfield County is also home to 97,460 acres of Moshannon State Forest north and west of Clearfield. S.B. Elliott and Parker Dam state parks combine for another 780 acres.

Food, lodging and services, contact: The Magic Forests of West Central PA Tourism & Travel Bureau, c/o Brookville Office, R.R. #5, Box 47, Brookville, PA 15825. Phone: (800) 348-9393, (814) 849-5197.

IN BRIEF

State Gamelands: 20,972 acres

State Parks & Forests: 98,240 acres

Farm-Game Co-op: 24,950 acres (263 farms)

Safety Zone Lands: 18,509 acres (125 tracts)

Forest-Game Co-op: 18,957 acres

1993 Buck/Doe Harvest: 5,783 / 7,799

1994 Doe Permit Allocation: 18,500

Deer Density/FSM: 34

Deer Density Goal/FSM: 21

Average Buck Harvest/FSM: 6.8

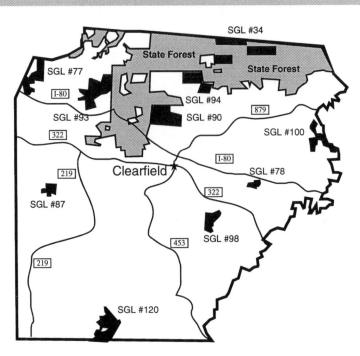

CLINTON COUNTY

Known as 'Black Forest County' by many sportsmen, Clinton's seemingly endless mountains, broad river valleys and steep gorges provide unlimited whitetail hunting opportunities.

The land in the southeast is characterized by long, narrow ridges. The northwest is hilly with broader ridges and dissected plateaus.

Covering 891 square miles with 87 percent supporting forests, Clinton's farmland is minimal. However, eight percent of the land base supports harvested cropland (corn, alfalfa, oats and soybeans) and livestock.

Public land is everywhere. Sproul State Forest, around Renovo, covers 190,964 acres, Bald Eagle State Forest near Mill Hall is 53,083 acres and Tiadaghton State Forest, north of Rauchtown, adds another 6,047 acres.

If that's not enough, look to three gamelands tracts. SGL No. 89 near Farrandville covers 10,571 acres and SGL No. 295, near Lamar, offers 10,072 acres.

It must be considered that Clinton's seemingly low rate of 2.7 bucks taken per square mile of forest land must be factored against the tremendous amount of woodland, much of it lightly hunted due to its ruggedness.

Food, lodging and services, contact: Clinton County Tourist Promotion Agency, Inc., Courthouse Annex, 151 Susquehanna Ave., Lock Haven, PA 17745. Phone: (717) 893-4037.

IN BRIEF

State Gamelands: 22,726 acres

State Parks & Forests: 250,794 acres

Farm-Game Co-op: 56,520 acres (401 farms)

Safety Zone Lands: 2,136 acres (18 tracts)

Forest-Game Co-op: 11,835 acres

1993 Buck/Doe Harvest: 1,939 / 1,605

1994 Doe Permit Allocation: 5,500

Deer Density/FSM: 17

Deer Density Goal/FSM: 16

Average Buck Harvest/FSM: 2.5

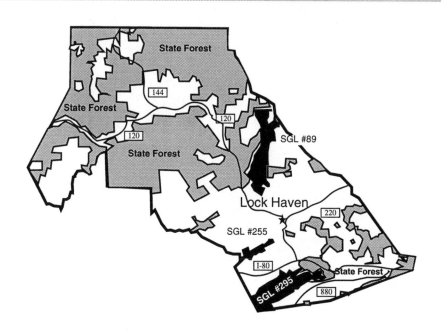

★ ELK COUNTY

Elk, as its name implies, is the home of Pennsylvania's 'other' deer — the Rocky Mountain elk. Tourists flock to the county during the September bugling season to watch and photograph the herd, which now numbers in excess of 150.

But whitetails are also abundant, as are public lands on which to hunt them. Fully 91 percent of the county's 830 square miles hold trees. Elevations here run from 900 to 2,376 feet.

Agricultural holdings cover only four percent of the county with cattle and poultry production dominating although some hay, corn and oats can be found.

Elk County holds 36,115 acres of Elk State Forest, north of Johnsonburg, and 37,129 acres of Moshannon State Forest, southeast of Medix Run.

In addition, 23,148-acre SGL No. 25 near Johnsonburg and 23,995-acre SGL No. 44 at Portland Mills entice whitetail hunters as do three other gamelands tracts totaling more than 14,000 acres. Add to that a large chunk of Allegheny National Forest (see Federal Hunting Lands.)

Like neighboring Cameron County, Elk County can be described as 'rugged' with high mountains and steep slopes leading to narrow, V-shaped valleys.

Food, lodging and services, contact: Elk County Recreation & Tourist Council, Inc., 159 Main St., P.O. Box 35, Ridgway, PA 15853. Phone: (814) 772-5502.

IN BRIEF

State Gamelands: 61,343 acres

State Parks & Forests: 73,244 acres

Farm-Game Co-op: None

Safety Zone Lands: 6,599 acres (36 tracts)

Forest-Game Co-op: 55,924 acres

1993 Buck/Doe Harvest: 2,995 / 2,653

1994 Doe Permit Allocation: 11,500

Deer Density/FSM: 26

Deer Density Goal/FSM: 21

Average Buck Harvest/FSM: 4.0

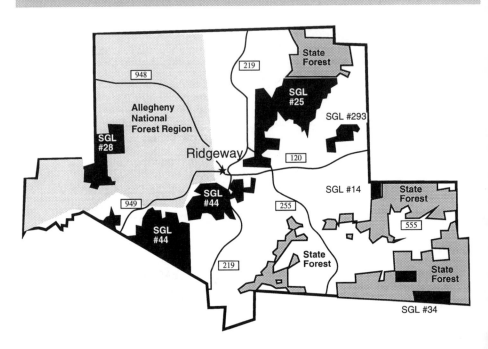

LYCOMING COUNTY

Lycoming often leads the state in black bear harvests and its whitetail numbers and popularity among hunters also rank it high on the deer harvest list.

The northern portion of the 1,237 square mile county is hilly with scattered mountains. To the south, mountains are more prevalent with numerous, narrow sandstone ridges. Elevations range from 460 to 2,403 feet.

Fully 77 percent of the county is forested. Farms compose 20 percent of the landscape with diversified interests ranging from corn, alfalfa, oats, wheat and soybeans to apple and cherry orchards and cattle operations.

Much of Tiadaghton State Forest, covering 172,313 acres near Jersey Mills and Ralston, draws deer hunters. Seven gamelands, including 25,447-acre SGL No. 75 near English Center, add to the unbroken forest.

Food, lodging and services, contact: Lycoming County Tourist Promotion Agency, 848 West Fourth St., Williamsport, PA 17701. Phone: (800) 358-9900, (717) 321-1200.

IN BRIEF

State Gamelands: 42,769 acres

State Parks & Forests: 172,313 acres

Farm-Game Co-op: 15,481 acres (152 farms)

Safety Zone Lands: 15,975 acres (107 tracts)

Forest-Game Co-op: 341 acres

1993 Buck/Doe Harvest: 3,901 / 4,336

1994 Doe Permit Allocation: 15,350

Deer Density/FSM: 27

Deer Density Goal/FSM: 19

Average Buck Harvest/FSM: 4.1

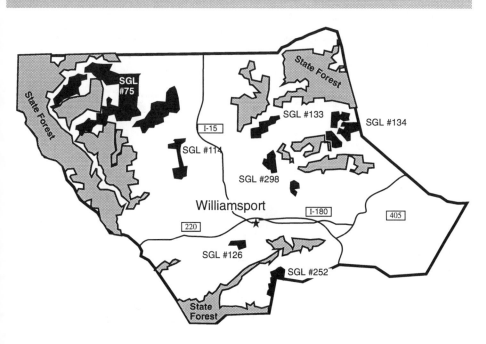

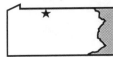

McKEAN COUNTY

Bordering New York, 81 percent of McKean's 979 square miles is forest-covered. Elevations range from 1,260 to 2,460 feet.

Farms occupy only eight percent of the county with cattle ranching predominating. Sparse croplands offer hay, wheat, oats and corn.

Angular ridgetops, sloping valleys and undulating hills describe McKean, which, along with Potter County, contributes to the headwaters of the Allegheny River.

Five gamelands and 5,619 acres of Susquehannock State Forest are within McKean's borders. SGL No. 30 near Betula sets aside 11,572 acres for hunters followed by 8,195-acre SGL No. 61 near Port Allegany.

Like many counties rimming New York, McKean annually produces harvests in excess of 4,000 bucks and as many as 7,500 or more antlerless deer.

Food, lodging and services, contact: Seneca Highlands Tourist Association, Inc., P.O. Box 698, Intersection Rts. #6 & U.S. #219, Mt. Jewett, PA 16740. Phone: (814) 778-9944.

IN BRIEF

State Gamelands: 21,682 acres

State Parks & Forests: 5,619 acres

Farm-Game Co-op: None

Safety Zone Lands: 51,027 acres (268 tracts)

Forest-Game Co-op: 126,686 acres

1993 Buck/Doe Harvest: 4,082 / 7,548

1994 Doe Permit Allocation: 15,300

Deer Density/FSM: 28

Deer Density Goal/FSM: 20

Average Buck Harvest/FSM: 5.0

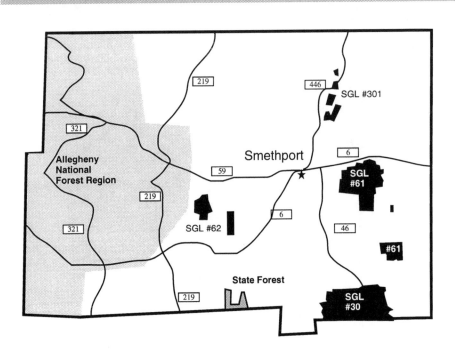

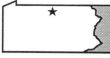

POTTER COUNTY

Appropriately dubbed 'God's Country,' Potter — and its county seat, Coudersport — is arguably the state's most widely known deer hunting county. For many years it produced the biggest buck and doe harvests and it still seesaws with several other northcentral counties for the annual honor.

In the heart of the Alleghenies on the New York border, much of Potter's steep slopes and broad ridges are far off the beaten path. Covering 1,801 square miles, its elevations range from 1,000 to 2,5687. The county hosts an abundance of black cherry trees, their fruits especially attractive to bears and whitetails in high production years.

Forests cover 86 percent of the county with numerous commercial holdings, much of which is leased to hunt groups and clubs. Farms cover 16 percent of Potter with potatoes, wheat, corn and oats grown on about one-third of the croplands. Cattle production dominates.

Visiting hunters frequent the 266,599 acres of Susquehanna State Forest within Potter's borders or any of three gamelands offering 4,028, 8,221 and 6,786 acres — the biggest SGL No. 64 near Galeton.

In a recent year Potter County hunters harvested more than 10,500 whitetails.

Food, lodging and services, contact: Potter County Recreation, Inc., P.O. Box 245, Coudersport, PA 16915. Phone: (814) 435-2290.

IN BRIEF

State Gamelands: 19,035 acres

State Parks & Forests: 267,199 acres

Farm-Game Co-op: 64,509 acres (357 farms)

Safety Zone Lands: 3,563 acres (24 tracts)

Forest-Game Co-op: 41,262 acres

1993 Buck/Doe Harvest: 4,405 / 6,152

1994 Doe Permit Allocation: 18,550

Deer Density/FSM: 26

Deer Density Goal/FSM: 20

Average Buck Harvest/FSM: 4.8

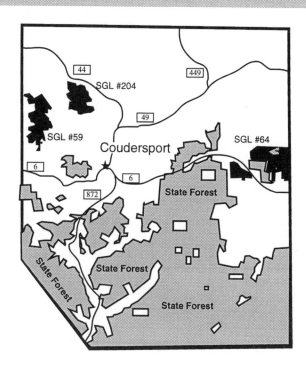

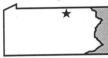

TIOGA COUNTY

Bordering Potter, Tioga is truly 'big woods' country with an abundance of public hunting areas for everything from bucks and bears to gobblers and grouse. Elevations across its 1,131 square miles span 840 to 2,543 feet. Two-thirds of the county is wooded.

Much of the remainder is in cattle, dairy, poultry and sheep production with hay, corn, oats and barley growing on tilled farmlands.

As one of the 'big woods' counties, thousands of hunters migrate to the rugged and scenic woods every fall. They find an abundance of public land in 148,940-acre Tioga State Forest at Wellsboro and Blossburg with another 1,000 acres at Colton Point and Leonard Harrison state parks, between Wellsboro and Galeton.

Three big gamelands include 13,232-acre SGL No. 37 at Tioga and 8,861-acre SGL No. 208 near Gaines.

Food, lodging and services, contact: Tioga Association for Recreation and Tourism, 114 Main St., Wellsboro, PA 16901. Phone: (800) 332-6718, (717) 724-1926 Ext. T.

IN BRIEF

State Gamelands: 24,487 acres

State Parks & Forests: 150,085 acres

Farm-Game Co-op: 20,605 acres (143 farms)

Safety Zone Lands: 29,211 acres (122 tracts)

Forest-Game Co-op: 1,300 acres

1993 Buck/Doe Harvest: 4,454 / 7,297

1994 Doe Permit Allocation: 20,600

Deer Density/FSM: 26

Deer Density Goal/FSM: 19

Average Buck Harvest/FSM: 5.9

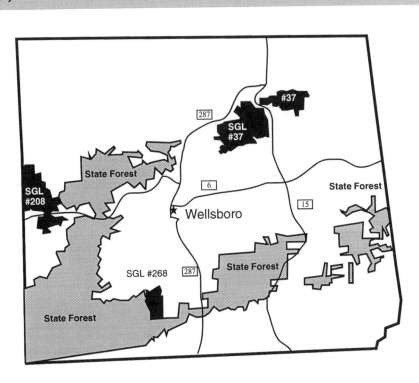

UNION COUNTY

Covering 317 square miles, Union County's elevations range from 440 to 2,160 feet across the north Appalachian ridge and valley landform. Forests cover 68 percent of the county.

Farms occupy much of the remainder with most in harvested crops, including corn, alfalfa, wheat and oats.

A vast stretch of Bald Eagle State Forest — 57,766 acres — can be found in the Laurelton region with only three small gamelands available in the remainder of the county. One is a 682-acre gameland transfer from the Dept. of Agriculture in Hartley Township in mid-1994.

Food, lodging and services, contact: Susquehanna Valley Visitors Bureau, 219D Hafer Rd., P.O. Box 268, Lewisburg, PA 17837. Phone: (800) 458-4748, (717) 524-7234.

IN BRIEF

State Gamelands: 1,274 acres
State Parks & Forests: 57,766 acres
Farm-Game Co-op: 33,242 acres (337 farms)
Safety Zone Lands: 2,694 acres (22 tracts)

Forest-Game Co-op: None
1993 Buck/Doe Harvest: 1,022 / 1,504
1994 Doe Permit Allocation: 4,100
Deer Density/FSM: 23
Deer Density Goal/FSM: 16
Average Buck Harvest/FSM: 4.8

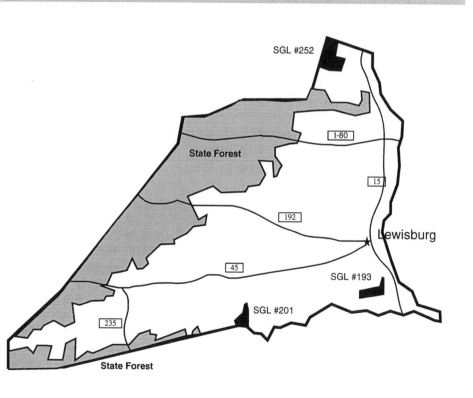

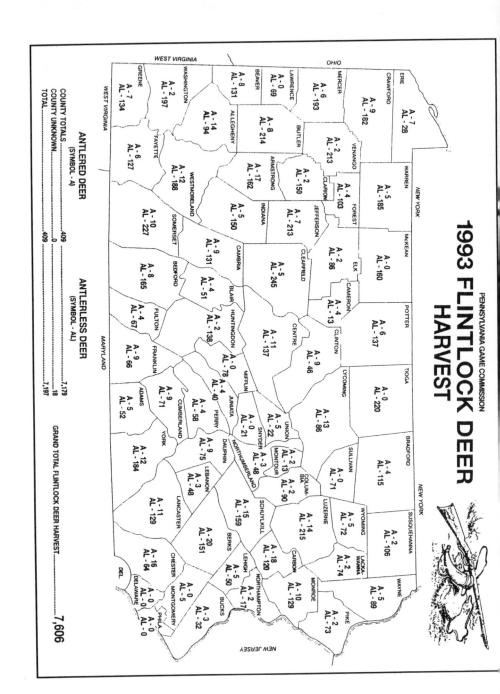

1993 FLINTLOCK DEER HARVEST

PENNSYLVANIA GAME COMMISSION

ANTLERED DEER
(SYMBOL - A)

COUNTY TOTALS 409
COUNTY UNKNOWN 0
TOTAL 409

ANTLERLESS DEER
(SYMBOL - AL)

COUNTY TOTALS 7,179
COUNTY UNKNOWN 18
TOTAL 7,197

GRAND TOTAL FLINTLOCK DEER HARVEST 7,606

WEST VIRGINIA
OHIO
NEW YORK
MARYLAND
NEW JERSEY

CRAWFORD A-7 AL-28
ERIE A-6 AL-193
MERCER A-9 AL-182
LAWRENCE A-0 AL-69
BEAVER A-2 AL-197
WASHINGTON A-2 AL-134
GREENE A-7
VENANGO A-8 AL-214
BUTLER A-2 AL-213
ALLEGHENY A-14 AL-94
WARREN A-5 AL-185
FOREST A-4 AL-103
CLARION A-2 AL-150
ARMSTRONG A-17 AL-162
WESTMORELAND A-12 AL-188
FAYETTE A-6 AL-127
SOMERSET A-10 AL-227
INDIANA A-5 AL-150
JEFFERSON A-7 AL-213
ELK A-2 AL-245
CLEARFIELD A-5 AL-245
CAMBRIA A-9 AL-131
BEDFORD A-8 AL-165
BLAIR A-4 AL-51
FULTON A-4 AL-67
HUNTINGDON A-2 AL-138
FRANKLIN A-9 AL-66
ADAMS A-5 AL-52
McKEAN A-0 AL-160
CAMERON A-4 AL-13
CLINTON A-6 AL-137
CENTRE A-11 AL-137
MIFFLIN A-0 AL-78
JUNIATA A-4 AL-40
CUMBERLAND A-9 AL-71
PERRY A-4 AL-58
YORK A-4 AL-184
POTTER A-6 AL-137
LYCOMING A-9 AL-46
UNION A-5 AL-22
SNYDER A-0 AL-21
DAUPHIN A-9 AL-75
NORTHUMBERLAND A-3 AL-48
LEBANON A-3 AL-48
LANCASTER A-11 AL-129
TIOGA A-0 AL-220
BRADFORD A-4 AL-115
SULLIVAN A-0 AL-71
MONTOUR A-2 AL-13
COLUM-BIA A-2 AL-90
SCHUYLKILL A-15 AL-159
BERKS A-20 AL-151
WYOMING A-5 AL-72
LUZERNE A-14 AL-215
LEHIGH A-5 AL-5
CARBON A-0 AL-129
NORTHAMPTON A-2 AL-17
MONROE A-10 AL-129
SUSQUEHANNA A-2 AL-106
LACKA-WANNA A-2 AL-74
WAYNE A-5 AL-89
PIKE A-2 AL-73
CHESTER A-16 AL-64
MONTGOMERY A-5 AL-5
DELAWARE A-0 AL-0
PHILA. A-0 AL-0
BUCKS A-3 AL-32
DEL. A-0 AL-0

SOUTHCENTRAL REGION

"The Southcentral Region is a land of diversity. Rugged game-filled ridges rising from broad farming valleys dominate much of South-central Pennsylvania. The fertile land of both field and forest supports abundant big and small game populations. The great contrast of ridges on one hand and rich farming land on the other is the key to the area's game resources. All 11 counties have ample whitetail populations but Huntingdon, Bedford and Perry counties normally have the highest kill. However, the agricultural counties, particularly Adams, generally produce the heaviest whitetails."

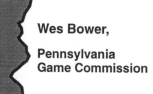

Wes Bower,

Pennsylvania
Game Commission

Pennsylvania Game Commission
Southcentral Region
P.O. Box 537, Huntingdon, PA 16652
Phone: (800) 422-7554 and (814) 643-1831
Adams, Bedford, Blair, Cumberland, Franklin, Fulton, Huntingdon, Juniata, Mifflin, Perry and Snyder counties.

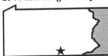

ADAMS COUNTY

Located on the southern border of Pennsylvania, Adams County covers 521 square miles with 59 percent in farmland, more than most other southwestern counties. Crops include corn, wheat and potatoes along with apples and peaches. Abundant pasture lands also rim its woodlands.

Availability of croplands provides Adams County hunters with, arguably, the heaviest whitetails in the Southcentral division.

The county holds broad highlands and ridges of primarily deciduous hardwoods. Compared to the rest of the region, however, it holds only one state gameland —SGL No. 249. Scattered tracts cover 1,942 acres near Biglerville.

A focal point for many hunters during the deer seasons is Michaux State Forest near Caledonia with 21,897 acres of public hunting grounds.

Food, lodging and services, contact: Gettysburg Travel Council, Inc., 35 Carlisle St., Gettysburg, PA 17325. Phone: (717) 334-6274.

IN BRIEF

State Gamelands: 1,942 acres

State Parks & Forests: 21,897 acres

Farm-Game Co-op: 25,178 acres (232 farms)

Safety Zone Lands: 42,452 acres (120 tracts)

Forest-Game Co-op: None

1993 Buck/Doe Harvest: 1,598 / 2,505

1994 Doe Permit Allocation: 11,900

Deer Density/FSM: 42

Deer Density Goal/FSM: 24

Average Buck Harvest/FSM: 9.2

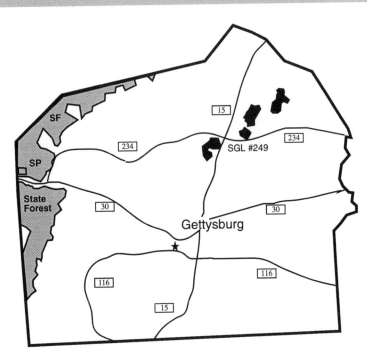

BEDFORD COUNTY

Wooded ridges and open valleys cut through Bedford in a northeast to south-west direction. Ridges covered in hardwoods and scattered groves of conifers rise 1,500 feet and more above valley floors,

Seventy-two percent of the county's 1,017 square miles is forested with eleva-tions varying from 740 to 3,136 feet. Portions of the county are dramatically steep and rocky.

Cattle production is king in farm country with alfalfa, corn and oats on harvest-ed lands.

Two state forest tracts, less than 3,000 acres each, and expansive Buchanan State Forest with 29,603 acres (near Chaneysville) hold numerous deer. Good white-tail hunting is also to be had on Bedford's eight gamelands varying in size from 2,626 acres to 13,878 acres. The largest is SGL No. 73 near Martinsburg. SGL No. 261 near Pavia stretches across 11,926 acres. From the Maryland border to the Pennsyl-vania Turnpike a hunter can roam contiguous, deer-rich forests.

Food, lodging and services, contact: Bedford County Tourist Promotion Agency, Inc., 137 East Pitt St., Bedford, PA 15522. Phone: (800) 765-3331 and (814) 623-1771.

IN BRIEF

State Gamelands: 62,477 acres

State Parks & Forests: 34,942 acres

Farm-Game Co-op: 42,792 acres (351 farms)

Safety Zone Lands: 69,011 acres (394 tracts)

Forest-Game Co-op: 123 acres

1993 Buck/Doe Harvest: 4,193 / 4,631

1994 Doe Permit Allocation: 20,000

Deer Density/FSM: 27

Deer Density Goal/FSM: 25

Average Buck Harvest/FSM: 5.8

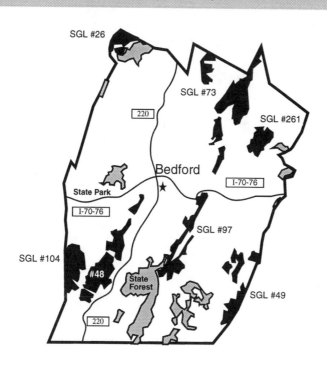

BLAIR COUNTY

★

Covering 527 square miles, Bedford's northwest is hilly, often mountainous. To the southwest, long valleys sweep through rugged mountain ridges. Many oak, maple and cherry ridges, rugged in many spots, have been ravaged by gypsy moths in recent years. Timber salvage operations have opened lands to sunlight and heavy undergrowth, prime for whitetails.

Some 64 percent of the county is forested with elevations ranging from 720 to 3,000 feet. Farms occupy about one-fourth of the county with over half in harvested croplands of corn, oats and alfalfa. The remainder holds cattle and poultry.

No state forest lands are available in Blair but nine gamelands take up the slack, ranging in acreage from 352 to 6,421. The largest is SGL No. 166 near Canoe Creek. SGL No. 147 near Martinsburg holds 6,073 acres with 5,932 acres composing SGL No. 118 near Williamsburg.

Food, lodging and services, contact: Convention and Visitors Bureau of Blair County, 1231 Eleventh Ave., Altoona, PA 16601. Phone: (800) 84-AL-TOONA and (814) 943-4183.

IN BRIEF

State Gamelands: 26,439 acres

State Parks & Forests: None

Farm-Game Co-op: 53,366 acres (398 farms)

Safety Zone Lands: 42,309 acres (225 tracts)

Forest-Game Co-op: 9,005 acres

1993 Buck/Doe Harvest: 1,918 / 1,356

1994 Doe Permit Allocation: 11,800

Deer Density/FSM: 31

Deer Density Goal/FSM: 22

Average Buck Harvest/FSM: 5.7

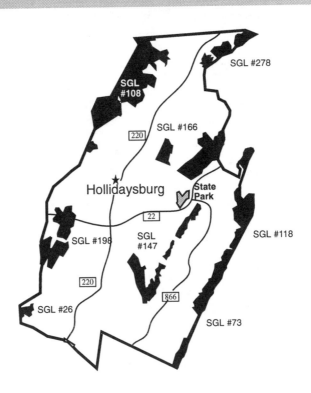

CUMBERLAND COUNTY

Located west of Harrisburg, the Appalachian Ridge cuts through Cumberland's 547 square miles. The region's rolling hills and rich, fertile, limestone valleys grow wheat, corn, barley and apples, providing desirable deer food in many areas.

Woodlands cover 35 percent of the county with farms occupying the rolling lowlands, making up 47 percent of the topography. Cumberland's 547 square miles range in elevation from 291 to 2,240 feet.

Michaux State Forest surrounding Pine Grove Furnace and Tuscarora State Forest near Doubling Gap combine for 34,665 acres of public land. Three state gamelands, one near Newville (No. 169 with 2,317 acres), another at Carlisle Springs (No. 230 containing 1,082 acres), and SGL No. 305 east of Mt. Holly Springs, offer additional hunting grounds.

Food, lodging and services, contact: Harrisburg-Hershey-Carlisle Tourism & Convention Bureau, 114 Walnut St., P.O. Box 969, Harrisburg, PA 17108. Phone: (800) 995-0969 and (717) 232-1377.

IN BRIEF

State Gamelands: 4,250 acres

State Parks & Forests: 34,665 acres

Farm-Game Co-op: 70,537 acres (623 farms)

Safety Zone Lands: 13,235 acres (78 tracts)

Forest-Game Co-op: 698 acres

1993 Buck/Doe Harvest: 1,184 / 1,989

1994 Doe Permit Allocation: 9,700

Deer Density/FSM: 27

Deer Density Goal/FSM: 17

Average Buck Harvest/FSM: 6.1

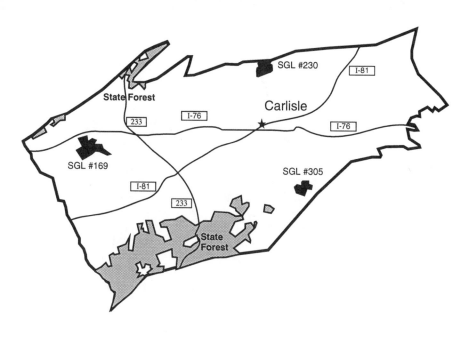

FRANKLIN COUNTY

Rimmed by Maryland, Franklin's 774 square miles are made up of 44 percent woodland and 50 percent farmland. Elevations range from 400 to 2,440 feet.

The landscape in the eastern portion of the county is largely fertile, rolling lowlands. The western section, holding the Appalachian's Blue Ridge, is considerably more mountainous with long, narrow sandstone ridges and shale and limestone valleys.

Farmland areas are diverse with stands of corn and alfalfa, apples and peaches or cattle and hogs.

Coincidentally, Franklin's 1993 deer season harvest of antlered and antlerless deer was split equally; 1,760 of each.

Michaux (at Caledonia) and Buchanan (at Upper Strasburg) state forests cover 38,258 acres of wooded public hunting grounds. SGL No. 235 at Fort Loudon stretches across 6,062 acres and SGL No. 76, near Roxbury, covers 4,323 acres.

The Letterkenny Army Depot's 8,000 acres is open for special deer hunts.

Food, lodging and services, contact: Cumberland Valley Visitors' Council, 565 Lincoln Way East, P.O. Box 394, Chambersburg, PA 17201. Phone: (717) 261-1322.

IN BRIEF

State Gamelands: 10,385 acres

State Parks & Forests: 38,258 acres

Farm-Game Co-op: 98,278 acres (712 farms)

Safety Zone Lands: 23,412 acres (92 tracts)

Forest-Game Co-op: 1,134 acres

1993 Buck/Doe Harvest: 1,760 / 1,760

1994 Doe Permit Allocation: 6,800

Deer Density/FSM: 29

Deer Density Goal/FSM: 27

Average Buck Harvest/FSM: 5.2

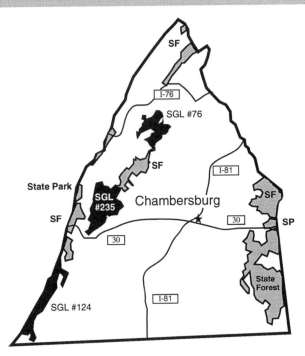

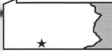

FULTON COUNTY

★

Bordered on the south by Maryland, Fulton's forests cover 69 percent of the 438 square mile county. Cattle and corn, alfalfa, oats and wheat dominate the numerous farmlands.

Wooded ridges and cleared, often deep, valleys, extend in a northeast to southwest direction across the county. Elevations range from 420 to 2,440 feet across the Appalachian Ridge.

Three tracts of Buchanan State Forest — at Sideling Hill, Cowans Gap and Big Cove Tannery — provide 29,187 acres of public whitetail country. Of Fulton's six gamelands, three exceed 5,900 acres. The largest is 6,835-acre SGL No. 124 near Mercersburg. SGL 53, locally called the 'Meadow Grounds,' is 5,927 acrse of regrown farmland, a popular hunting tract. Add to that the 6,073-acre SGL No. 65 near Warfordsburg.

Food, lodging and services, contact: Fulton County Tourist Promotion Agency, P.O. Box 141, McConnellsburg, PA 17233. Phone: (717) 485-4064.

IN BRIEF

State Gamelands: 20,530 acres

State Parks & Forests: 29,187 acres

Farm-Game Co-op: 14,693 acres (90 farms)

Safety Zone Lands: 16,293 acres (73 tracts)

Forest-Game Co-op: 6,379 acres

1993 Buck/Doe Harvest: 1,788 / 2,517

1994 Doe Permit Allocation: 6,400

Deer Density/FSM: 25

Deer Density Goal/FSM: 20

Average Buck Harvest/FSM: 5.9

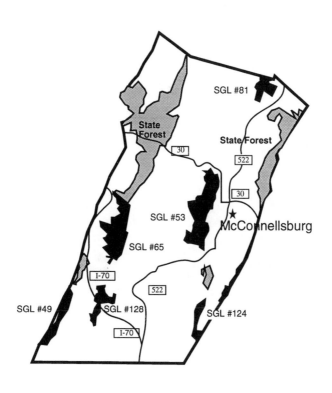

HUNTINGDON COUNTY

Best known for Raystown Lake and its surrounding, game-rich mountains, Huntingdon's 877 square miles range in elevation from 520 to 2,400 feet.

Three-fourths of the county is forested with the 'lay of the land' notably a series of ridges and valleys running in a northeast-southwest direction. Corn, grain, alfalfa, oats and wheat comprise a portion of the scattered farmlands although cattle lands dominate.

There's never a problem finding accessible public hunting lands here. Within Rothrock State Forest, south of State College, 66,272 acres are available with 20,000 acres of Corps of Engineers land bordering Raystown Lake.

Eight gamelands all hold viable deer populations. The most notable include 5,724-acre SGL No. 67 around Broad Top City, 5,679-acre SGL No. 112 near Huntingdon and 4,121-acre SGL No. 71 near Mapleton Depot.

Food, lodging and services, contact: Huntingdon County Tourist Promotion Agency, 241 Mifflin St., Huntingdon, PA 16652. Phone: (814) 643-3577.

IN BRIEF

State Gamelands: 27,354 acres

State Parks & Forests: 66,452 acres

Farm-Game Co-op: 33,552 acres (203 farms)

Safety Zone Lands: 36,701 acres (158 tracts)

Forest-Game Co-op: 19,896 acres

1993 Buck/Doe Harvest: 4,221 / 5,737

1994 Doe Permit Allocation: 18,250

Deer Density/FSM: 31

Deer Density Goal/FSM: 21

Average Buck Harvest/FSM: 6.4

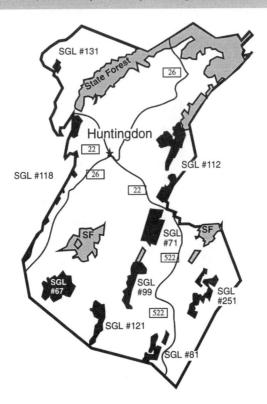

JUNIATA COUNTY

Northwest of Harrisburg, Juniata's 392 square miles are mountainous with long, narrow sandstone ridges alternating with equally long valleys. Elevations go from 383 to 2,260 feet.

Two-thirds of the county is forested with the remainder largely in cattle, fruit and field crop production. Apple and peach orchards and corn, alfalfa, oats and wheat are the main crops.

Tuscarora State Forest holds 17,337 acres north of Reeds Gap with four game-lands tracts inside county borders. The biggest is SGL No. 107 near Mifflintown with 5,560 acres. The Tuscarora Mountain region of Juniata links it with four other counties. Much of it is in public hunting lands which attract sportsmen in the bow, buck and doe seasons.

Food, lodging and services, contact: Juniata-Mifflin County Tourist Promotion Agency, 19 South Wayne St., Lewistown, PA 17044. Phone: (717) 248-5713.

IN BRIEF

State Gamelands: 8,909 acres
State Parks & Forests: 17,337 acres
Farm-Game Co-op: 13,731 acres (94 farms)
Safety Zone Lands: 38,826 acres (196 tracts)

Forest-Game Co-op: 5,117 acres
1993 Buck/Doe Harvest: 1,432 / 2,617
1994 Doe Permit Allocation: 5,800
Deer Density/FSM: 25
Deer Density Goal/FSM: 18
Average Buck Harvest/FSM: 5.5

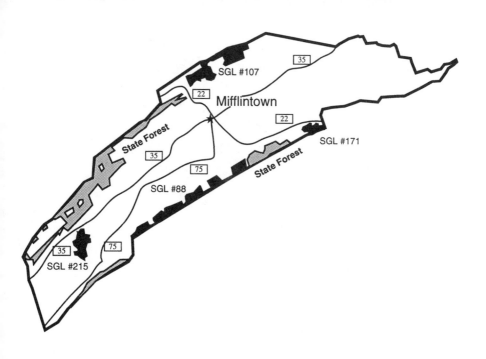

MIFFLIN COUNTY

Southeast of State College, Mifflin's 413 square miles lie in the rich Appalachian Ridge and Valley Region. The mountain-valley terrain ranges from 440 to 2,340 feet.

Long, narrow sandstone ridges and long valleys with deep soils hold rich, deciduous forest vegetation. Farms occupy about 34 percent of the land with over half in livestock and livestock products. Primary vegetables are corn and tomatoes with apples and peaches on orchard lands.

Two state forests — Bald Eagle and Tuscarora — provide more than 57,000 acres of public deer hunting grounds. One gameland of 534 acres is located near Stroder Mills and a portion of 6,560-acre SGL No. 107 is shared with Juniata County.

Mifflin's Farm-Game and Safety Zone cooperators allow hunting on private lands, which exceed 57,000 acres. Mifflin's deer numbers in the mid-1990s were close to its goal of 22 whitetails per square forested mile.

Food, lodging and services, contact: Juniata-Mifflin County Tourist Promotion Agency, 19 South Wayne St., Lewistown, PA 17044. Phone: (717) 248-6713.

IN BRIEF

State Gamelands: 534 acres

State Parks & Forests: 57,361 acres

Farm-Game Co-op: 8,275 acres (54 farms)

Safety Zone Lands: 61,971 acres (455 tracts)

Forest-Game Co-op: 581 acres

1993 Buck/Doe Harvest: 1,372 / 2,287

1994 Doe Permit Allocation: 3,550

Deer Density/FSM: 23

Deer Density Goal/FSM: 22

Average Buck Harvest/FSM: 4.6

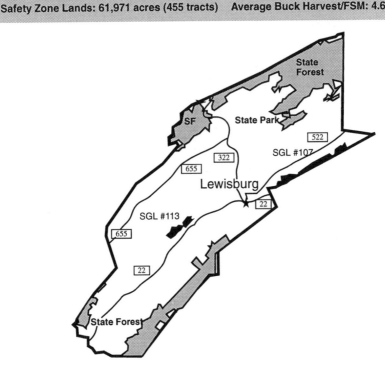

PERRY COUNTY

★

Elevations here range from 310 to 2,240 feet within the Appalachian Ridge and alley Region of the state. Of Perry's 557 square miles, 64 percent is wooded. The ountain country holds long, narrow sandstone ridges penetrated by long valleys.

Farms occupy nearly one-third of the county with corn, alfalfa, oats and wheat n most harvest lands. More than 500 of these private holdings are in Game Commission co-op programs.

Tuscarora State Forest's 41,098 acres in the New Germantown area and seven amelands comprise Perry County's public hunting lands. Of the latter, SGL No. 170 ear Marysville is the most expansive followed by SGL No. 88 at Ickesburg with ,930 acres.

Food, lodging and services, contact: Perry County Tourist and Recreation 3ureau, Cook Rd., Duncannon, PA 17020. Phone: (717) 834-4912.

IN BRIEF

State Gamelands: 20,461 acres

State Parks & Forests: 41,098 acres

Farm-Game Co-op: 30,204 acres (248 farms)

Safety Zone Lands: 43,141 acres (285 tracts)

Forest-Game Co-op: 1,415 acres

1993 Buck/Doe Harvest: 2,638 / 4,099

1994 Doe Permit Allocation: 16,050

Deer Density/FSM: 33

Deer Density Goal/FSM: 17

Average Buck Harvest/FSM: 7.4

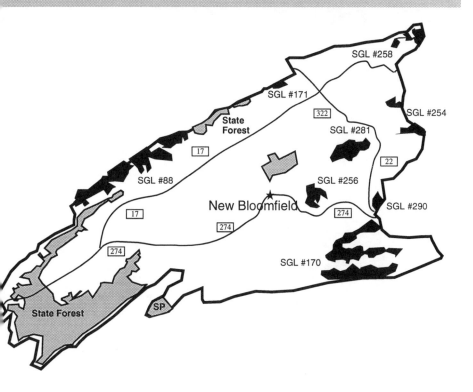

SNYDER COUNTY

As is typical of the region, Snyder's mountainous landscape is sliced by long ridges and narrow valleys. Half of the county is forested with abut 45 percent of the 329 square miles in farmland. Crops include tobacco and apples with hog and cattle raising on some parcels.

Elevations range from 400 to 2,165 feet.

Units at Beaver Springs and Troxelville, parts of Bald Eagle State Forest, provide 28,684 acres of deer habitat. Three gamelands combine for over 25,000 additional hunting territory; the largest SGL No. 188 near Beavertown.

Annual buck and doe harvests average about 2,500 with deer numbers above carrying capacity, according to commission biologists.

Food, lodging and services, contact: Susquehanna Valley Visitors Bureau, 219D Hafer Rd., P.O. Box 268, Lewisburg, PA 17837. Phone: (800) 458-4747 and (717) 524-7234.

IN BRIEF

State Gamelands: 2,714 acres

State Parks & Forests: 28,684 acres

Farm-Game Co-op: 53,823 acres (460 farms)

Safety Zone Lands: 26,706 acres (196 tracts)

Forest-Game Co-op: 224 acres

1993 Buck/Doe Harvest: 992 / 1,551

1994 Doe Permit Allocation: 5,200

Deer Density/FSM: 28

Deer Density Goal/FSM: 18

Average Buck Harvest/FSM: 5.9

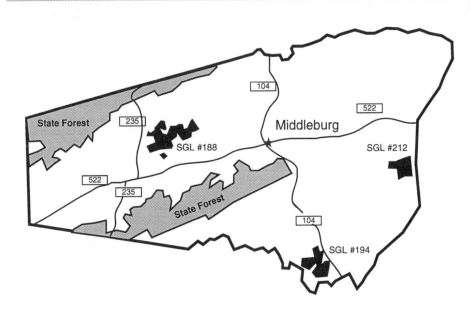

NORTHEAST REGION

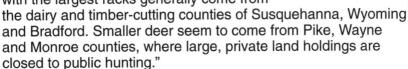

"Northeastern Pennsylvania is a land of great contrasts, from the gutted terrain of stripmines to some of the state's most picturesque scenes of white birch, blue lakes and moss-covered woodland floors. [It's] a land of mountains, meadows, deep forested woodlands and farms planted to corn and wheat. The best nourished [deer] with the largest racks generally come from the dairy and timber-cutting counties of Susquehanna, Wyoming and Bradford. Smaller deer seem to come from Pike, Wayne and Monroe counties, where large, private land holdings are closed to public hunting."

Ed Sherlinski, Pennsylvania Game Commission

Pennsylvania Game Commission
Northeast Region
P.O. Box 220, Dallas, PA 18612-0220
Phone: (800) 228-0789 and (717) 675-1143
Bradford, Carbon, Columbia, Lackawanna, Luzerne, Monroe, Montour, Northumberland, Pike, Sullivan, Susquehanna, Wayne and Wyoming counties.

BRADFORD COUNTY

Bradford provides the best of both worlds for the deer hunter, offering farm-pasture habitats and forested mountains and valleys. The county's north, approaching the New York border, is rolling and hilly with the south largely rugged with high plateaus. The county covers 1,152 square miles with elevations ranging from 640 to 2,420 feet.

Fifty-nine percent of Bradford is wooded with numerous beef cattle and dairy farms throughout, typically in scenic valleys rimmed by highland forests. Hay, corn, alfalfa and oats comprise the harvestable crops with pasture lands supporting a thriving dairy business.

Bradford typically makes the state's annual top 10 list in both deer harvest numbers and the amount of bucks taken per square mile of woodland.

Some 3,838 acres of Tioga State Forest, north of Canton, overlap into Bradford but the lack of public forest land is made up by 11 state gamelands. Near Tioga S.F. is SGL No. 12 with 23,289 acres. SGL No. 36 near Towanda covers 18,929 acres with 5,618-acre SGL No. 219 at Warren Center.

Food, lodging and services, contact: Endless Mountains Visitors Bureau, RR 6, Box 132A, Tunkhannock, PA 18657. Phone: (717) 836-5431.

IN BRIEF

State Gamelands: 55,178 acres

State Parks & Forests: 3,838 acres

Farm-Game Co-op: 14,544 acres (79 farms)

Safety Zone Lands: 95,322 acres (538 tracts)

Forest-Game Co-op: None

1993 Buck/Doe Harvest: 5,044 / 8,258

1994 Doe Permit Allocation: 14,950

Deer Density/FSM: 30

Deer Density Goal/FSM: 22

Average Buck Harvest/FSM: 7.5

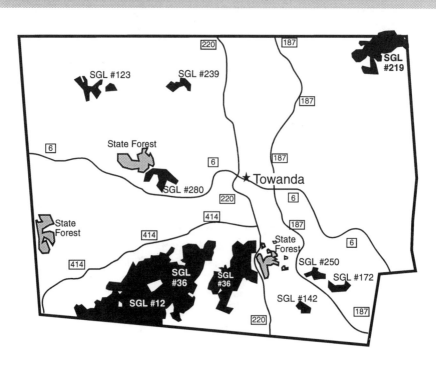

CARBON COUNTY

This Appalachian Mountain county covers only 384 square miles but it offers abundant public hunting lands. With elevations of 370 to 2,220 feet, Carbon's landscape is 75 percent wooded with only eight percent occupation by farms. Corn, oats, barley and hay are the chief crops with cattle farming a secondary business.

Bordered on the south by the Blue Mountain with heavily glaciated uplands, Carbon is both scenic and rugged. The Lehigh River cuts through the county and gamelands.

Hickory Run State Park is popular year-round with anglers, campers and sight-seers and a fall and winter attraction for hunters. The park east of White Haven, totals 15,398 acres.

Five gamelands, the largest SGL No. 141 near Jim Thorpe, spans 17,047 acres. SGL No. 40 at White Haven offers another 6,118 acres.

Food, lodging and services, contact: Pocono Mountains Vacation Bureau, Inc., 1004 Main St., Stroudsburg, PA 18360. Phone: (800) 762-6667 or (717) 424-6050.

IN BRIEF

State Gamelands: 26,337 acres

State Parks & Forests: 17,351 acres

Farm-Game Co-op: 983 acres (6 farms)

Safety Zone Lands: 37,842 acres (87 tracts)

Forest-Game Co-op: 5,811 acres

1993 Buck/Doe Harvest: 1,450 / 1,824

1994 Doe Permit Allocation: 5,800

Deer Density/FSM: 28

Deer Density Goal/FSM: 23

Average Buck Harvest/FSM: 5.1

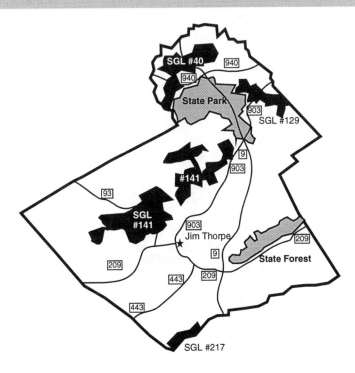

COLUMBIA COUNTY

Mountainous Columbia County holds long, narrow ridges with elevations of 460 to 2,450 feet. Spanning only 486 square miles with 53 percent of its surface forested, little Columbia produces abundant and occasional big bucks.

Farms cover about 39 percent of the terrain, mostly in croplands yielding oats, soybeans, corn and hay.

In terms of buck harvest per square mile of forest, Columbia ranks exceptionally high, particularly for a "mountain" county.

Despite being heavily forested, no state forest or park lands are present in the county. However, hunters are welcome on 12,538-acre SGL No. 58 near Catawissa, 4,335-acre SGL No. 226 near Millville and on three smaller tracts.

More than 30,000 acres of private holdings are open to hunters on safety zone and farm-game cooperatives.

Food, lodging and services, contact: Columbia-Montour Tourist Promotion Agency, Inc., 121 Paper Mill Rd., Bloomsburg, PA 17815. Phone: (800) VISIT-10 or (717) 784-8279.

IN BRIEF

State Gamelands: 20,345 acres

State Parks & Forests: None

Farm-Game Co-op: 13,892 acres (145 farms)

Safety Zone Lands: 16,641 acres (130 tracts)

Forest-Game Co-op: None

1993 Buck/Doe Harvest: 2,006 / 3,809

1994 Doe Permit Allocation: 12,650

Deer Density/FSM: 36

Deer Density Goal/FSM: 19

Average Buck Harvest/FSM: 7.8

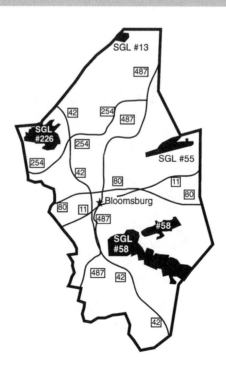

LACKAWANNA COUNTY

Encompassing Scranton, Lackawanna provides good hunting within a short drive of the city. The county's 461 square miles are 68 percent forested.

This is the heart of the anthracite region with its trademarked high, upland, dissected character. Farms cover only 16 percent of the county with both croplands and cattle operations to be found. The main crops include hay, corn, oats and wheat.

Three gamelands — the biggest 3,984-acre SGL No. 300 near Carbondale and 3,430-acre SGL No. 135 near Gouldsboro — are open to deer hunters. Lackawanna State Forest provides another 6,024 acres, west of Thornhurst.

Food, lodging and services, contact: Pennsylvania's Northeast Territory Visitor's Bureau, Airport Aviation Center, Hangar Rd., Avoca, PA 18641. Phone: (800) 245-7711 or (717) 457-1320.

IN BRIEF

State Gamelands: 8,913 acres

State Parks & Forests: 6,024 acres

Farm-Game Co-op: None

Safety Zone Lands: 14,697 acres (100 tracts)

Forest-Game Co-op: None

1993 Buck/Doe Harvest: 1,806 / 2,451

1994 Doe Permit Allocation: 6,200

Deer Density/FSM: 31

Deer Density Goal/FSM: 23

Average Buck Harvest/FSM: 5.8

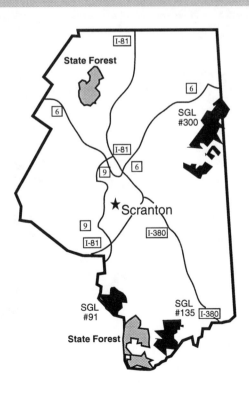

LUZERNE COUNTY

Luzerne's 891 square miles include the city of Wilkes-Barre and plentiful mountain and valley woodlands. Forests encompass two-thirds of the county throughout the rugged, dissected plateaus. Elevations range from 480 to 2,463 feet.

Farmland covers 12 percent of the county with just over half in harvested crops and the remainder in cattle production. Potatoes, alfalfa, corn and oats lead the 'grocery' list.

Luzerne is rich in both state forests and gamelands. The public woodlands include 8,085 acres of Ricketts Glen State Park at Red Rock and 1,416 acres of Lackawanna State Forest west of Plymouth.

Ten gamelands are scattered about the county. The most notable is SGL No. 91 at Bear Creek with 14,390 acres followed by SGL No. 187 near White Haven (8,186 acres), SGL No. 119 at Mountain Top (7,963 acres), and SGL No. 57 near Red Rock (28,242 acres) shared with Wyoming County.

Food, lodging and services, contact: Pennsylvania's Northeast Territory Visitor's Bureau, Airport Aviation Center, Hangar Rd., Avoca, PA 18641. Phone: (800) 245-7711 or (717) 457-1320.

IN BRIEF

State Gamelands: 47,278 acres

State Parks & Forests: 9,501 acres

Farm-Game Co-op: 15,193 acres (159 farms)

Safety Zone Lands: 20,527 acres (176 tracts)

Forest-Game Co-op: None

1993 Buck/Doe Harvest: 3,693 / 5,217

1994 Doe Permit Allocation: 16,000

Deer Density/FSM: 33

Deer Density Goal/FSM: 17

Average Buck Harvest/FSM: 6.3

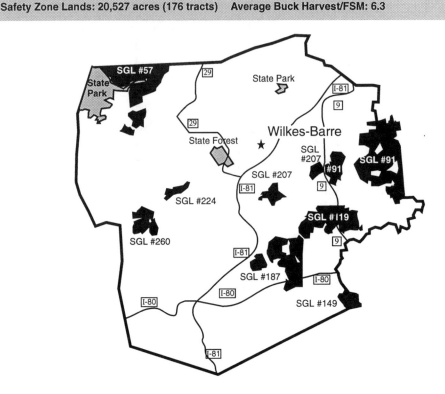

MONROE COUNTY

In the heart of the tourist-rich Poconos, Monroe borders the Delaware River and New Jersey. The land in the northern portion of the county is hilly with more mountainous features along the Blue Mountain, rimming its southern line. Elevations go from 300 to 2,220 feet.

This is not an area of rugged mountains and tall peaks. Its high, forested upland is interspersed with numerous glacial lakes. Forests cover three-fourths of Monroe County.

Only eight percent of the county is farmland, planted in hay, corn, wheat and oats or used for cattle production.

In the Canadensis-Tannersville region is the 8,637-acre tract of Delaware State Forest. State parklands at Tobyhanna and Gouldsboro offer hunters 5,485 acres with Big Pocono State Park contributing another 1,017 huntable public grounds.

Six gamelands, topped by 25,527-acre SGL No. 127 near Tannersville also offer visiting hunters good whitetail habitat.

Food, lodging and services, contact: Pocono Mountains Vacation Bureau, Inc., 1004 Main St., Stroudsburg, PA 18360. Phone: (800) 762-6667 or (717) 424-6050.

IN BRIEF

State Gamelands: 38,378 acres

State Parks & Forests: 15,139 acres

Farm-Game Co-op: 10,935 acres (108 farms)

Safety Zone Lands: 433 acres (6 tracts)

Forest-Game Co-op: None

1993 Buck/Doe Harvest: 1,803 / 2,141

1994 Doe Permit Allocation: 8,750

Deer Density/FSM: 22

Deer Density Goal/FSM: 18

Average Buck Harvest/FSM: 3.9

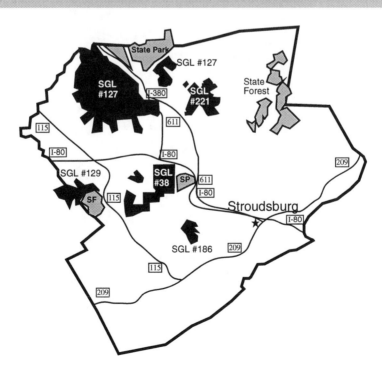

MONTOUR COUNTY

One of the state's smallest counties with only 131 square land miles, tiny Montour is a consistent buck and doe producer. It is a mountainous region with 27 percent woodland, producing a relatively high buck harvest.

Fifty-eight percent of Montour is in farmland, accounting for well-fed and numerous deer. Nearly two-thirds of the farms are in crop production (tobacco, alfalfa, corn, oats and soybeans) with the remainder hosting hogs and cattle.

Elevations here run from 440 to 1,380 feet.

As might be expected, no state forest lands penetrate the county and only one small (227-acre) gameland (SGL No. 115 near Danville) is available. Deer hunting here is best done by contacting private landowners, as those in farm co-op and safety zone programs.

Due to the abundance of farmland with adjacent woods, buck harvests are exceptionally high, in some years exceeding 11 bucks taken per square mile of woodland.

Food, lodging and services, contact: Columbia-Montour Tourist Promotion Agency, Inc., 121 Paper Mill Rd., Bloomsburg, PA 17815. Phone: (800) VISIT-10 or (717) 784-8279.

IN BRIEF

State Gamelands: 227 acres

State Parks & Forests: None

Farm-Game Co-op: 10,260 acres (67 farms)

Safety Zone Lands: 7,253 acres (53 tracts)

Forest-Game Co-op: None

1993 Buck/Doe Harvest: 361 / 344

1994 Doe Permit Allocation: 1,900

Deer Density/FSM: 55

Deer Density Goal/FSM: 30

Average Buck Harvest/FSM: 9.6

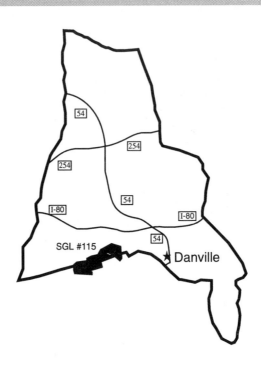

NORTHUMBERLAND COUNTY

Northumberland's 461 square miles are 50 percent forested. Elevations range from 400 to 1,760 feet across the northern Appalachian Ridge countryside.

Broad valleys broken by north-south running ridges characterize the land. Farm country composes about 42 percent of the landscape with cropland dominating. Wheat, soybeans, corn and alfalfa are the chief crops with pig farming another important business.

As with neighboring Montour, Northumberland has no state park or state forest holdings. However, three gamelands, with SGL No. 84 near Treverton the biggest at 8,154 acres, are available, all with good deer populations. Montour also has more farm-game cooperatives than any other Northeast Region county.

Food, lodging and services, contact: Susquehanna Valley Visitors Bureau, 219D Hafer Rd., P.O. Box 268, Lewisburg, PA 17837. Phone: (800) 458-4748 or (717) 524-7234.

IN BRIEF

State Gamelands: 10,735 acres

State Parks & Forests: None

Farm-Game Co-op: 66,716 acres (741 farms)

Safety Zone Lands: 11,019 acres (44 tracts)

Forest-Game Co-op: None

1993 Buck/Doe Harvest: 1,020 / 1,446

1994 Doe Permit Allocation: 5,300

Deer Density/FSM: 23

Deer Density Goal/FSM: 23

Average Buck Harvest/FSM: 4.5

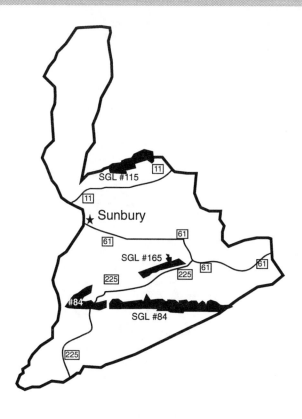

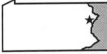

PIKE COUNTY

Another Pocono Mountain county with numerous lakes, ponds and public hunting lands, Pike borders portions of New Jersey and New York to the east. It spans 550 square miles. Numerous wetlands penetrate the 82 percent of the countryside with forests, serving as home for plentiful black bears as well as whitetails.

Many private hunting clubs and woodland vacation and resident developments cover the county, accounting for an under-harvest of deer and animals smaller in size than many other counties. This is one of few counties in the state which, in the mid-1990s, held deer numbers below carrying capacity.

Only two percent of the county is in farms, mainly holding livestock. Crops include hay, corn and oats.

Many deer hunters head to the county's scattered tracts, totaling 62,983-acres, of Delaware State Forest lands for buck season. Also popular is the 1,450-acre bear and deer-rich Promised Land State Park, north of Canadensis.

Four state gamelands offer another 21,000-plus acres with SGL No. 180 near Greely the most expansive.

Food, lodging and services, contact: Pocono Mountains Vacation Bureau, Inc., 1004 Main St., Stroudsburg, PA 18360. Phone: (800) 762-6667 or (717) 424-6050.

IN BRIEF

State Gamelands: 21,564 acres

State Parks & Forests: 64,433 acres

Farm-Game Co-op: None

Safety Zone Lands: 85 acres (1 tract)

Forest-Game Co-op: None

1993 Buck/Doe Harvest: 1,543 / 2,209

1994 Doe Permit Allocation: 5,150

Deer Density/FSM: 18

Deer Density Goal/FSM: 19

Average Buck Harvest/FSM: 3.4

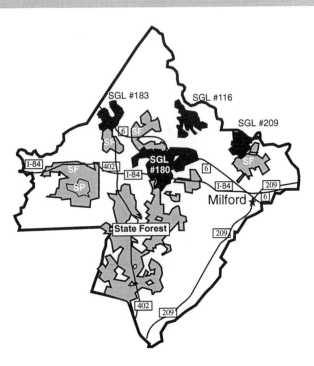

SULLIVAN COUNTY

This is the second least populous county in the state, made up of 86 percent forest land. Covering 451 square miles, elevations run from 779 to 2,593 square feet.

Deep gorges and varying valleys cover Sullivan although much of its forests are elevated, accounting for geologists' descriptions as a 'high relief' area.

Farms occupy about 12 percent of the land, most holding livestock. Crops include hay, corn and oats.

Sullivan's deer numbers far outnumber its human residents although populations swell in the hunting seasons as visitors escape to their backwoods cabins and lodges.

Wyoming State Forest's 39,013 acres, in the Forksville and Hillsgrove areas, entice many visiting sportsmen with a few preferring the 920-acres of scenic World's End State Park next to Forksville.

State gamelands number four with extensive (45,529 acres) SGL No. 13 near Sonestown the largest. SGL No. 66 near Lopez is another popular deer hunting site.

Food, lodging and services, contact: Endless Mountains Visitors Bureau, RR 6, Box 132A, Tunkhannock, PA 18657-9232. Phone: (717)-836-5431.

IN BRIEF

State Gamelands: 57,182 acres

State Parks & Forests: 39,933 acres

Farm-Game Co-op: None

Safety Zone Lands: 12,648 acres (47 tracts)

Forest-Game Co-op: None

1993 Buck/Doe Harvest: 1,650 / 2,104

1994 Doe Permit Allocation: 9,600

Deer Density/FSM: 28

Deer Density Goal/FSM: 16

Average Buck Harvest/FSM: 4.3

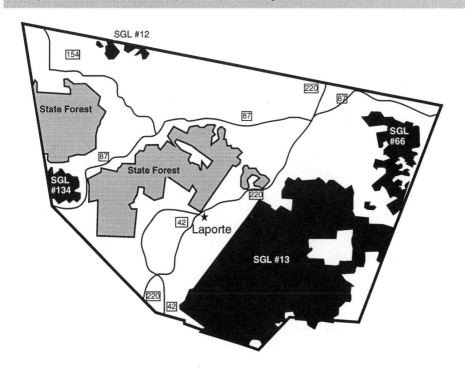

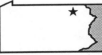

SUSQUEHANNA COUNTY

Bordering New York on the north, Susquehanna County's 826 square miles are 65 percent forested. Mountain elevations span 760 to 2,693 feet.

Another completely rural county, cattle and dairy products are the focus on most of the 34 percent of landscape in farmland. Hay, corn and oats are the main crops.

Rolling and hilly, Susquehanna, like neighboring Bradford, has larger deer than most northern tier counties because of crop and pasture lands and numerous timbercuts. The latter yield the sapling and second growth habitat which is more conducive to good deer country than mature forests.

No state forests are found here but there's plenty of hunting grounds — more than 60,000 acres — on safety zone and co-op farms. Add to that five gamelands open to public hunting. SGL No. 35 near Hallstead with 7,739 acres is the biggest although two others exceed 2,000 acres.

Food, lodging and services, contact: Endless Mountains Visitors Bureau, RR 6, Box 132A, Tunkhannock, PA 18657. Phone: (717) 836-5431.

IN BRIEF

State Gamelands: 14,324 acres

State Parks & Forests: None

Farm-Game Co-op: 41,277 acres (256 farms)

Safety Zone Lands: 20,450 acres (89 tracts)

Forest-Game Co-op: None

1993 Buck/Doe Harvest: 3,462 / 4,032

1994 Doe Permit Allocation: 7,000

Deer Density/FSM: 29

Deer Density Goal/FSM: 25

Average Buck Harvest/FSM: 6.5

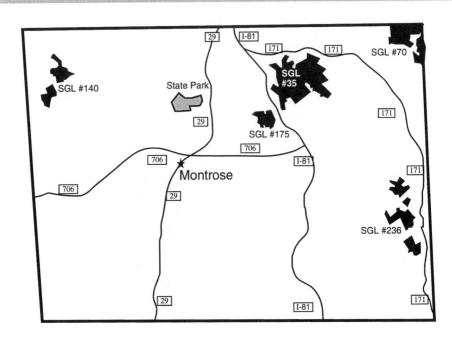

WAYNE COUNTY

Bordering New York on its east, Wayne covers 731 square miles with elevations from 680 to 2,654 feet. Two-thirds of the county is wooded.

Farms occupy much of the remainder of the county with livestock and livestock products dominating. Hay, oats and corn are the main crops.

Wayne's topography, typical of the Poconos, consists of high wooded hills with hundreds of small, forest-encircled glacial lakes.

Prompton State Park, northeast of Honesdale, is the county's only state-owned parkland with 850 acres. The biggest public tract (9,367 acres) is SGL No. 159 at Lookout. SGL No. 70 near Susquehanna contributes another 3,766 acres. Two other smaller gamelands are located at Starlight and Archbald. More than 14,000 acres of private farms are also available to sportsmen.

Food, lodging and services, contact: Pocono Mountains Vacation Bureau, Inc., 1004 Main St., Stroudsburg, PA 18360. Phone: (800) 762-6667 or (717) 424-6050.

IN BRIEF

State Gamelands: 14,167 acres

State Parks & Forests: 850 acres

Farm-Game Co-op: 734 acres (8 farms)

Safety Zone Lands: 13,314 (90 tracts)

Forest-Game Co-op: None

1993 Buck/Doe Harvest: 3,215 / 5,284

1994 Doe Permit Allocation: 9,350

Deer Density/FSM: 34

Deer Density Goal/FSM: 20

Average Buck Harvest/FSM: 6.7

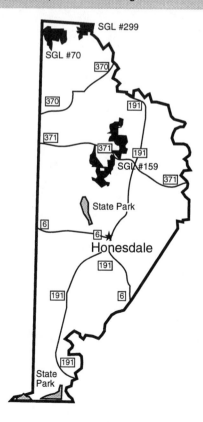

WYOMING COUNTY

Another totally rural county, Wyoming covers 399 square miles with 62 percent in forest. Elevations range from 560 to 2,380 feet.

About 30 percent of the county is in farmland, primarily used for livestock. Hay, corn and oats are grown on tilled lands.

Northeast of the Susquehanna River, this county duplicates the ecological and geographic features of neighboring Bradford and Susquehanna counties. Southwest of the river, topography rises rapidly to 2,000 feet, forming a rugged, forested plateau interrupted by stream-bottom gorges.

The southwest corner of the county offers extensive public hunting with good numbers of whitetails. The biggest tract is SGL No. 57, near Noxen, offering 28,242 acres. More than 20,000 acres of co-op lands can also be found.

Food, lodging and services, contact: Endless Mountains Visitors Bureau, RR 6, Box 132A, Tunkhannock, PA 18657. Phone: (717) 836-5431.

IN BRIEF

State Gamelands: 28,272 acres

State Parks & Forests: 1,273 acres

Farm-Game Co-op: 9,258 acres (46 farms)

Safety Zone Lands: 10,942 acres (56 tracts)

Forest-Game Co-op: 1,350 acres

1993 Buck/Doe Harvest: 1,570 / 2,701

1994 Doe Permit Allocation: 5,300

Deer Density/FSM: 25

Deer Density Goal/FSM: 23

Average Buck Harvest/FSM: 6.4

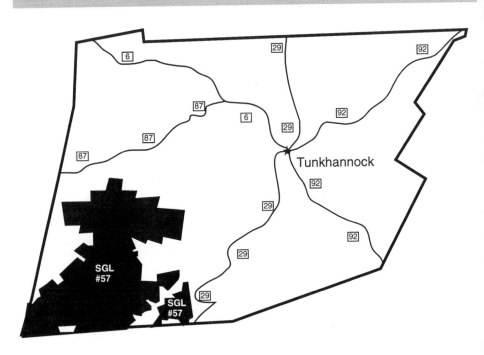

SOUTHEAST REGION

"Nearly a third of the hunting licenses sold in the commonwealth are purchased in this region, which isn't too surprising as it contains nearly half of the state's population. The Southeast's deer population is excellent. Many areas are suffering from an overabundance of whitetails. Countless resident hunters annually travel to the more popular deer hunting territory of the northern tier counties when deer season opens. More often than not, they leave behind farm-fed whitetails which weigh more and have larger antlers than those found farther north. Farmers here often complain about excessive crop damage and posting is often the cause. If hunters don't have access, they can't harvest deer causing the damage."

Mike Schmit, Pennsylvania Game Commission

Pennsylvania Game Commission
Southeast Region
RD 2, Box 2584Reading, PA 19605
Phone: (800) 228-0791 and (610) 926-3136

Berks, Bucks, Chester, Dauphin, Delaware, Lancaster, Lebanon, Lehigh, Montgomery, Northampton, Philadelphia, Schuylkill and York counties.

BERKS COUNTY

★

In terms of bucks taken by hunters per square mile of woodland, Berks leads the list just about every year. Abundant and fertile farmland plays no small part in the county's deer populations and sizes. Add to that (unusual in the Southeast) abundant public hunting grounds totaling nearly 27,000 acres and another 70,000 in landowner-game commission co-ops.

Covering 861 square miles with 134 to 1,680-foot elevations, the county is 35 percent forested. The rolling lowlands of southern Berks contrast sharply with the Blue Mountain on its northern edge.

Farms occupy about 47 percent of the county, nearly three-quarters in cropland and the remainder cattle holdings. Alfalfa, hay, wheat, corn and barley are the chief crops.

French Creek State Park near Birdsboro and a small tract of Weiser State Forest are the sole Dept. of Environmental Resources holdings here. State gamelands on the Blue Mountain at Shartlesville (SGL No. 110 with 10,093 acres) and Eckville (SGL No. 106 holding 9,197 acres) and three others are popular deer hunting grounds.

Food, lodging and services, contact: Berks County Visitors Information Association, V.F. Factory Outlet Complex, Park Road & Hill Ave., P.O. Box 6677, Reading, PA 19610. Phone: (800) 443-6610 and (610) 375-4085.

IN BRIEF

State Gamelands: 21,130 acres

State Parks & Forests: 5,790 acres

Farm-Game Co-op: 64,164 acres (576 farms)

Safety Zone Lands: 5,773 acres (49 tracts)

Forest-Game Co-op: 4,300 acres

1993 Buck/Doe Harvest: 3,162 / 5,201

1994 Doe Permit Allocation: 18,900

Deer Density/FSM: 44

Deer Density Goal/FSM: 21

Average Buck Harvest/FSM: 10.5

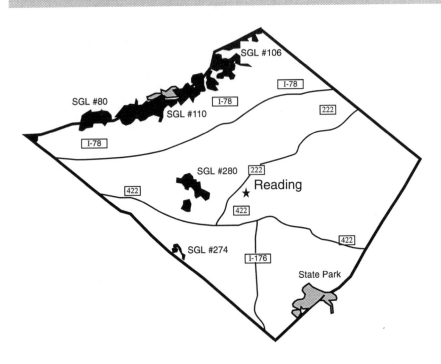

BUCKS COUNTY

Bucks, the fifth most populous county in the state, holds a surprisingly large number of whitetails. Those avoiding vehicles may grow to 3-4 years of age and more, making the county a haven for some monster bucks within its 610 square miles. The biggest human population is in the southern townships.

Set north of Philadelphia and bordering the Delaware River, Bucks county's gently rolling hills, with elevations running from sea level to 980 feet, is 26 percent forested. Farmland composes 29 percent and the remainder is covered with towns, cities and sprawling suburbia. Crops include soybeans, wheat and corn.

A part of the Special Regulations Area, season lengths here are liberal as is the issuance of as many as five antlerless deer tags to hunters with access to overpopulated habitats. Rifles are not permitted here for whitetails.

As might be expected, public hunting lands are minimal. Nockamixon State Park west of Quakertown covers 3,000 acres. Four gamelands (two under 310 acres each) are within county borders. SGL No. 56 at Upper Black Eddy covers 1,740 acres with SGL No. 157 near Harrow offering 2,010 acres.

Food, lodging and services, contact: Bucks County Tourist Commission, Inc., P.O. Box 912, Dept., 56, Doylestown, PA 18901. Phone: (215) 345-4552.

IN BRIEF

State Gamelands: 4,320 acres

State Parks & Forests: 3,000 acres

Farm-Game Co-op:9,125 acres (119 farms)

Safety Zone Lands: 2,064 acres (25 tracts)

Forest-Game Co-op: None

1993 Buck/Doe Harvest: 1,317 / 3,585

1994 Doe Permit Allocation: 19,350

Deer Density/FSM: 25

Deer Density Goal/FSM: 5

Average Buck Harvest/FSM: 8.2

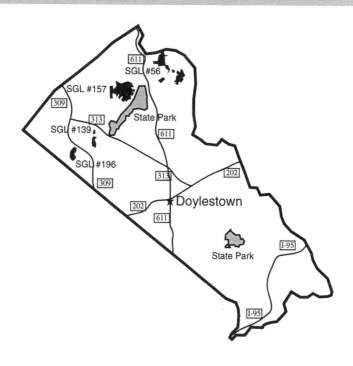

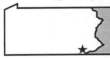

CHESTER COUNTY

A personal note here: Given one county on which to have hunting access in buck season, I'll choose Chester. Not a big woods county (28 percent is forested), the many 'gentlemen's farms' — some sizable — provide haven for big-racked bucks and fat does with ready access to crops and the protection of posted refuges. Finding land on which to hunt here is difficult. Seasons and doe tags here are liberal, as part of the Special Regulations Area.

Chester's elevations range from 66 to 1,020 feet across its vast 758 square miles. The north is largely composed of broad highlands and ridges with gently rolling lowlands to the south. Farms occupy 45 percent of the county with tobacco, soybeans, corn, alfalfa and barley the prime money-crops.

Marsh Creek State Park's 1,000 acres near Eagle is the only Dept. of Environmental Resources holding in the county. The sole gameland is SGL No. 43 at Elverson, totaling 1,819 acres.

Food, lodging and services, contact: Chester County Tourist Bureau, 601 Westtown Rd., West Chester, PA 19382. Phone: (800) 228-9933 and (610) 344-6365.

IN BRIEF

State Gamelands: 1,819 acres

State Parks & Forests: 1,000 acres

Farm-Game Co-op: 18,685 acres (187 farms)

Safety Zone Lands: 307 acres (3 tracts)

Forest-Game Co-op: None

1993 Buck/Doe Harvest: 1,821 / 4,285

1994 Doe Permit Allocation: 16,000

Deer Density/FSM: 34

Deer Density Goal/FSM: 5

Average Buck Harvest/FSM: 8.8

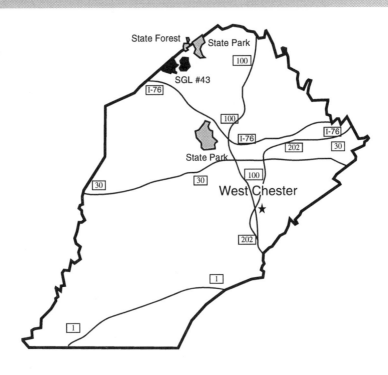

DAUPHIN COUNTY

Encompassing the state capital, Dauphin's 528 square miles vary from mountains in its central and north to rolling lowlands in its south.

Elevations range from 280 to 1,760 feet with fully half of the county in forest. Ridge country typifies northern Dauphin with rich farmlands and rolling hills southward. Livestock and crops are grown on the 33 percent of the county in farmland. Tobacco, barley, corn and hay grow on nearly two-thirds of the harvest soils.

The biggest of three public deer hunting tracts in the county is 41,392-acre SGL No.211 near Dauphin. SGL No. 210 at Lykens provides another 11,061 acres. Two tracts of Weiser State Forest are within Dauphin's borders, both adjoined by SGL 210.

Food, lodging and services, contact: Harrisburg-Hershey-Carlisle Tourism & Convention Bureau, 114 Walnut St., P.O. Box 969, Harrisburg, PA 17108. Phone: (800) 995-0969 and (717) 232-1377

IN BRIEF

State Gamelands: 54,273 acres

State Parks & Forests: 8,357 acres

Farm-Game Co-op: 39,624 (402 farms)

Safety Zone Lands: 10,040 acres (62 tracts)

Forest-Game Co-op: None

1993 Buck/Doe Harvest: 1,577 / 2,408

1994 Doe Permit Allocation: 10,550

Deer Density/FSM: 28

Deer Density Goal/FSM: 23

Average Buck Harvest/FSM: 6.0

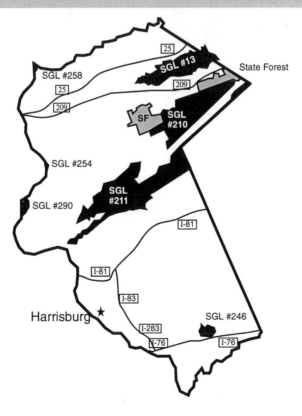

LANCASTER COUNTY

This is farm-country pure and simple with many handsome Amish farms dotting the county. A full 69 percent of the land is in farms, accounting for vast acreage in corn, tobacco, alfalfa, wheat, barley and corn plus pastures and orchards.

Lancaster's 952 square miles are characterized by broad highlands and ridges in the north and rolling lowlands to the south. It's bordered by the Susquehanna River to the west.

Woodland covers only 13 percent of the county which ranges in elevation from 109 to 1,200 feet. Its deer density per forested square mile is among the highest in the state.

Six gamelands tracts are scattered across this Pennsylvania Dutch landscape. The biggest is SGL No. 46 (5,027 acres) near Hopeland with another 4,537-acres inside the borders of SGL No. 156 at Elstonville.

More than 100,000 acres are available through co-op and safety zone projects.

Food, lodging and services, contact: Pennsylvania Dutch Convention & Visitors Bureau, 501 Greenfield Rd., Lancaster, PA 17601. Phone: (800) 735-2629 and (717) 299-8901.

IN BRIEF

State Gamelands: 11,287 acres

State Parks & Forests: None

Farm-Game Co-op: 82,320 acres (987 farms)

Safety Zone Lands: 19,848 acres (181 tracts)

Forest-Game Co-op: 3,500 acres

1993 Buck/Doe Harvest: 1,457 / 2,261

1994 Doe Permit Allocation: 13,700

Deer Density/FSM: 54

Deer Density Goal/FSM: 19

Average Buck Harvest/FSM: 11.7

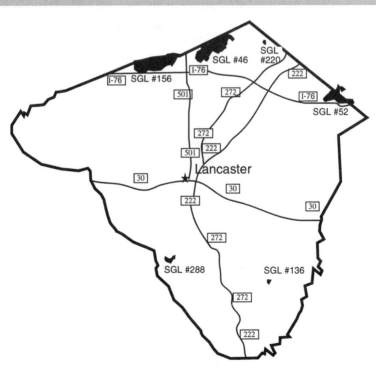

LEBANON COUNTY

Half of Lebanon's 363 square miles is devoted to farming with another 34 percent in woodlands. Its southern three-quarters consists of rolling lowlands dotted with farms. The northern part of the county is more mountainous with elevations spanning 340 to 1,660 feet.

Farms make up half of the fertile, limestone land, mainly in harvestable crops including tobacco, corn, barley and soybeans with plentiful cattle lands, as well.

A portion of Swatara State Park's 3,600 acres is shared with Schuylkill County. SGL No. 145 at Mt. Gretna with its 2,792 acres and SGL No. 211 to the north are popular hunting grounds.

Food, lodging and services, contact: Lebanon Valley Tourist and Visitors Bureau, P.O. Box 329, 625 Quentin Rd., Lebanon, PA 17042. Phone: (717) 272-8555.

IN BRIEF

State Gamelands: 3,539 acres

State Parks & Forests: 3,000 acres

Farm-Game Co-op: 24,678 acres (242 farms)

Safety Zone Lands: 8,882 acres (68 tracts)

Forest-Game Co-op: 600 acres

1993 Buck/Doe Harvest: 701 / 829

1994 Doe Permit Allocation: 5,600

Deer Density/FSM: 29

Deer Density Goal/FSM: 23

Average Buck Harvest/FSM: 5.8

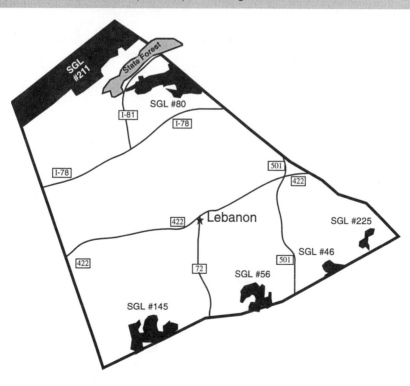

LEHIGH COUNTY

Lehigh's 348 square miles include 43 percent farmland and 29 percent woods, ranging in elevations from 220 to 1,640 feet. Gently rolling hills and farmlands are rimmed in the north by the Blue Mountain. The south is also hilly with abundant farms and country homesites.

Harvested cropland yields wheat, potatoes, barley and corn with numerous peach and apple orchards scattered across the county.

There aren't any state parks or forests here and only two gamelands — SGL No. 217 near Slatedale (4,070 acres) and SGL 205 near Schnecksville (1,303 acres).

Lehigh annually yields some large corn-fed whitetails including trophy quality bucks, among them the state record non-typical bowbuck. It regularly ranks in the top 10 counties for bucks taken per square mile of county woodland.

Food, lodging and services, contact: Lehigh Valley Convention and Visitors Bureau, Inc., P.O. Box 20785, Lehigh Valley, PA 18002. Phone (800) 747-0561 and (610) 882-9200.

IN BRIEF

State Gamelands: 5,373 acres

State Parks & Forests: None

Farm-Game Co-op: 15,369 acres (184 farms)

Safety Zone Lands: 3,126 acres (23 tracts)

Forest-Game Co-op: None

1993 Buck/Doe Harvest: 824 / 1,617

1994 Doe Permit Allocation: 7,100

Deer Density/FSM: 32

Deer Density Goal/FSM: 22

Average Buck Harvest/FSM: 8.2

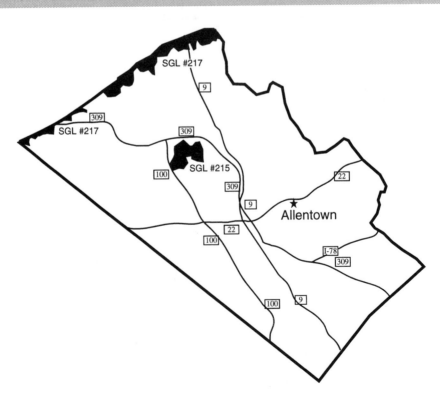

MONTGOMERY COUNTY

Characterized by a belt of ridges and broad highlands, Montgomery is 18 percent forested with another 24 percent in farms. As the third most populous county in the state (more than 1,300 people per square mile), little public hunting land is available even though whitetails live throughout the region.

Elevations within the 486 square mile county run from 20 to 700 feet. Soybeans, corn, hay and wheat cover much of the farm region.

Evansburg State Park's 1,000 acres near Collegeville is the only Dept. of Environmental Resources land in Montgomery and only one small gameland is to be found. The county is part of the Special Regulations Area.

Food, lodging and services, contact: Valley Forge Convention and Visitors Bureau, P.O. Box 311, Norristown, PA 19404. Phone (800) 441-3549 and (610) 278-3558.

IN BRIEF

State Gamelands: 158 acres

State Parks & Forests: 1,000 acres

Farm-Game Co-op: 10,992 acres (128 farms)

Safety Zone Lands: 4,459 acres (31 tracts)

Forest-Game Co-op: None

1993 Buck/Doe Harvest: 638 / 1,104

1994 Doe Permit Allocation: 10,000

Deer Density/FSM: 32

Deer Density Goal/FSM: 5

Average Buck Harvest/FSM: 7.2

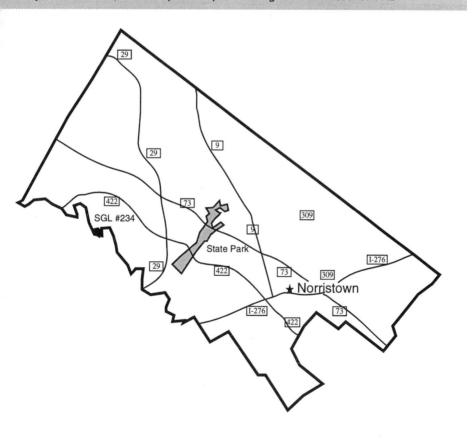

NORTHAMPTON COUNTY

Bordering the Delaware River and New Jersey to the east, Northampton County's 376 square miles are covered 34 percent in forest and 42 percent in farms. Elevations range from 140 to 1,660 feet from its rolling, farm-country lowlands north to the rim of the Appalachian (Blue) Mountains.

Farms support beef and dairy cattle, primarily, with croplands growing wheat, corn, alfalfa, oats and soybeans. Numerous peach, apple and pear orchards can also be found.

With neighboring Lehigh, Northampton County annually ranks in the top 10 counties for bucks harvested per square wooded mile.

Jacobsburg State Park near Belfast is the sole Dept. of Environmental Resources land in the county, offering hunters 1,000 acres. SGL No. 168 near Wind Gap stretches along the Blue Mountain across 5,173 acres.

Food, lodging and services, contact: Lehigh Valley Convention and Visitors Bureau, Inc., P.O. Box 20785, Lehigh Valley, PA 18002. Phone (800) 747-0561 and (610) 882-9200.

IN BRIEF

State Gamelands: 5,173 acres

State Parks & Forests: 1,000 acres

Farm-Game Co-op: 40,297 acres (435 farms)

Safety Zone Lands: 3,924 acres (17 tracts)

Forest-Game Co-op: None

1993 Buck/Doe Harvest: 949 / 910

1994 Doe Permit Allocation: 7,750

Deer Density/FSM: 36

Deer Density Goal/FSM: 27

Average Buck Harvest/FSM: 7.5

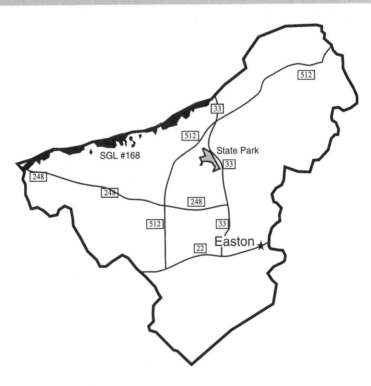

PHILADELPHIA COUNTY

To many people's surprise, deer hunting (bowhunting only) is permitted within the city's borders. Covering 136 square miles, the county (city) ranges in elevation from sea level to 440 feet.

As the ninth most populated city in the nation it seems incongruous that whitetails would be present, but they cause severe damage to vegetation in some places and present hazards when crossing thoroughfares. A few farms within city limits produce corn, a special attractant to whitetails.

In1993, bowhunters tagged 37 deer within city limits, hardly denting its growing herd.

No public lands are available for hunting nor does the Game Commission attempt to manage whitetails in Philadelphia. Most bowhunting is done on private estates.

Food, lodging and services, contact: Philadelphia Convention and Visitors Bureau, 1515 Market St., Suite 2020, Philadelphia, PA 19102. Phone: (800) 312-WKND and (215) 636-1666.

IN BRIEF

State Gamelands: None

State Parks & Forests: None

Farm-Game Co-op: None

Safety Zone Lands: None

Forest-Game Co-op: None

1993 Buck/Doe Harvest: 26 / 11

1994 Doe Permit Allocation: 500

Deer Density/FSM: N/A

Deer Density Goal/FSM: N/A

Average Buck Harvest/FSM: N/A

DELAWARE COUNTY

With more than 3,000 residents per square mile, Delaware County's minimal (11 percent) amount of woodland and six percent of farmland offers little space for free-roaming deer. Nevertheless, the county, like most of the far Southeast, has an over-abundance of the adaptable animals and few open lands on which to hunt them.

Sportsmen with permission of private landowners and farmers take only about 500-600 deer annually. Many are bucks, accounting for a variable 'per wooded square mile' harvest which in recent years has ranged from 5.9 to a phenomenal 13.1.

Elevations rise from the flat lowlands at sea level with rolling lowlands rising to 500 feet. Crops produced here include alfalfa, hay, corn and soybeans.

The relatively small, densely populated suburban county offers no farm-game or safety zone programs. It's in the Southeast's Special Regulations Area.

Food, lodging and services, contact: Delaware County Convention and Visitors Bureau, Inc., 200 East State St., Suite 100, Media, PA 19063. Phone (800) 343-3983 and (610) 565-3679.

IN BRIEF

State Gamelands: None

State Parks & Forests: None

Farm-Game Co-op: None

Safety Zone Lands: None

Forest-Game Co-op: None

1993 Buck/Doe Harvest: 284 / 840

1994 Doe Permit Allocation: 5,000

Deer Density/FSM: 52

Deer Density Goal/FSM: 5

Average Buck Harvest/FSM: 8.4

SCHUYLKILL COUNTY

More like the northeastern counties in some of its natural and topographic features, 71 percent of Schuylkill's 782 square miles hold forests. The land is mountainous yielding in many places to gently rolling farmlands. Elevations span 380 to 2,094 feet.

Agricultural interests occupy 20 percent of the land with nearly two-thirds in crops including potatoes, corn, hay, oats and wheat along with peach and apple orchards.

In a recent year more than three dozen Schuylkill farms registered as "deer damage farms,"' permitting January hunting for antlerless deer while attesting to the their raids on crops.

Locust Lake State Park near Mahanoy City (1,045 acres), Tuscarora State Park near Barnesville (1,100 acres) and more than 9,000 acres in scattered tracts of Weiser State Forest, all offer good whitetail numbers.

Ten gamelands are scattered across Schuylkill. The largest include: SGL No. 110 near Auburn with 10,093 acres; SGL No. 106 at Drehersville, 9,197 acres; and SGL No. 80 near Rock with 8,236 acres.

Food, lodging and services, contact: Schuylkill County Visitors Bureau, P.O. Box 237, Pottsville, PA 17901. Phone: (800) 765-7282 and (717) 622-7700.

IN BRIEF

State Gamelands: 38,099 acres

State Parks & Forests: 11,878 acres

Farm-Game Co-op: 68,880 acres (669 farms)

Safety Zone Lands: 10,317 acres (76 tracts)

Forest-Game Co-op: 20,236 acres

1993 Buck/Doe Harvest: 3,098 / 4,993

1994 Doe Permit Allocation: 15,100

Deer Density/FSM: 32

Deer Density Goal/FSM: 20

Average Buck Harvest/FSM: 5.6

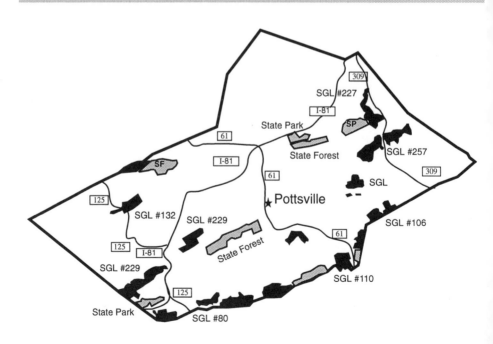

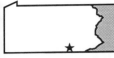

YORK COUNTY

York's hilly and mountainous north yields to rolling lowlands in its south. It's bordered by the Susquehanna River on its west. Elevations run from 109 to 1,440 feet.

Woodland covers 27 percent of the county which is largely farm country. Cattle and croplands compose 52 percent of its 906 square miles. York's rich fields produce barley, soybeans, corn, potatoes, and tobacco.

Four gamelands, including 1,517-acre SGL No. 242 at Rossville and 1,166-acre SGL No. 243 at Franklintown, hold deer. York County has no state parks or forest lands.

In terms of buck kills per square wooded mile, York annually ranks among the top counties. The county's woods and farms support an overpopulation of whitetails according to Game Commission biologists, to the dismay of most farmers.

Food, lodging and services, contact: York County Convention and Visitors Bureau, 1 Market Way East, York, PA 17401. Phone: (800) 673-2429 and (717) 848-4000.

IN BRIEF

State Gamelands: 4,014 acres

State Parks & Forests: None

Farm-Game Co-op: 74,232 acres (667 farms)

Safety Zone Lands: 25,808 acres (194 tracts)

Forest-Game Co-op: None

1993 Buck/Doe Harvest: 2,572 / 5,310

1994 Doe Permit Allocation: 23,300

Deer Density/FSM: 43

Deer Density Goal/FSM: 18

Average Buck Harvest/FSM: 10.5

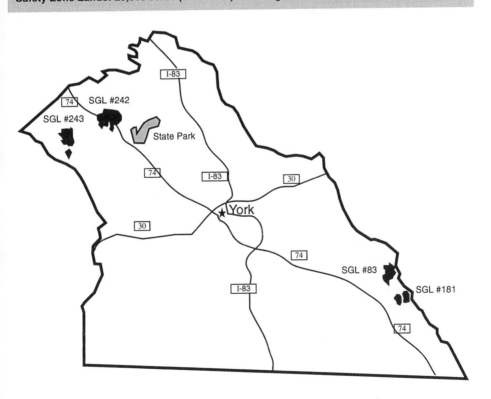

FEDERAL HUNTING LANDS

U.S. Army Corps of Engineers

The U.S. Army Corps of Engineers owns and manages 23 facilities in Pennsylvania open to recreational use. While fishing is the main attraction on Corps' impoundments, some facilities also offer hunting lands surrounding the lakes and dams. Many of the properties adjoin or are within state forests, parks and gamelands.

Federal properties open to hunting include: Raystown Lake (Huntingdon County), Francis Walter Dam (Carbon-Luzerne), Crooked Creek lake (Armstrong), Blue Marsh Lake (Berks), Cowanesque Lake (Tioga), Loyalhanna Lake (Westmoreland), Mahoning Creek Lake (Armstrong, Jefferson and Indiana), Shenango River Lake (Mercer), Tioga-Hammond Lakes (Tioga), Tionesta Lake (Forest), Woodcock Creek Lake (Crawford) and Youghiogheny Lake (Somerset and Fayette).

For additional information and brochures, call or write the office closest to the specific facility.

▶ *U.S. Army Engineer Dist., POB Box 1715, Baltimore, MD 21203-1715. Phone: (301) 962-3693.*

▶*U.S. Army Engineer Dist., Wanamaker Bldg., 1001 Penn Square East, Philadelphia, PA 19107-3390. Phone: (215) 656-6515.*

▶ *U.S. Army Engineer Dist., Wm. S. Moorhead Federal Bldg., 1000 Liberty Ave., Pittsburgh, PA 15222-4186. Phone: (412) 644-6924.*

Military Installations

Two military installations in the state permit deer hunting, with restrictions. Officers may also conduct controlled hunts to reduce deer numbers within the federal lands. These are not 'public' lands in the true sense of the word, rather restricted grounds with access by permit.

Beginning in 1994, the Pennsylvania Game Commission issued 'deer control permits' to military bases. This allows the bases to conduct deer hunts without requiring participating hunters to have doe licenses from the counties in which the facilities are located. Drawings are conducted whenever applications exceed available permits. If applicants are fewer than the license allotment, individuals are allowed more than one permit.

By law, military installations may set their own seasons, typically for limited periods between October and February.

Military bases offering hunting opportunities include:

▶ *Fort Indiantown Gap, USAG, Annville, PA 17003-5011. Phone (717) 865-5444 or (717) 865-2362. (18,000 acres in Lebanon County)*

▶ *Letterkenny Army Depot, Chambersburg, PA 17201-4150. Phone (717) 267-8300. (19,000 acres in Franklin County)*

National Wildlife Refuges

Two National Wildlife Refuges are found within Pennsylvania borders. Tinicum N.W.R. is an urban sanctuary in Philadelphia. Hunting is not permitted.

Erie National Wildlife Refuge in Guys Mills, Crawford County, east of Meadville, permits hunting on much of its 8,516 acres. The refuge is divided into the Seneca Di-

vision and Sugar Lake Division, each with different ecological attributes.
For information write: Erie N.W.R., RD1, Wood Duck Lane, Guys Mills, PA 16327. Phone: (814) 789-3585.

Delaware Water Gap National Recreation Area

The Delaware Water Gap National Recreation includes the Delaware River in Monroe and Pike counties and New Jersey. Under jurisdiction of the National Park Service, hunting is permitted on portions of the 70,000-acre facility, about half of which is in Pennsylvania.

For information, write: Delaware Water Gap N.R.A., Bushkill, PA 18324. Phone: (717) 588-2435.

Allegheny National Forest

The most notable federal parcel in the state is Allegheny National Forest, spanning more than a half-million acres south of the New York border in Warren, McKean, Elk and Forest counties. The multiple-use, 512,000-acre forest is a whitetail, small game and turkey hunter's delight.

The focal point for anglers, boaters and some hunters, who gain access to the backwoods via boats and canoes, is the Allegheny Reservoir. The high-walled Kinzua Dam blocks the waters of the Allegheny River, backing the lake 27 miles into New York's Allegany State Park and the Seneca Indian Reservation.

Black bear, deer, grouse, squirrel, snowshoe hare and waterfowl abound in the region and many hunters utilize the numerous motels and bed-and-breakfast operations nearby (see individual county listings for information sources).

More than 65 million board feet of timber is harvested from the Allegheny N. F. each year, creating a diverse array of second growth habitat, prime for whitetails. The forest stands include black cherry, yellow poplar, white ash, red maple, sugar maple and scatterings of softwoods.

It should be noted that numerous in-holdings are found within the federal property. Free maps, available from the forest service, designate the private lands as do signs and other markers along backwoods roads and within the woodlands.

Nearby towns of Warren, Bradford, Kane and Ridgway offer food, lodging and shopping. Numerous private campgrounds are also located within or adjacent to the national forest. A few national forest campgrounds stay open through the deer season.

For hunting information and maps, write: Allegheny National Forest, P.O. Box 847, Warren, PA 16365. Phone: (814) 723-5150.

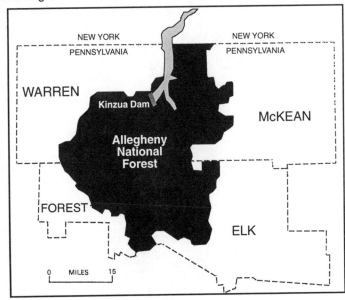

PART
V
MEMORIES OF THE HUNT

Chapter
27

HOW TO SCORE YOUR BUCK

"How many points?"

That's the question thousands of Pennsylvanians ask one another each deer season and after when they compare notes on their annual trophies.

Before that, probably at camp, someone will argue about the actual number of points on a buck's headgear.

"Hang a ring on it," someone will advise upon scrutinizing a short point.

That's long been the been the standard by which Pennsylvania hunters decide whether or not a "cheater," brow configuration or elongated burr projection qualifies as a countable "point."

Any hunter who's been in the troop for a year or two knows there are "8-pointers" and there are "8-POINTERS." More than a mere count of tine-tips is necessary for assessing the quality of a rack.

Today's deer hunters are becoming increasingly sophisticated and more sportsmen and women are curious as to the Boone & Crockett score that a particularly large trophy might garner. Bowhunters refer to it as the Pope & Young score. Measurement methods are the same for both groups.

So how do you go about determining the score of your best buck?

As only a few certified Boone & Crockett measurers live in Pennsylvania (many game commission personnel are official scorers), there's no need to have your rack scored officially unless it approaches record book size. But if you're able to follow directions, anyone can get a rough score of his or her personal trophy.

While the B&C system may seem, at first, complex, it's simply a matter of jotting down measurements of specific segments on a set of antlers, then adding up the score.

It takes time and concentration but it's not as complex as might be imagined. I've never been a math whiz but I've scored dozens of racks and after tabulating the first its relative simplicity is understood.

But, as fair warning, don't attempt to score your antlers on a night when your patience is at a low ebb or some disturbance from family, friends or telephone is likely. Have a friend join you for the scoring session. Not only will his or her interest be piqued but an extra set of hands is always helpful in achieving an accurate reading.

While some of the directions may have to be read two or three times, by following the guidelines and the sketches on the official score sheet, anyone can get a close accounting of the B&C score of a rack, big or small.

Racks and skulls must undergo a 60-day drying period before being measured. But that shouldn't matter much for your personal tabulations.

First, understand that whitetail comparisons are made in two categories: typical and non-typical. The majority of antlers will be "typical" in that the two sides are somewhat symmetrical and the tines grow off the main beam in normal fashion, even though they may be somewhat unbalanced.

Non-typical racks may have unusual curvature, jut from the main beam in varied angles and numbers or simply show great imbalance from one side to the other. While measurements of non-typical antlers may take a bit more time, techniques for scoring both are the same. Only certain additions and subtractions differ. That will be explained later.

To qualify for the record book, a B&C typical buck must measure at least 170 points; 140 for the P&Y book. Non-typical minimum is 195 for B&C and 170 for a bowhunter's P&Y consideration.

For listing in the Pennsylvania Game Commission's records a 140 typical gun-buck will make "the book." Non-typical gun-bucks must measure at least 160 B&C points. For Keystone bowhunters, a typical buck must measure a minimum 115 and non-typical, 160.

No matter. Most of us will never need worry about qualifying for either halls of fame. But many buck hunters would like to know how their trophies — no matter what the size — "measure up."

Oh yes. One more caution. Don't be shocked upon learning that your biggest buck may fall far short of your expectations. Learning that your trophy only tapes out to a 99 brings more respect for those humongous wall-hangers that most of us only see in magazines.

So grab your best rack, a tape measure, a copy of the scoring form, a pencil and a cold drink — and get started.

How To Score Your Rack

First, you'll need a flexible steel tape. Cloth tapes can be used but aren't as accurate.

Keep in mind that measurements are made to the nearest 1/8th inch (rounded off to the next highest 1/8th inch when necessary). To avoid confusion, record all fractional measurements in eighths (Example: 3/4-inch would be written as 6/8; 1/2-inch would be 4/8, etc.)

When it's necessary to change the direction of measurement, as when a beam or long tine takes a sharp turn or curve, use a pencil to mark a "control point" and swing the tape at this point.

Copy the official B&C Score Sheet on which to record the following measurements (refer to diagram on the form for the varied measurement sectors):

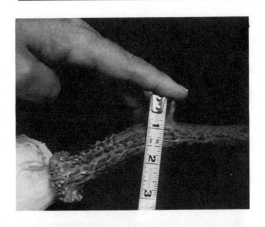

(A) Number of points on each antler

To be counted as a point, a projection must be at least one inch long and its length must exceed the width of its base. All points are measured from the tip of point to the nearest edge of the beam. (Although the beam tip is counted as a point, it is not measured as a point as its score is taken into account when measuring the main beam.)

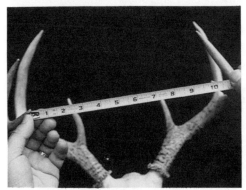

(B) Tip to tip spread

Easy enough. Simply measure the spread between the tips of the main beams. This point (photo) does not qualify.

(C) Greatest (outside) spread

Make this measurement parallel to the top of the skull (more properly at a right angle to the centerline from the skull's nose to the crown) at the widest spread. Do not hold the tape diagonally or your measurement will be flawed.

An official Boone & Crockett Scoring form can be found on page 298. It is recommended that several copies be made for use during scoring sessions

(D) Inside spread of main beams
Make this measurement at the beams' widest spread. (Note: After measuring the lengths of the main beams (Category F) return to this category to determine Spread Credit. Spread Credit is given if the inside spread is less than or equal to the length of the longest antler. If applicable, enter the spread measurement under Column 1.

But if the spread exceeds the longer antler's length, enter the antler measurement under Column 1. (Example: Assume a rack holds an 18-inch inside spread and the longest main beam is 19 inches. The figure (18) should be recorded in Column 1. But if the rack has an 18-inch inside spread and the longest main beam is 17 inches, enter 17 in Column A. Finally, if the spread exceeds the (longest) beam length, subtract the numbers. In this example (18-17=1) enter in Column D.)

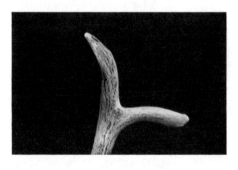

(E) Total lengths of all abnormal points
Abnormal points include drop tines and other peculiar growths that may poke from the sides or bottom of the main beams or from other places. Measure in the usual manner, add the total score and enter in Column E-4.

If no abnormal points exist, ignore this category. (Note: On a rack being measured as "typical," the total lengths of these points will be deducted at the end of the scoring session. On a non-typical rack, abnormal points are added.)

(F) Length of main beams
This measurement is taken from the lowest outside edge of the burr (at a point directly above the eyes or eye sockets) along each beam's outer curve to its very tip.

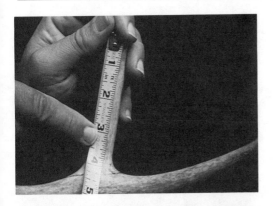

(G) Length of each point (G-1 to G-7)

Remember, a point must be at least an inch long to be included in the G category. The brow tines (if present) are measured as G-1. Points G-2, G-3, etc. are the points progressively farther from the skull (see diagram).To measure precisely, draw a line where the tine intersects the beam.

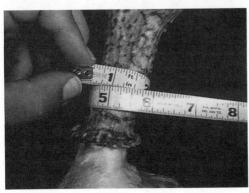

(H) Circumferences (H-1 to H-4)

Circumferences are taken at their narrowest spots between the points. If the brow tine is missing, take measurements H-1 and H-2 at the smallest circumference between the burr and point G-2.

The measuring is now complete.

For all categories F through H, subtract the right antler/left antler numbers and enter the figure as the total in Column 4.

If the rack is being scored as "typical," add Columns, 1, 2 and 3 and subtract Column 4. That's your final rough score.

If the rack is to be scored as "non-typical," do the same but instead of subtracting the score of all abnormal points (E), add it.

Some racks may be scored as either typical or non-typical. The non-typical rack will always have the greatest point-value as no deductions are made.

To avoid the inherent complexity of determining your own B&C score, some minor measurement details that could cause confusion have been ignored here. That's why trained measurers are certified by the B&C and P&Y clubs for trophies potentially eligible for making "the book."

Even the pros will often disagree upon measurements of especially notable trophies and must sometimes remeasure a dozen times or more to determine an honest and accurate rating.

For additional information on scoring and whitetail records, write:

* Boone & Crockett Club, 205 S. Patrick St., Alexandria, VA 22314.
* Pope & Young Club, 1804 Borah, Moscow, ID 83843.

Chapter 28

HOW TO AGE YOUR DEER

How hard is it to estimate the age of the bucks or does hanging on the camp meat pole?

"It's really not all that difficult," suggests Mike Ondik. "Up until about 3-1/2 years, at least."

Ondik, a well-known whitetail deer lecturer with the National Rifle Association's Whitetail Superclinic seminar series and former technician at the Penn State Cooperative Wildlife Research Unit, has aged thousands of deer in the past 30 years.

"At 3-1/2 the teeth will have a significant amount of wear," Ondik explained. Notably, more of the dark dentine will be visible. Aging deer, particularly those over 3-1/2 years old, is an "iffy" matter. Then again, few hunters ever shoot deer that old. Younger deer can be aged by anyone willing to spend the time to learn how.

Number of teeth, tooth wear and the exposure of dentine are the three criteria for judging age, Ondik explained. However, it must be understood that variables will occur, resulting in an incorrect analysis. Diet is the prime influence.

"Deer that live in areas with sandy soil wear their teeth down a whole lot faster than those living where there's silt or loam," said Ondik. "The sand on vegetation they eat will wear down the teeth faster over a period of a few years."

The tooth-reading method is the only one by which a hunter and most biologists can age a deer in the field. Contrary to a long-standing belief still held by some people, says Ondik, antler points mean absolutely nothing in establishing a buck's age.

A costly cross-section microscopic method is more reliable than visibly studying a jawbone but even that is seldom necessary and often inaccurate, according to Ondik.

So how's it done?

Let's begin with the easiest deer to age — fawns and yearlings.

Whitetails are born with 20 teeth — eight front teeth in the lower jaw and 12 molars (three on the top and lower jaws on each side). All are "milk teeth," soft, sharp structures which are replaced within 17 months. As the jaw grows, more room is provided for additional teeth. An adult deer has 32.

Through 1-1/2 years, these grinding teeth provide a simple, accurate method for determining age. All anyone needs to look at are the teeth on one of the lower jawbones.

In addition to the teeth lining the jawbone, deer also have teeth in the front of the mouth called pincers — four on each side including a canine tooth and three incisors. There are no teeth on the front of the upper jaw.

It must be pointed out that confusion in counting teeth can be a problem for anyone who gazes into a deer's mouth or studies a jawbone the first time. That's largely because individual molars are composed of *cuspids* — prominences or "points" on the crown of each tooth. At first glance, the cuspids look like individual teeth. Look closely and the individual molars are easily discerned.

Here's a simplified method for aging your deer.

* Fawns will be 5-6 months of age by the archery season. At this stage their relatively small sizes or the presence of "buttons" on the heads of young bucks will reveal their general ages. By the gun season, most fawns will be at least seven months old. By then they have permanent pincers at the very front of the jaw and the early growth stage of the second permanent molar (cheek tooth) can be seen.

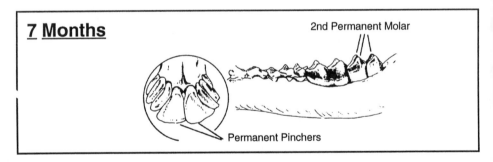

7 Months

2nd Permanent Molar

Permanent Pinchers

* A 1-1/2-year-old buck or doe will have lost its milk teeth and will show a third cheek tooth. It may be just beginning to "erupt" or as much as half-grown and show little dentine.

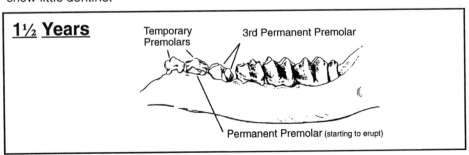

1½ Years

Temporary Premolars

3rd Permanent Premolar

Permanent Premolar (starting to erupt)

* A 2-1/2-year old whitetail begins to show some tooth wear, which increases as a deer ages. The ratio of light (enamel) and dark (dentine) areas continues to change as a deer ages. The older the deer, the more visible dentine. By 2-1/2 the dentine on the first molar (nearest the front of the jaw) and the enamel are about equal. The second and third molars show more enamel than dentine.

2½ Years

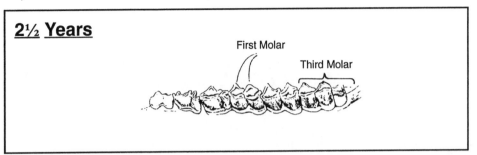

*By age 3-1/2, dentine on the first molar is greater than the amount of enamel. Both are about equal on the second molar and the third molar will show less dentine than enamel.

3½ Years

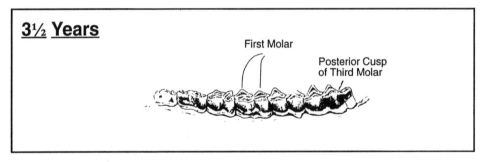

*Older deer are extremely difficult to age, and few of us will ever have the opportunity to do it. By the time all three molars show more of the brownish-black dentine than enamel, a deer is probably 4-1/2 years or older. With age the crests and enamel are ground away. The darker and more stunted (from wear) the teeth, the older the deer.

After studying a few jawbones (which, on a recently harvested deer, are exposed by slitting the cheek skin) most hunters can make an educated and accurate guess as to a deer's age.

Quick Venison Meatball Stew

Chapter
29

VENISON
Double Your Pleasure

Thousands of Pennsylvania families rely on a deer or two in the freezer each year. This low-cholesterol meat is healthy and nutritious, no matter how it's prepared.

In our home, venison shows up in everything from hamburgers and spaghetti sauces to grilled steaks and chops, chip steak sandwiches, ring bologna and gourmet meals when "company comes."

Our kids grew up with venison and now are serving it on their own tables.

Of course, this entire book could be filled with venison recipes and many books contain just that. To whet your tastebuds a bit, try one or all of these delights from the Fegely dinner table.

...........Betty Lou Fegely

BASIC VENISON MEATBALLS

2 eggs
1/2 cup milk
2 lbs. ground venison
1 cup chopped onions
1/4 cup dry bread crumbs
1 tsp. salt
1/4 tsp. McCormick's pepper
1 tsp. Worchestershire sauce

Heat oven to 400 F. In large bowl combine eggs and milk; blend well. Stir in remaining ingredients; mix well. Shape into balls 1 to 1 1/2 inches in diameter. Place in an ungreased 15x10x1-inch pan and bake at 400 F. for 15-20 minutes or until lightly browned and thoroughly cooked. Can be frozen and used later in various recipes. Great for parties and appetizers.

GRILLED VENISON CHOPS

Marinade
Combine the following for marinade:
1/2 cup butter
3 tb. brown sugar
6 oz. red wine
1 tb. Worchestershire sauce
dash of garlic powder
8 venison chops or tenderloin cut into 1 1/2-inch thick slices

Place the venison and marinade in a zip-lock type bag and refrigerate for at least three hours (or up to three days). Spray grill with Pam, preheat and place venison over hot coals for 3-5 minutes on each side. Baste with leftover marinade and extra garlic or brush lightly with bottled barbecue sauce. Be careful not to overcook. This cut is best served medium rare to medium and tends to dry out quickly on the grill. Serve with baked potato and fresh tossed salad. Easy, but delicious.

VENISON SHISHKABOB

Marinade
1 cup salad oil
1 clove garlic, smashed
3/4 cup white wine
1 tsp. oregano
1 tsp. basil
parsley
salt and pepper
1 1/2 lb. boneless venison steak, cut in 2 inch cubes

Mix all seven ingredients and place in zip-lock type bag with venison cubes. Marinade at least three hours in refrigerator.

10 cubes sweet onions
10 cubes green pepper
10 cherry tomatoes
10 mushroom caps

Alternate cubes of venison, onion, green pepper, mushroom caps and cherry tomatoes on skewers. Brush lightly with marinade. Grill, turning once, for 3-5 min. on each side. Serves four. Serve with grilled potatoes, carrots and salad. Great for company.

QUICK VENISON MEATBALL STEW

1 (10 1/2-oz) can condensed beef broth
1 1/3 cups water
1 (16-oz) pkg New England style frozen vegetables
16 frozen venison meatballs (see basic venison meatball recipe)
1 medium onion, chopped
1 tsp. basil
1 tsp. McCormick's seasoned pepper
1/4 cup flour
1/4 cup cold water

In 4-quart saucepan or Dutch oven, combine all ingredients except flour and 1/4 cup water. Bring to a boil. Reduce heat; cover and simmer 10 minutes or until meatballs are thoroughly heated and vegetables are tender, stirring occasionally. In a small jar with a tight fitting lid, combine water and flour. Shake well. Gradually stir into stew mixture and cook until thickened, stirring frequently. Serve in individual bowls. Serves four.
Great with applesauce and warm Italian bread.

CAROL'S VENISON FINGERS

Marinade
1/2 cup olive oil
1/4 cup red wine vinegar
1 tsp. dried oregano
1 tsp. dried basil
1 clove garlic,crushed
1 lb. venison steaks
1 cup unseasoned cracker-meal
1/4 cup olive oil
4 tb. margerine- butter will burn too easily

Combine oil, vinegar, garlic, and seasoning for marinade. Cut steak into finger-sized strips. Place single layer in a glass dish or in a sealable bag and cover with marinade. Marinate in refrigerator overnight or a few days. Remove the meat and dredge in cracker-meal. Pat the meal firmly into meat on all sides. Bring olive oil and margarine to 325 degrees (medium heat) in an electric frying pan. Saute the strips until golden. Drain on paper towels. Serve hot as an appetizer or in larger pieces for entree. Serves 4 as an entree. 6-8 as appetizer.
Unique and delicious.

Chapter 30

DEER CAMP REVISITED
Palaces In The Popple

Pennsylvania deer camps, like the hunters who inhabit them, come in a variety of sizes, shapes, smells, sounds and personalities. But they share one characteristic: They're palaces to hunters who annually migrate to them for buck hunts.

No matter if the "camp" is carpeted, water flows at the twist of a handle and the bathroom is walled with tile or the structure is subject to northwinds that sneak through holes in the siding, water's carted from a nearby spring and the nearest "relief room" is a tumbledown outhouse 25 cold and snowy paces from the cabin door, or it's simply a tent set on the edge of the deer woods, countless sportsmen know them as the places where memories are born.

Today, unlike the past, many deer camps also have ladies in residence. Once totally a male bastion, an increasing number of girls and women are now sharing in the joys of deer camp.

Here, in Pennsylvania, deer camp is solid tradition. While referred to as "camps," few can hold up to the turn-of-the-century whitetail encampments when canvas tents or log shacks, open fires and oak meat poles were standard items. Creature comforts, such as beds with mattresses and spigots with water, were luxuries.

I'm not old enough to have experienced deer camps of the 1920's and earlier. Few of us are. But I vividly recall the more modern versions of the buckskin camps where blaze orange would have been scorned, duck coats or Woolrich suits being the standard dress for the hunt.

Today, I'm pleased to report, the camp in which several friends and I spend the opening days of the annual hunt is considerably more comfortable.

But I'm privileged to have experienced a sampling of the rough 'n tough deer camp of the past when several friends and I set up shop in tents for a buck season hunt.

Like heirlooms handed down generation to generation, kids exposed to deer camps seldom throw away the memories, themselves adopting their own friends and camps as they grow older.

Most hunters gain entry to a camp courtesy of a father, uncle or some special person who thought enough of them to share the experience and the mystique — passing on the tradition.

I can still remember my first night at Dad's deer camp, the same in which my late grandfather was a member. I was 18 and a freshman at Lock Haven State College (now University) in Clinton County. Dad hosted me for the opening day of buck season at Tall Maples Hunting Lodge in Sullivan County, about a 90-minute drive east of school. (I even managed a second day of hunting by getting lost along the Loyalsock on the opener, wandering around in the dark for over four hours, and finally being found too late to go back to school that night.)

As I vividly recall, the camp was alive with action, from long-johned members making hasty runs to the two-holer to cigar munching poker players surrounding the long wooden dining table. Another contingent sitting in the small living room, near the woodstove, told tales which grew taller by the year. Bucks got bigger and wiser and hunters grew hardier and smarter as the night wore on.

Hands caringly stroked the stocks of guns new and old as they were polished and oiled. The old standards, largely .32 Winchester Specials or some other type of "brush guns," many without the high-power scopes that today top deer rifles, lined a stand-up rack along the far wall like soldiers at attention, awaiting their call.

On the eve of the opener talk was always of past hunts and happenings that took place in camp before and after the actual hunting expeditions. Jokes and pranks flowed as easily as the Seagrams and Ballantine stocked in the camp refrigerator.

With it all there was a certain anxiety; an experience one seeks to savor and not let go until the early hours of morning when the subconscious finally relinquishes dreams of big-racked bucks and sleep comes reluctantly. Most often it's an abrupt nap with the dreamer jarred to consciousness by the clanging of a broad-faced alarm clock.

The smells of bacon and fresh-brewed coffee drifted up the spiraling stairs, expediting the task of dressing on a morning where a peek through the window revealed a new-fallen blanket of tracking snow.

As I write this it's that time of year again. Tonight the fires will burn bright, curling woodsmoke into the crisp night throughout the northwoods. Tomorrow, before first light, the bobbing beams of flashlights will pilot orange-coated hunters to their favored stands in the woods and field edges. By dusk camp poles will hang heavy with deer. If not, talk of the day's misses and the ritual of snipping shirt-tails will fill the hours and thereafter sleep will come more gently.

I'd like to have been part of a 1900 deer camp, mainly to verify my belief that little has changed among avid deer hunters and the spirit of deer camp over the near century. Certainly, accommodations are more comfortable now and camps are easier to access. Four-wheel-drive trucks and Jeeps now fill the front yards of the mountain camps. No longer need anyone curse getting stuck in the snow and mud with the Old Model T, or hiking and mule-tripping into the hinterlands as our forefathers did.

Hunters dress differently, too, and deer are more abundant than when our great-grandfathers took to the forests. Variable scopes enhance shiny guns, some with plastic stocks of which my grandfather would surely make comment. The arsenal is stacked on the camp rack and the line-up of Cordura and Goretex boots in front of the door underscores a modern time.

But I'll bet anticipation's the same as it was in those wind-blown tents of a century past. And the smells are similar, too. Whether the alluring odor of Hoppes No. 9 or the addictive scent of frying bacon and black coffee wafting through the camp kitchen, an escape to deer camp satisfies and stimulates all of the senses.

I like it that way. It takes me back to the time of the lumberjacks, miners and hard-working townsfolk who labored hard above ground and under to feed their families. But once each year they'd band together to play hard in the backwoods deer camps, bringing home venison as a bonus.

This is the season that urges me to draw John Madson's "The White-Tailed Deer" (Winchester, 1961) from my bookshelf and once again read his poem, "Palace In The Popple," shared here with John's personal blessing.

"Palace In The Popple"

It's a smoky, raunchy boars' nest
With an unswept, drafty floor
And pillowticking curtains
And knife scars on the door.
The smell of a pine-knot fire
From a stovepipe that's come loose
Mingles sweetly with the bootgrease
And the Copenhagen snoose.
There are work-worn 30-30s
With battered, steel-shod stocks,
And drying lines of longjohns
And of steaming, pungent socks.
There's a table for the Bloody Four
And their game of two-card draw,
And there's deep and dreamless sleeping
On bunk ticks stuffed with straw.
Jerry and Jake stand by the stove,
Their gun talk loud and hot.
Bogie has drawn a pair of kings
And is raking in the pot.
Frank's been drafted again as cook
And is peeling some spuds for stew
While Bruce wanders by in baggy drawers

Reciting "Dan McGrew."
No where on earth is fire so warm
Nor coffee so infernal
Nor whiskers so stiff, jokes so rich
Nor hope blooming so eternal.
A man can live for a solid week
In his old underbritches
And walk like a man and spit when he wants
And scratch himself where he itches.
I tell you, boys, there's no place else
Where I'd rather be, come fall,
Where I eat like a bear and sing like a wolf
And feel like I'm bull-pine tall.
In that raunchy cabin out in the bush
In the land of the raven and loon,
With a tracking snow lying new to the ground
At the end of the Rutting Moon.

Deer camp!
May woodsmoke forever curl from its chimney.

(Right) Woolrich clothing, as worn here by Ed Kaufmann prior to the state's more restrictive blaze orange law, has been a standard on the deer camp scene for more than 150 years. The company continues to make quality hunting wear at its Clinton County plant.

ORGANIZATIONS

SPORTSMEN'S ORGANIZATIONS/CONSERVANCIES

Pennsylvania organizations whose interests and work touch on deer management, deer hunting, youth education and legislative and conservation interests were asked to provide profiles of their group's purposes and activities.

The following organizations responded. For more information, write or call the addresses provided.

PENNSYLVANIA DEER ASSOCIATION, INC.

The Pennsylvania Deer Association was formed in 1978 and today has more than 1,000 members. Our purpose is to educate ourselves and the public regarding the ecological, recreational and economic importance of the Pennsylvania white-tailed deer. We strongly emphasize ethics and the inclusion of youth in the sport. Each year we are involved in youth events/programs that promote a better understanding of our outdoor heritage.

Publications: "The Browse Line" (Quarterly) and "The Yearling" (Quarterly-Youth).

For Information, write: Pennsylvania Deer Association, 215 Hunters Rd., Newville, PA 17241. Phone: (717) 776-7248.

PENNSYLVANIANS FOR THE RESPONSIBLE USE OF ANIMALS

Pennsylvanians for the Responsible Use of Animals (PRUA) is a federation of Pennsylvania agricultural, biomedical/veterinary research, entertainment and professional wildlife management organizations that support continued, responsible use of animals.

PRUA offers a forum for member organizations to work together in communicating their concerns for humane animal handling issues. The coalition also provides factual information to the public, media, elected officials and those responsible for the care of animals. Sponsors of Hunters Sharing the Harvest, a program to supply venison to the homeless and soup kitchens statewide.

Publication: Newsletter and PRUA Briefs published 3-4 times annually.

For more information, contact Kenneth Brandt, P.O. Box 61, Elizabethtown, PA 17022. Phone: (717) 367-5223.

PENNSYLVANIA SPORTSMEN FOR THE DISABLED, INC.

In March, 1989, a sportsmen's group was formed with the primary purpose and goals of securing accessible hunting and fishing facilities, public & private, for all disabled, handicapped and blind individuals in Pennsylvania. This a premier outdoor organization securing access for all outdoor recreation. Activities include Awards Dinner, Christmas Party, "Special Day For Special Kids" and Family Day.

Publication: "Sportsmen's Newsletter" (Monthly)

For information, write: PA Sportsmen for the Disabled, Inc., R.D. #1, Box 470, New Alexandria, PA 15670. Phone: (412) 668-7439, (800) 484-7505 PIN 1989.

PENNSYLVANIA FEDERATION OF SPORTSMEN'S CLUBS, INC.

Since 1932, the PFSC has been an aggressive advocate for the sportsmen of the Commonwealth and of quality conservation practices of all of Pennsylvania's natural resources. Headquartered in Harrisburg, the federation is the most effective voice of the sportsmen on Capitol Hill. Its proud tradition of legislative accomplishments can be traced to 1937 when PFSC was the driving force behind the passage of Pennsylvania's Clean Streams Act.

Publication: "On Target" (Bi-monthly)

For Information, write: Pennsylvania Federation of Sportsmen's Clubs, 2426 N. Second St., Harrisburg, PA 17110. Phone: (717) 232-3480.

UNIFIED SPORTSMEN OF PENNSYLVANIA

The Unified Sportsmen of Pennsylvania was founded in 1983 as a non-profit, corporate body for the purpose of bringing comprehensive attention to important problems related to hunting, fishing and trapping. The organization also promotes and maintains the highest standards in conservation of our natural resources. USP works with other sportsmen's organizations to protect and achieve the compatible needs of both wildlife and sportsmen and to defend out heritage rights to hunt, fish and trap as well as protecting our constitutional rights to keep and bear arms.

For information, write: Unified Sportsmen of Pennsylvania, POB 687, Harrisburg, PA 17108-0687. (Phone: (717) 923-2644.

UNITED BOWHUNTERS OF PENNSYLVANIA

The purpose of the United Bowhunters of Pennsylvania is to protect and promote bowhunting opportunities for the sportsmen and women of the Commonwealth. Current membership, 3500. Our goals include: fighting the anti-hunting movement, bowhunter education for first-time bowhunters, support of youth programs, an archery bear season and the wise use of our natural resources. Activities include a State-wide convention, carp shoots, golf shoots, 3-D shoots, regional and county meetings.

Publication: Club News in "Bowhunting News" (Monthly)

For information, write: United Bowhunters of PA, Box 732, Bryn Athyn, PA 19009. Phone: (215) 947-1510.

PENNSYLVANIA STATE ARCHERY ASSOCIATION

Over 100 archery clubs scattered throughout Pennsylvania make up the Pennsylvania State Archery Association. Founded in 1931, the PSAA has become a model archery organization because of its bowhunting interest and tournament archery activities. The PSAA was instrumental in Pennsylvania becoming the first state to legalize bowhunting. Tournament archery is regulated by PSAA rules. There is room in our organization for anyone who shoots a bow.

For information, write: Barbara Goss, Executive Administrator, R.D. 1, Box 247A, Lewistown, PA 17044. Phone: (717) 248-9203.

PENNSYLVANIA FEDERATION OF BLACK POWDER SHOOTERS, INC.

The Pennsylvania Federation of Black Powder Shooters is the spokes-group for the blackpowder hunters of the state. The group also sponsors state championship matches, the state muzzleloading team and is involved in legislation and Game Commission affairs concerning muzzleloading.

Publication: "Cap & Flint Newsletter"

For more information, write: Tiny VanSant, Treasurer, PFBPS, 506 Franklin St., Shoemakersville, PA 19555.

WILDLANDS CONSERVANCY/WILDLANDS TRUST FUND

Begun in 1980, the Wildlands Trust Fund, land preservation arm of the Wildlands Conservancy, has aided the Pennsylvania Game Commission in adding more than 16,000 acres of public game lands in 14 counties of eastern Pennsylvania. Tax deductible contributions provide the money differences between what the Commonwealth, limited by law, can provide and what we feel is a fair market price of the wildlife habitat to be preserved.

Publication: "Update" (10 times a year)

For information, write: Wildlands Trust Fund, 3701 Orchid Place, Emmaus, PA 18049. Phone: (610) 965-4397.

WESTERN PENNSYLVANIA CONSERVANCY

With nearly 20,000 members, the Western Pennsylvania Conservancy is the state's largest private land conservation organization. It has one essential purpose: to conserve water, land and wildlife. Since 1932, the Conservancy has protected nearly 200,000 acres of prime natural lands throughout western Pennsylvania for parks, forests, nature reserves and game lands.

Publication: "Conserve" (Quarterly)

For information, write: Western Pennsylvania Conservancy, 316 Fourth Ave., Pittsburgh, PA 15222. Phone: (412) 288-2777.

PHOTO CREDITS

All photographs by the author unless otherwise credited.

Betty Lou Fegely 2, 21, 32, 37, 40 (left), 45, 50, 58, 61, 62, 65, 76 (bottom right), 96, 104, 108, 115, 121, 124, 129, 146, 148, 158, 178, 182, 183, 274, 277, 278, 279, 284, 299

Pennsylvania Historic and Museum Commission 8, 35, 180

Bear Archery 46

Wally Taber 49

Remington Arms Co. 55 (top)

Olin-Winchester 55 (bottom)

Horton Manufacturing Co. 70, 71
Haas Outdoors 83 (left)
Spartan Realtree (right)
Fieldline 84
Imperial-Schrade 85
Simmons Outdoor Corp. 86 (top)
Nikon 86 (bottom)
Ranging 87
Vince Fugazzotto 92
John Phillips 102
Keith Kaeppel 107
Wellington Outdoors 113
Primos Wild Game Calls 122
The Morning Call 173
Other photos courtesy of hunters listed in cutlines.

BIBLIOGRAPHY

Bell, Bob, Betsy Maugans, Bob Mitchell. *Pennsylvania Big Game Records (1965-1986)*. Harrisburg: Pennsylvania Game Commission, 1988.

Doutt, J., C. Heppenstall, J. Guilday. *Mammals of Pennsylvania*. Harrisburg: Pennsylvania Game Commission, 1977.

Flying The Colors: Pennsylvania Facts. Dallas, TX: Clements Research, Inc., 1987.

Lewis, Don. *The Shooter's Corner*. Harrisburg: Pennsylvania Game Commission, 1989.

Liscinsky, S., C. Cushwa, M. Puglisi and M. Ondik. *What Do Deer Eat? Pennsylvania Game News*. Harrisburg: Pennsylvania Game Commission.

Merritt, Joseph F. *Guide to the Mammals of Pennsylvania*. Pittsburgh: University of Pittsburgh Press, 1987.

Powell, D. and T. Considine. *An Analysis of Pennsylvania's Forest Resources*. United States Department of Agriculture: Resource Bulletin NE-69, 1982.

Rue, Leonard Lee, III. *The Deer of North America*. Danbury: Grolier Book Clubs, Inc., 1989.

Shissler, Bryon. *White-tailed Deer Biology and Management In Pennsylvania*. Conestoga: Wildlife Managers, 1985.

Weiss, John. *The Advanced Deer Hunter's Bible*. New York: Doubleday, 1993.

Boone & Crockett Club
Official Scoring System
For North American
Big Game Trophies

205 S. Patrick Street
Alexandria, VA 22314

Detail of Point Measurement

H-4
H-3
H-2
H-1

G-2 G-3 G-4 G-5 G-6 G-7
G-1

A
B
C
D
E
F

DEER TAKEN BY: ☐ BOW ☐ GUN ☐ MUZZLELOADER

	Supplementary Data	Col. 1 Spread Credit	Col. 2 Right Antler	Col. 3 Left Antler	Col. 4 Diff.
A. Number of points on each antler:	R L				
B. Tip to tip spread:					
C. Greatest Spread:					
D. Inside Spread of Main Beams:	Spread credit may equal but not exceed length of longer antler:				
If Inside Spread of main beams exceeds longer antler, enter difference:					
E. Total length of all abnormal points:					
F. Length of main beam:					
G-1. Length of first point, if present:					
G-2. Length of second point:					
G-3. Length of third point:					
G-4. Length of fourth point, if present:					
G-5. Length of fifth point, if present:					
G-6. Length of sixth point, if present:					
G-7. Length of seventh point, if present:					
H-1. Circumference at smallest point between first point and burr:					
H-2. Circumference at smallest point between first point and second point:					
H-3. Circumference at smallest point between second and third point:					
H-4. Circumference at smallest point between third and fourth point or ½ way between third point and beam tip if fourth point missing:					
TOTALS:					

ADD	Col. 1	
	Col. 2	
	Col. 3	
	TOTAL	
Substract Col. 4		
FINAL SCORE		

Location of Kill:
Date of Kill:
Big Game License No.
Name of Taker:
Address:

(scoring developed by Boone & Crockett Club)

SCORED BY: